Matthew Brown

The Life of
ELIJAH

A. W. Pink

D1427736

THE BANNER OF TRUTH TRUST

THE BANNER OF TRUTH TRUST

3 Murrayfield Road, Edinburgh EH12 6EL

PO Box 621, Carlisle, Pennsylvania 17013, USA

★

First published 1956

British revised edition by

courtesy of I. C. Herendeen

June 1963

Reprinted 1968

Reprinted 1976

★

ISBN 0 85151 041 8

Set in 10/12pt Plantin
Printed and bound in Great Britain by
Hazell Watson & Viney Ltd
Aylesbury, Bucks

Contents

Preface

From one generation to another, the servants of the Lord have sought to edify their fellow-believers by commenting on the Old Testament narrative. In such ministries expositions of the life of Elijah have always been prominent. His sudden appearance out of complete obscurity, his dramatic interventions in the national history of Israel, his miracles, his departure from earth in a chariot of fire, all serve to captivate the thought of preacher and writer alike. The New Testament sustains this interest. If Christ Jesus is the Prophet 'like unto Moses,' Elijah, too, has his New Testament counterpart in John – the greatest of the prophets. And even more remarkably, Elijah himself in living person re-appears to view when, with Moses, he stands on the mount of 'the excellent glory,' 'to speak of the strife that won our life with the incarnate Son of God.' What a superb honour was this! As Moses and Elijah are the names which shine in dual grandeur in the closing chapters of the Old Testament, they likewise appear as living representatives of the Lord's redeemed host – the resurrected and the translated – on 'the holy mount,' their theme the exodus which their Saviour and Lord was to accomplish at the time appointed by the Father.

It is the 'translated' representative, the second of the two marvellous Old Testament exceptions to the universal reign of death, who is portrayed in the following pages. 'He comes in like a tempest, who went out in a whirlwind' (says the 17th century Bishop Hall); 'the first that we hear from him is an oath and a threat.' His words, like lightnings, seem to cleave the firmament of Israel. On one famous occasion, the God of Abraham, Isaac and Israel answered them by fire upon the altar of burnt offering. Throughout Elijah's astonishing career judgment and mercy were mingled. From the moment when he steps forth, 'without father, without mother,' 'as if he had been a son of the earth,' to the day when his mantle fell from him and he crossed the river of death without tasting death, he exercised a ministry only paralleled by that of Moses, his companion on the mount. 'He was,' says Bishop Hall, 'the eminentest prophet reserved for the corruptest age.'

It is therefore fitting that the lessons which may legitimately be drawn from Elijah's ministry should be presented afresh to our own generation. The agelessness of prophecy is a striking witness to its divine origin. The prophets are withdrawn but their messages give a light to each succeeding age. History repeats itself. The wickedness and idolatry rampant in Ahab's reign live on in our gross 20th century profanities and corruptions. The worldliness and ungodliness of a Jezebel, in all their painted hideousness, have not only intruded into the present-day scene, but have become ensconced in our homes and our public life.

A. W. Pink (1886-1952), author of this 'Life of Elijah,' had a wide experience of conditions in the English-speaking world. Before finally settling in Britain during the 'thirties, he had exercised his ministry in Australia and the United States of America. Thereafter he devoted himself to Biblical exposition largely carried on by means of the magazine which he established. His study of Elijah is particularly suited to the needs of the present day. Our lot is cast in a time of widespread and deep departure from the ancient landmarks of the people of the Lord. Truths which were dear to our forefathers are now trodden underfoot as the mire of the streets. Many, indeed, claim to preach and re-publish truth in a new garb, but the new garb has proved to be the shroud of truth rather than its authentic 'beautiful garments' as known to the ancient prophets.

Mr. Pink clearly felt called to the task of smiting the ungodliness of the age with the rod of God's anger. With this object he undertakes the exposition of Elijah's ministry, applying it to the contemporary situation. He has a message for his own nation, and also for the people of God. He shows that the ancient challenge, 'Where is the Lord God of Elijah?' is no mere rhetorical question. Where indeed? Have we lost our faith in Him? Has effectual fervent prayer no place in our hearts? Can we not learn from the life of a man subject to like passions as we are? If we possess the wisdom which is from above we shall say with Josiah Conder:

> 'Lord, with this grace our hearts inspire:
> Answer our sacrifice with fire;
> And by Thy mighty acts declare
> Thou art the God who heareth prayer.'

If such aspirations are ours, the 'Life of Elijah' will fan the sacred flame. If we lack them, may the Lord use the work to bring conviction to our sluggish spirits, and to convince us that the test of Carmel is still completely valid: 'The God that answers by fire, let Him be God.'

S. M. HOUGHTON

January, 1963.

CHAPTER ONE

Elijah's Dramatic Appearance

Elijah appeared on the stage of public action during one of the darkest hours of Israel's sad history. He is introduced to us at the beginning of 1 Kings 17, and we have but to read through the previous chapters to discover what a deplorable state God's people were then in. Israel had grievously and flagrantly departed from Jehovah, and that which directly opposed Him had been publicly set up. Never before had the favoured nation sunk so low. Fifty-eight years had passed since the kingdom had been rent in twain following the death of Solomon. During that brief period no less than seven kings had reigned over the ten tribes, and all of them without exception were wicked men. Painful indeed is it to trace their sad course, and still more tragic to behold how there has been a repetition of the same in the history of Christendom.

The first of those seven kings was Jeroboam. Concerning him we read that he 'made two calves of gold,' and said unto the people, 'It is too much for you to go up to Jerusalem: behold thy gods, O Israel, which brought thee up out of the land of Egypt. And he set the one in Bethel, and the other put he in Dan. And this thing became a sin: for the people went to worship before the one, even unto Dan. And he made an house of high places, and made priests of the lowest of the people, which were *not* of the sons of Levi. And Jeroboam ordained a feast in the eighth month, on the fifteenth day of the month, like unto the feast that is in Judah, and he offered upon the altar. So did he in Bethel, sacrificing unto the calves that he had made: and he placed in Bethel the priests of the high places which he had made . . .' 1 Kings 12. 28-32. Let it be duly and carefully noted that the apostasy began with *the corrupting of the priesthood*, by installing into the Divine service men who were never called and equipped by God!

Of the next king, Nadab, it is said, 'And he did evil in the sight of the Lord, and walked in the way of his father, and in his sin wherewith he made Israel to sin,' 1 Kings 15. 26. He was succeeded on the throne by the very man who murdered him, Baasha, 1 Kings 15. 27. Next came Elah, a drunkard, who in turn was a murderer, 1 Kings 16. 8, 9. His successor, Zimri, was guilty of 'treason,' 1 Kings 16. 20. He was followed by a military adventurer of the name of Omri, and of him we are told, 'but Omri wrought evil in the eyes of the Lord, and did worse than all that were before him. For he walked in all the way of Jeroboam the son of Nebat, and in his sin wherewith he made Israel to sin, to provoke the Lord God of Israel to anger with their vanities,' 1 Kings 16. 25, 26. The evil cycle was completed by Omri's son, for he was even more vile than those who had preceded him.

'And Ahab the son of Omri did evil in the sight of the Lord above all that were before him. And it came to pass, as if it had been a light thing for him to walk in the sins of Jeroboam the son of Nebat, that he took to wife Jezebel the daughter of Ethbaal king of the Zidonians, and went and served Baal, and worshipped him,' 1 Kings 16. 30, 31. This marriage of Ahab to a heathen princess was, as might fully be expected (for we cannot trample God's Law beneath our feet with impunity), fraught with the most frightful consequences. In a short time all trace of the pure worship of Jehovah vanished from the land and gross idolatry became rampant. The golden calves were worshipped at Dan and Bethel, a temple had been erected to Baal in Samaria, the 'groves' of Baal appeared on every side, and the priests of Baal took full charge of the religious life of Israel.

It was openly declared that Baal lived and that Jehovah ceased to be. What a shocking state of things had come to pass is clear from, 'And Ahab made a grove; and Ahab did more to provoke the Lord God of Israel to anger than all the kings of Israel that were before him,' 1 Kings 16. 33. Defiance of the Lord God and blatant wickedness had now reached their culminating point. This is made still further evident by, 'in his days did Hiel the Bethelite build Jericho,' v. 34. Awful effrontery was this, for of old it had been recorded, 'Joshua adjured them at that time, saying, Cursed be the man before the Lord, that riseth up and buildeth this city Jericho: he shall lay the foundation thereof in his firstborn and in his youngest son shall be set up the gates of it,' Josh. 6. 26. The rebuilding of the accursed Jericho was open defiance of God.

Now it was in the midst of this spiritual darkness and degradation that there appeared on the stage of public action, with dramatic suddenness, a solitary but striking witness to and for the living God. An eminent commentator began his remarks upon 1 Kings 17 by saying, 'The most illustrious prophet Elijah was raised up in the reign of the most wicked of the kings of Israel.' That is a terse but accurate summing up of the situation in Israel at that time: not only so, but it supplies the key to all that follows. It is truly saddening to contemplate the awful conditions which then prevailed. Every light had been extinguished, every voice of Divine testimony was hushed. Spiritual death was spread over everything, and it looked as though Satan had indeed obtained mastery of the situation.

'And Elijah the Tishbite, who was of the inhabitants of Gilead, said unto Ahab, As the Lord God of Israel liveth, before whom I stand, there shall not be dew nor rain these years, but according to my word,' 1 Kings 17. 1. God, with a high hand, now raised up a powerful witness for Himself. Elijah is here brought to our notice in a most abrupt manner. Nothing is recorded of his parentage or previous manner of life. We do not even know to which tribe he belonged, though the fact that he was 'of the inhabitants of Gilead' makes it likely that he pertained either to Gad or Manasseh, for Gilead was divided between them. 'Gilead lay east of the Jordan: it was wild and rugged; its hills were covered with shaggy forests; its awful solitudes were only broken by the dash of mountain streams; its valleys were the haunt of fierce wild beasts.'

As we have pointed out above, Elijah is introduced to us in the Divine narrative in a strange manner, without anything being told us of his ancestry or early life. We believe there is a *typical reason* why the Spirit made no reference to Elijah's origin. Like Melchizedek, the beginning and close of his history is shrouded in sacred mystery. As the absence of any mention of Melchizedek's birth and death was Divinely designed to foreshadow the eternal Priesthood and Kingship of Christ, so the fact that we know nothing of Elijah's father and mother, and the further fact that he was supernaturally translated from this world without passing through the portals of death, mark him as the typical forerunner of the everlasting Prophet. Thus the omission of such details adumbrated the *endlessness* of Christ's *prophetic* office.

The fact that we are told Elijah 'was of the inhabitants of Gilead' is no doubt recorded as a sidelight upon his natural training – one which ever exerts a powerful influence on the forming of character. The people of those hills reflected the nature of their environment: they were rough and rugged, solemn and stern, dwelling in rude villages and subsisting by keeping flocks of sheep. Hardened by an open-air life, dressed in a cloak of camel's hair, accustomed to spending most of his time in solitude, possessed of sinewy strength which enabled him to endure great physical strain, Elijah would present a marked contrast with the town dwellers in the lowland valleys, and more especially would he be distinguished from the pampered courtiers of the palace.

What age he was when the Lord first granted Elijah a personal and saving revelation of Himself we have no means of knowing, as we have no information about his early religious training. But there is one sentence in a later chapter which enables us to form a definite idea of the spiritual calibre of the man – 'I have been very jealous for the Lord God of hosts,' 1 Kings 19. 10. Those words cannot mean less than that he had God's glory greatly at heart and that the honour of *His* name meant more to him than anything else. Consequently, he must have been deeply grieved and filled with holy indignation as he became more and more informed about the terrible character and wide extent of Israel's defection from Jehovah.

There can be little room for doubt that Elijah must have been thoroughly familiar with the Scriptures, especially the first books of the Old Testament. Knowing how much the Lord had done for Israel, the signal favours He had bestowed upon them, he must have yearned with deep desire that they should please and glorify Him. But when he learned that this was utterly lacking, and as tidings reached him of what was happening on the other side of the Jordan, as he became informed of how Jezebel had thrown down God's altars, slain His servants, and replaced them with the idolatrous priests of heathendom, his soul must have been filled with horror and his blood made to boil with indignation, for he was 'very jealous for the Lord God of hosts.' Would that more of such righteous indignation filled and fired us today!

Probably the question which now most deeply exercised Elijah was, How should he act? What could *he* do, a rude, uncultured, child of the desert? The more he pondered it, the more difficult the situation must have seemed; and no doubt Satan whispered in his ear, 'You can do nothing, conditions are hopeless.' But there *was* one thing he could do: betake himself to that grand resource of all deeply tried souls – he could *pray*. And he did: as James 5. 17 tells us, 'he prayed earnestly.' He prayed because he was assured that the Lord God lived and ruled over all. He prayed because he realized that God is almighty and that with Him all things are possible. He prayed because he felt his own weakness and insufficiency and therefore turned to One who is clothed with might and is infinitely self-sufficient.

But in order to be effectual, prayer must be grounded on the Word of God, for without faith it is impossible to please Him, and 'faith cometh by hearing, and hearing by the Word of God,' Rom. 10. 17. Now there was one particular passage in the earlier books of Scripture which seems to have been specially fixed on Elijah's attention: 'Take heed to yourselves, that your heart be not deceived, and ye turn aside, and serve other gods, and worship them; and then the Lord's wrath be kindled against you, and He shut up the heaven, *that there be no rain*, and that the land yield not her fruit,' Deut. 11. 16, 17. That was exactly the crime of which Israel was now guilty: they had turned aside to worship false gods. Suppose, then, that this Divinely-threatened judgment should not be executed, would it not indeed appear that Jehovah was but a myth, a dead tradition? And Elijah was 'very jealous for the Lord God of hosts,' and accordingly we are told that 'he prayed earnestly that it might not rain,' James 5. 17. Thus we learn once more what true prayer is: it is faith laying hold of the Word of God, pleading it before Him, and saying, 'do as Thou hast said,' 2 Sam. 7. 25.

'He prayed earnestly that it might not rain.' Do some of our readers exclaim, 'What a terrible prayer'? Then we ask, Was it not far more terrible that the favoured descendants of Abraham, Isaac and Jacob should despise and turn away from the Lord God and blatantly insult Him by worshipping Baal? Would they desire the thrice Holy One to wink at such enormities? Are His righteous laws to be trampled upon with impunity? Shall He refuse to enforce their just penalties? What conception would men form of the Divine character if He ignored their open defiance of Himself? Let Scripture answer: 'Because sentence against an evil work is not executed speedily, therefore the heart of the sons of men is fully set in them to do evil,' Eccl. 8. 11. Yes, and not only so, but as God declared, 'These things hast thou done, and I kept silence; thou thoughtest that I was altogether such an one as thyself: but I will reprove thee, and set them in order before thine eyes,' Psa. 50. 21.

Ah, my reader, there is something far more dreadful than physical calamity and suffering, namely, moral delinquency and spiritual apostasy. Alas, that this is so rarely perceived today! What are crimes against man in comparison with high-handed sins against God? Likewise what are national reverses in comparison with the loss of God's favour? The fact is that Elijah had a true sense of values: he was 'very jealous for the Lord God of hosts,' and therefore he prayed earnestly that it might not rain. Desperate diseases call for drastic measures. And as he prayed, Elijah obtained assurance that his petition was granted, and that he must go and acquaint Ahab. Whatever danger the prophet might personally incur, both the king and his subjects should learn the direct connection between the terrible drought and their sins which had occasioned it.

The task which now confronted Elijah was no ordinary one, and it called for more than common courage. For an untutored rustic of the hills to appear uninvited before a king who defied Heaven was sufficient to quell the bravest; the more so when his heathen consort shrank not from slaying any who opposed her will, in fact who had already put many of God's servants to death. What likelihood, then, was there of this lonely Gileadite escaping with his life? 'But the righteous are bold as a lion,' Prov. 28. 1: they who are right with God are neither daunted by difficulties nor dismayed by dangers. 'I will not be afraid of ten thousands of people, that have set themselves against me round about,' Psa. 3. 6; 'Though a host should encamp against me, my heart shall not fear,' Psa. 27. 3: such is the blessed serenity of those whose conscience is void of offence and whose trust is in the living God.

The hour for the execution of his stern task had arrived, and Elijah leaves his home in Gilead to deliver unto Ahab his message of judgment. Picture him on his long and lonely journey. What were the subjects which engaged his mind? Would he be reminded of the similar mission on which Moses had embarked, when he was sent by the Lord to deliver his ultimatum to the haughty monarch of Egypt? Well, the message which *he* bore would be no more palatable to the degenerate king of Israel. Yet such a recollection need in nowise deter or intimidate him: rather should the remembrance of the sequel strengthen his faith. The Lord God had not failed his servant Moses, but had stretched forth His mighty arm on his behalf, and in the end had given him full success. The wondrous works of God in the past should ever hearten His servants and saints in the present.

CHAPTER TWO

The Heavens Shut Up

'When the enemy shall come in like a flood, the Spirit of the Lord shall lift up a standard against him,' Isa. 59. 19. What is signified by the enemy coming in 'like a flood?' The figure used here is a graphic and expressive one: it is that of an abnormal deluge which results in the submerging of the land, the imperilling of property and life itself, a deluge threatening to carry everything before it. Aptly does such a figure depict the moral experience of the world in general, and of specially-favoured sections of it in particular, at different periods in their history. Again and again a flood of evil has broken loose, a flood of such alarming dimensions that it appeared as though Satan would succeed in beating down everything holy before him, when, by an inundation of idolatry, impiety and iniquity, the cause of God upon earth seemed in imminent danger of being completely swept away.

'When the enemy shall come in like a flood.' We have but to glance at the context to discover what is meant by such language. 'We wait for light, but behold obscurity; for brightness, but we walk in darkness. We grope for the wall like the blind, and we grope as if we had no eyes . . . For our transgressions are multiplied before Thee, and our sins testify against us . . . In transgressing and lying against the Lord, and departing away from our God, speaking oppression and revolt, conceiving and uttering from the heart words of falsehood. And judgment is turned away backward, and justice standeth afar off: for truth is fallen in the street, and equity cannot enter. Yea, truth faileth; and he that departeth from evil is accounted mad,' Isa. 59. 9-15, see margin of v. 15. Nevertheless, when the Devil has brought in a flood of lying errors, and lawlessness has become ascendant, the Spirit of God intervenes and thwarts Satan's vile purpose.

The solemn verses quoted above accurately describe the awful conditions which obtained in Israel under the reign of Ahab and his heathen consort, Jezebel. Because of their multiplied transgressions God had given up the people to blindness and darkness, and a spirit of falsehood and madness possessed their hearts. In consequence, truth was fallen in the street – ruthlessly trampled underfoot by the masses. Idolatry had become the state religion: the worship of Baal was the order of the day: wickedness was rampant on every side. The enemy had indeed come in like a flood, and it looked as though there was no barrier left which could stem its devastating effects. Then it was that the Spirit of the Lord lifted up a standard against him, making public demonstration that the God of Israel was highly displeased with the sins of the people, and would now visit their iniquities upon them. That heavenly standard was raised aloft by the hand of Elijah.

God has never left Himself without witnesses on earth. In the darkest seasons of human history the Lord has raised up and maintained a testimony for Himself. Neither persecution nor corruption could entirely destroy it. In the days of the antediluvians, when the earth was filled with violence and all flesh had corrupted its way, Jehovah had an Enoch and a Noah to act as His mouthpieces. When the Hebrews were reduced to abject slavery in Egypt, the Most High sent forth Moses and Aaron as His ambassadors, and at every subsequent period in their history one prophet after another was sent to them. So also has it been throughout the whole course of Christendom: in the days of Nero, in the time of Charlemagne, and even in the dark ages – despite the incessant opposition of the Papacy – the lamp of truth was never extinguished. And so here in 1 Kings 17 we behold again the unchanging faithfulness of God to His covenant, by bringing upon the scene one who was jealous for His glory and who feared not to denounce His enemies.

Having already dwelt upon the significance of the particular office which Elijah exercised, and taken a look at his mysterious personality, let us now consider the meaning of *his name*. A most striking and declarative one it was, for Elijah may be rendered 'my God is Jehovah' or 'Jehovah is my God.' The apostate nation had adopted Baal as their deity, but our prophet's name proclaimed the true God of Israel. Judging from the analogy of Scripture we may safely conclude that this name was given to him by his parents, probably under prophetic impulse or in consequence of a divine communication. Nor will this be deemed a fanciful idea by those acquainted with the Word. Lamech called his son Noah, 'saying, This same shall comfort us (or be a rest to us) concerning our work,' Gen. 5. 29 – 'Noah' signifying 'rest' or 'comfort.' Joseph gave names to his sons expressive of God's particular providences to him, Gen. 41. 51, 52. Hannah's name for her son, 1 Sam. 1. 20, and the wife of Phinehas for hers, 1 Sam. 4. 19-22, are further illustrations.

We may observe that the same principle holds good in connection with many of the *places* mentioned in the Scriptures: Babel, Gen. 11. 9; Beersheba, Gen. 21. 31; Massah and Meribah, Ex. 17. 7; and Cabul, 1 Kings 9. 13 margin, being cases in point; indeed no one who desires to understand the sacred writings can afford to neglect a careful attention to proper names. The importance of this receives confirmation in the example of our Lord Himself, for when bidding the blind man to wash in the pool of Siloam it was at once added: 'which is *by interpretation*, Sent,' John 9. 7. Again, when Matthew records the angel's command to Joseph that the Saviour was to be named Jesus, the Spirit moved him to add, 'All this was done that it might be fulfilled which was spoken of the Lord by the prophet, saying, Behold, a virgin shall be with child, and shall bring forth a son, and they shall call His name Emmanuel, which *being interpreted is*, God with us,' 1. 21, 23. Compare also the words, 'which is, being interpreted,' in Acts 4. 36; Hebrews 7. 1, 2.

It will thus be seen that the example of the apostles warrants us to educe instruction from proper names (for if not all of them, many embody important truths), yet this must be done with modesty and according to the analogy of Scripture, and not with dogmatism or for the purpose of establishing any new doctrine.

How aptly the name Elijah corresponded to the prophet's mission and message is at once apparent, and what encouragement every consideration of it would afford him! We may also couple with his striking name the fact that the Holy Spirit has designated Elijah 'the Tishbite,' which significantly enough denotes *the stranger here*. And we must also take note of the additional detail that he was 'of the inhabitants of Gilead,' which name means *rocky* – because of the mountainous nature of that country. It is ever such a one whom God takes up and uses in a critical hour: a man who is out and out for Him, in separation from the religious evil of his day, and who dwells on high; a man who in the midst of fearful declension carries in his heart the testimony of God.

'And Elijah the Tishbite, who was of the inhabitants of Gilead, said unto Ahab, As the Lord God of Israel liveth, before whom I stand, there shall not be dew nor rain these years, but according to my word,' I Kings 17. 1. This memorable event occurred some eight hundred and sixty years before the birth of Christ. For the dramatic suddenness, the exceeding boldness, and the amazing character of it, there are few of a like nature in sacred history. Unannounced and unattended, a plain man, dressed in humble garb, appeared before Israel's apostate king as the messenger of Jehovah and the herald of dire judgment. No one in the court would know much, if anything, about him, for he had just emerged from the obscurity of Gilead, to stand before Ahab with the keys of Heaven in his hand. Such are often the witnesses to His truth which God has employed. At His bidding they come and go: not from the ranks of the influential and learned do they issue. They are not the products of this world system, nor does the world place any laurels on their brow.

'As the Lord God of Israel liveth, before whom I stand, there shall not be dew nor rain these years, but according to my word.' There is much more in this expression, 'the Lord God of Israel liveth,' than meets the eye at first glance. Observe that it is not simply 'the Lord God liveth,' but 'the Lord God of Israel,' which is also to be distinguished from the wider term, 'the Lord of hosts.' At least three things were signified thereby. First, 'the Lord God of Israel' threw particular emphasis upon His special relationship to the favoured nation: Jehovah was their King, their Ruler, the One with whom they had to do, the One with whom they had entered into a solemn covenant. Second, Ahab is thereby informed that He *liveth*. This grand fact had evidently been called in question. During the reigns of one king after another Israel had openly mocked and defied Jehovah, and no dire consequences had followed; and so the false idea had come to prevail that the Lord had no real existence. Third, this affirmation, 'the Lord God of Israel liveth,' pointed a striking contrast with the lifeless idols whose impotency should now be made apparent – unable to defend their deluded votaries from the wrath of God.

Though, for wise reasons of His own, God 'endured with much longsuffering the vessels of wrath fitted to destruction,' Rom. 9. 22, yet He affords clear and sufficient proof throughout the course of human history that He is even now the governor of the wicked and the avenger of sin. Such a proof was then given to Israel. Notwithstanding the peace and prosperity which the kingdom had long enjoyed, the Lord was highly incensed at the gross manner in which He had been publicly insulted, and the time had arrived for Him severely to chasten the wayward people. Accordingly He sent Elijah to Ahab to announce the nature and duration of His scourge. It is to be duly noted that the prophet came with his awe-inspiring message, not to the people, but to the king himself – the responsible head, the one who had it in his power to rectify what was wrong by banishing all idols from his dominions.

Elijah was now called upon to deliver a most unpalatable message unto the most powerful man in all Israel, but conscious that God was with him he flinched not from such a task. Suddenly confronting Ahab, Elijah at once made it evident that he was faced by one who had no fear of him, king though he were. His first words informed Israel's degenerate monarch that he had to do with the living God. 'As the Lord God of Israel liveth' was an outspoken confession of the prophet's faith, as it also directed attention to the One whom Ahab had forsaken. 'Before whom I stand': (that is, whose servant I am – cf. Deut. 10. 8; Luke 1. 19) in whose

Name I approach you, in whose veracity and power I unquestioningly rely, in whose ineffable presence I am now conscious of standing, and to whom I have prayed and obtained answer.

'There shall not be dew nor rain these years, but according to my word.' Frightful prospect was that! From the expression 'the early and the latter rain,' Deut. 11. 14; Jer. 5. 24, we gather that, normally, Palestine experienced a dry season of several months' duration: but though no rain fell then, heavy dews descended at night which greatly refreshed vegetation. But for neither dew nor rain to fall, and that for a period of years, was a terrible judgment indeed. That land so rich and fertile as to be designated one which 'flowed with milk and honey,' would quickly be turned into one of drought and barrenness, entailing famine, pestilence and death. And when God withholds rain, none can create it. 'Are there any among the vanities (false gods) of the Gentiles that can cause rain?' Jer. 14. 22 – how *that* reveals the utter impotency of idols, and the madness of those who render them homage!

The exacting ordeal facing Elijah in confronting Ahab and delivering such a message called for no ordinary moral strength. This will be the more evident if we direct attention to a detail which seems to have quite escaped the commentators, one which is only apparent by a careful comparison of Scripture with Scripture. Elijah told the king, 'there shall be no dew nor rain these years,' while in 1 Kings 18. 1 the sequel says, 'And it came to pass after many days, that the word of the Lord came to Elijah *in the third* year, saying, Go, shew thyself unto Ahab; and I will send rain upon the earth,' 1 Kings 18. 1. On the other hand, Christ declared 'many widows were in Israel in the days of Elias (Elijah), when the heaven was shut up three years *and six months*, when great famine was throughout all the land,' Luke 4. 25. How, then, are we to explain those extra six months? In this way: there had *already been* a six months' drought when Elijah visited Ahab: we can well imagine how furious the king would be when told that the terrible drought was to last another three years!

Yes, the unpleasant task before Elijah called for no ordinary resolution and boldness, and well may we inquire, What was the secret of his remarkable courage, how are we to account for his strength? Some of the Jewish rabbis have contended that he was an angel, but that cannot be, for the New Testament expressly informs us that he was 'a man subject to like passions as we are,' James 5. 17. Yes, he was but 'a man,' nevertheless he trembled not in the presence of a monarch. Though a man, yet he had power to close heaven's windows and dry up earth's streams. But the question returns upon us, How are we to account for the full assurance with which he foretold the protracted drought, his confidence that all would be according to his word? How was it that one so weak in himself became mighty through God to the pulling down of strongholds?

We suggest a threefold reason as to the secret of Elijah's strength. First, *his praying*. 'Elijah was a man subject to like passions as we are, and he prayed earnestly that it might not rain, and it rained not on the earth by the space of three years and six months,' James 5. 17. Let it be duly noted that the prophet did not begin his fervent supplications *after* his appearance before Ahab, but six months before! Here, then, lies the explanation of his assurance and boldness before the king. Prayer in private was the source of his power in public: he could stand unabashed in the presence of the wicked monarch because he had knelt in humility before God. But let it also be carefully observed that the prophet had 'prayed earnestly': no formal and spiritless devotion that accomplished nothing was his, but whole-hearted, fervent and effectual.

Second, *his knowledge of God*. This is clearly intimated in his words to Ahab, 'As the Lord God of Israel liveth.' Jehovah was to him a living reality. On all sides the open recognition of God had ceased: so far as outward appearances went there was not a soul in Israel who believed in His existence. But Elijah was not swayed by public opinion and practice. Why should he be, when he had within his own breast an experience which enabled him to say with Job, "I know that my Redeemer liveth!' The infidelity and atheism of others cannot shake the faith of one who has apprehended God for himself. It is this which explains Elijah's courage, as it did on a later occasion the uncompromising faithfulness of Daniel and his three fellow Hebrews. He who really knows God is strong, Dan. 11. 32, and fears not man.

Third, *his consciousness of the Divine presence*: 'As the Lord God of Israel liveth, before whom I stand.' Elijah was not only assured of the reality of Jehovah's existence, but he was conscious of being in His presence. Though appearing before the person of Ahab, the prophet knew he was in the presence of One infinitely greater than any earthly monarch, even Him before whom the highest angels bow in adoring worship. Gabriel himself could not make a grander avowal, Luke 1. 19. Ah, my reader, such a blessed assurance as this lifts us above all fear. If the Almighty was with him, why should the prophet tremble before a worm of the earth! The Lord God of Israel liveth: 'before whom I stand' clearly reveals the foundation on which his soul rested as he executed his unpleasant task.

CHAPTER THREE

The Brook Cherith

———

'Elijah was a man subject to like passions as we are, and he prayed earnestly that it might not rain, and it rained not on the earth by the space of three years and six months,' James 5. 17. Elijah is here brought before us as an example of what may be accomplished by the earnest prayers of one 'righteous man,' v. 16. Ah, my reader, mark well the descriptive adjective, for it is not every man, nor even every Christian, who obtains definite answers to his prayers. Far from it! A 'righteous man' is one who is right with God in a practical way: one whose conduct is pleasing in His sight, one who keeps his garments unspotted from the world, who is in separation from religious evil, for there is no evil on earth half so dishonouring and displeasing to God as *religious evil* (see Luke 10. 12-15; Rev. 11. 8). Such a one has the ear of Heaven, for there is no moral barrier between his soul and a sin-hating God. 'Whatsoever we ask, we receive of Him, because we keep His commandments, and do those things that are pleasing in His sight,' 1 John 3. 22.

'He prayed earnestly that it might not rain.' What a terrible petition to present before the Majesty on high! What incalculable privation and suffering the granting of such a request would entail! The fair land of Palestine would be turned into a parched and sterile wilderness, and its inhabitants would be wasted by a protracted famine with all its attendant horrors. Then was this prophet a cold and callous stoic, devoid of natural affection? No indeed! the Holy Spirit has taken care to tell us in this very verse that he was 'a man subject to like passions as we are,' and *that* is mentioned immediately before the record of his fearful petition.

And what does that description signify in *such* a connection? Why, this: that though Elijah was endowed with tender sensibilities and warm regard for his fellow-creatures, yet in his prayers he rose above all fleshly sentimentality.

Why was it Elijah prayed 'that it might not rain?' Not because he was impervious to human suffering, not because he took a fiendish delight in witnessing the misery of his neighbours, but because he put *the glory of God* before everything else, even before his own natural feelings. Recall what has been pointed out in an earlier chapter concerning the spiritual conditions that then obtained in Israel. Not only was there no longer any public recognition of God, no, not throughout the length and breadth of the land, but on every side He was openly insulted and defied by Baal worshippers. Daily the tide of evil rose higher and higher, until it had now swept practically everything before it. And Elijah was 'very jealous for the Lord God of hosts,' 1 Kings 19. 10, and longed to see His great Name vindicated and His backslidden people restored. Thus it was the glory of God and true love for Israel which actuated his petition.

Here, then, is the outstanding mark of a 'righteous man' whose prayers prevail with God: though one of tender sensibilities, yet he puts the honour of the Lord before every other consideration. And God has promised, 'them that honour *Me* I will honour,' 1 Sam. 2. 30. Alas, how frequently these words are true of us: 'Ye ask, and receive not; because ye ask amiss, that ye may consume it upon your lusts,' James 4. 3. We 'ask amiss' when natural feelings sway us, when carnal motives move us, when selfish considerations actuate us. But how different was it with Elijah! He was deeply stirred by the horrible indignities against his Master and longed to see Him given His rightful place again in Israel. 'And it rained not on the earth for the space of three years and six months.' The prophet failed not of his object. God never refuses to act when faith addresses Him on the ground of His own glory, and clearly it was on that ground Elijah had supplicated Him.

'Let us therefore come boldly unto the throne of grace, that we may obtain mercy and find grace to help in time of need,'

Heb. 4. 16. It was there at that blessed throne that Elijah obtained the strength which he so sorely needed at that time. Not only was he required to keep his own skirts clear from the evil all around him, but he was called upon to exercise a holy influence upon others, to act for God in a degenerate age, to make a serious effort to bring back the people to the God of their fathers. How essential it was, then, that he should dwell much in the secret place of the Most High, that he should obtain that grace from Him which alone could fit him for his difficult and dangerous undertaking: only thus could he be delivered from evil himself, and only thus could he hope to be instrumental in delivering others. Thereby equipped for the conflict, he entered upon his path of service endued with Divine power.

Conscious of the Lord's approbation, assured of the answer to his petition, sensible that the Almighty was with him, Elijah boldly confronted the wicked Ahab and announced the Divine judgment on his kingdom. But let us pause for a moment so that this weighty fact may sink into our minds, for it explains to us the more-than-human courage displayed by the servants of God in every age. What was it made Moses so bold before Pharaoh? What was it that enabled the young David to go forth and meet the mighty Goliath? What was it that gave Paul such strength to testify as he did before Agrippa? From whence did Luther obtain such resolution that 'though every tile on the roofs were a devil' he would continue his mission? In each case the answer is the same: supernatural strength was obtained from a supernatural source: only thus can we be energized to wrestle with the principalities and powers of evil.

'He giveth power to the faint; and to them that have no might He increaseth strength. Even the youths shall faint and be weary, and the young men shall utterly fall: But they that wait upon the Lord shall renew their strength; they shall mount up with wings as eagles; they shall run, and not be weary; and they shall walk, and not faint,' Isa. 40. 29-31. But where had Elijah learned this all-important lesson? Not in any seminary or Bible-training college, for if there were such in that day they were like some in our own degenerate time – in the hands of the Lord's enemies. Nor can the schools of orthodoxy impart such secrets: even godly men cannot teach themselves this lesson, much less can they impart it to others. Ah, my reader, as it was at 'the backside of the desert,' Ex. 3. 1, that the Lord appeared to and commissioned Moses, so it was in the solitudes of Gilead that Elijah had communed with Jehovah and had been trained by Him for his arduous duties: there he had 'waited' upon the Lord, and there had he obtained 'strength' for his task.

None but the living God can effectually say unto His servant, 'Fear thou not; for I am with thee: be not dismayed; for I am thy God: I will strengthen thee; yea, I will help thee; yea, I will uphold thee with the right hand of my righteousness,' Isa. 41. 10. Thus granted the consciousness of the Lord's presence, His servant goes forth 'as bold as a lion,' fearing no man, kept in perfect calm amid the most trying circumstances. It was in such a spirit that the Tishbite confronted Ahab: 'as the Lord God of Israel liveth, before whom I stand.' But how little that apostate monarch knew of the secret exercises of the prophet's soul ere he thus came forth to address his conscience! 'There shall not be dew nor rain these years, but according to *my* word.' Very striking and blessed is that. The prophet spoke with the utmost assurance and authority, for he was delivering God's message – the servant identifying himself with his Master. Such should ever be the demeanour of the minister of Christ: 'we speak that we do know, and testify that we have seen.'

'And the word of the Lord came unto him,' v. 2. How blessed! yet this is not likely to be perceived unless we ponder the same in the light of the foregoing. From the preceding verse we learn that Elijah had faithfully discharged his commission, and here we find the Lord speaking anew to His servant: thus we regard the latter as a gracious reward of the former. This is ever the Lord's way, delighting to commune with those who delight to do His will. It is a profitable line of study to trace this expression throughout the Scriptures. God does not grant fresh revelations until there has been a compliance with those *already* received: we may see a case of this in the early life of Abraham. 'The Lord had said unto Abraham, Get thee . . . unto the land that I will show thee,' Gen. 12. 1; but instead, he went only half way and settled in Haran, 11. 31, and it was not until he left there and fully obeyed that the Lord again appeared to him, 12. 4-7.

'And the word of the Lord came unto him, saying, Get thee hence, and turn thee eastward, and hide thyself by the brook Cherith,' vv. 2, 3. An important practical truth is hereby exemplified. God leads His servants step by step. Necessarily so, for the path which they are called to tread is that of faith, and faith is opposed to both sight and independency. It is not the Lord's way to reveal to us the whole course which is to be traversed: rather does He restrict His light to one step at a time, that we may be kept in continual dependence upon Him. This is a most salutary lesson, yet it is one that the flesh is far from relishing, especially in those who are naturally energetic and zealous. Before he left Gilead for Samaria to deliver his solemn message, the prophet would no doubt wonder what he should do as soon as it was delivered. But *that* was no concern of his, then: he was to obey the Divine order and leave God to make known what he should do next.

'Trust in the Lord with all thine heart; and lean not unto thine own understanding. In all thy ways acknowledge Him and He shall direct thy paths,' Prov. 3. 5, 6. Ah, my reader, had Elijah then leaned unto his own understanding, we may depend upon it that hiding himself by the brook Cherith is the last course he would have selected. Had he followed his instincts, yea had he done that which he considered most glorifying to God, would he not have embarked upon a preaching tour throughout the towns and villages of Samaria? Would he not have felt it was his bounden duty to do everything in his power calculated to awaken the slumbering conscience of the public, so that his subjects – horrified at the prevailing idolatry – would bring pressure to bear upon Ahab to put a stop to it? Yet that was the very thing God would not have him to do: what then are reasoning and natural inclinations worth in connection with Divine things? Nothing.

'And the word of the Lord came to him.' Note that it is not said, 'the *will* of the Lord was revealed to him' or 'the *mind* of God was made known'; we would particularly emphasize this detail, for it is a point on which there is no little confusion to-day. There are numbers who mystify themselves and others by a lot of pious talk about 'obtaining the Lord's mind' or 'discovering God's will' for them, which when carefully analysed amounts to nothing better than a vague uncertainty or a personal impulse. God's 'mind' or 'will,' my reader, is made known in *His Word,* and He never 'wills' anything for us which to the slightest degree clashes with that heavenly Rule. Changing the emphasis, note, 'the Word of the Lord *came to him*:' there was no need for him to go and search for it! See Deut. 30. 11-14.

And what a 'word' it was that came to Elijah! 'Get thee hence, and turn thee eastward, and hide thyself by the brook Cherith, that is before Jordan,' v. 3. Verily God's thoughts and ways are indeed entirely different from ours: yes, and He alone can 'make known,' Psa. 103. 7, the same unto us. It is almost amusing to see how commentators have quite wandered from the track here, for almost all of them explain the Lord's command as being given for the purpose of providing *protection* for His servant. As the death-dealing drought continued, the perturbation of Ahab would increase more and more, and as he remembered the prophet's language that there should be neither dew nor rain but according to *his* word, his rage against him would know no bounds: Elijah, then, must be provided with a refuge if his life was to be spared. Yet Ahab made no attempt to slay him when next they met, 1 Kings 18. 17-20! Should it be answered, 'That was because God's restraining hand was upon the king,' we answer, granted, but was not God able to restrain him all through the interval?

No, the reason for the Lord's order to His servant must be sought elsewhere, and surely that is not far to ascertain. Once it be recognized that next to the bestowment of His Word and the Holy Spirit to apply the same, the most valuable gift He grants any people is the sending of His own qualified servants among them, and that the greatest possible calamity which can befall any land is God's withdrawal of those whom He appoints to minister unto the soul, then no uncertainty should remain. The drought on Ahab's kingdom was a Divine scourge and in keeping therewith the Lord bade His prophet 'get thee hence.' The removal of the ministers of His truth is a sure sign of God's displeasure, a token that He is dealing in judgment with a people who have provoked Him to anger.

It should be pointed out that the Hebrew word for 'hide,' 1 Kings 17. 3, is an entirely different one from that which is found in Joshua 6, 17, 25 (Rahab's hiding of the spies) and in 1 Kings 18. 4, 13. The word used in connection with Elijah might well be rendered 'turn thee eastward and *absent* thyself,' as it is in Genesis 31. 49. Of old the Psalmist had asked, 'O God, why hast Thou cast us off for ever? why doth Thine anger smoke against the sheep of Thy pasture?' 74. 1. And what was it that caused him to make this plaintive inquiry? what had happened to make him realize that the anger of God was burning against Israel? This: 'They have cast fire into Thy sanctuary . . . they have burned up all the synagogues of God in the land. We see not our signs: *there is no more any prophet,*' vv. 7-9. It was the doing away with the public means of grace which was the sure sign of the Divine displeasure.

Ah, my reader, little as it may be realized in our day, there is no surer and more solemn proof that God is hiding His face from a people or nation than for Him to *deprive them* of the inestimable blessings of those who faithfully minister His holy Word to them, for as far as heavenly mercies excel earthly so much more dreadful are spiritual calamities than material ones. Through Moses the Lord had declared, 'My doctrine shall drop as the rain, my speech shall distil as the dew, as the small rain upon the tender herb, and as the showers upon the grass,' Deut. 32. 2. And now all dew and rain was to be withheld from Ahab's land, not only literally so, but spiritually so as well. Those who ministered His Word were removed from the scene of public action, cf. 1 Kings 18. 4.

If further proof of the Scripturalness of our interpretation of 1 Kings 17. 3 be required, we refer the reader to: 'And though the Lord give you the bread of adversity, and the water of affliction, yet shall not thy teachers be *removed into a corner* any more, but thine eyes shall see thy teachers,' Isa. 30. 20. What could be plainer than that? For the Lord to remove His teachers into a corner was the sorest loss His people could suffer, for here He tells them that His wrath shall be tempered with mercy, that though He gave them the bread of adversity and the water of affliction yet He would not again deprive them of those who ministered unto their souls. Finally, we would remind the reader of Christ's statement that there was 'great famine' in the land in Elijah's time, Luke 4. 25, and link up with the same: 'Behold, the days come, saith the Lord God, that I will send a famine in the land, not a famine of bread, nor a thirst for water, but of *hearing the words of the Lord*: and they shall wander from sea to sea, and from the north even to the east, they shall run to and fro to seek the word of the Lord, and shall not find it,' Amos 8. 11, 12.

CHAPTER FOUR

The Trial of Faith

'And the word of the Lord came unto him, saying, Get thee hence, and turn thee eastward, and hide thyself by the brook Cherith, that is before Jordan,' 1 Kings 17. 2, 3. As pointed out in our last chapter, it was not merely to provide Elijah with a safe retreat, to protect His servant from the wrath of Ahab and Jezebel, that Jehovah so commanded the prophet, but to signify His sore displeasure against His apostate people: the withdrawal of the prophet from the scene of public action was an additional judgment on the nation. We cannot forbear pointing out that tragic analogy which now obtains more or less in Christendom. During the past two or three decades God has removed some eminent and faithful servants of His by the hand of death, and not only has He not replaced them by raising up others in their stead, but an increasing number of those who still remain are being sent into seclusion by Him.

It was both for God's glory and the prophet's own good that the Lord bade him 'get thee hence . . . hide thyself.' It was a call to separation. Ahab was an apostate, and his consort was a heathen. Idolatry abounded on every side. Jehovah was publicly dishonoured. The man of God could have no sympathy or communion with such a horrible situation. Isolation from evil is absolutely essential if we are to 'keep ourselves unspotted from the world,' James 1. 27: not only separation from secular wickedness *but from religious corruption also*. 'Have no fellowship with the unfruitful works of darkness,' Eph. 5. 11, has been God's demand in every dispensation. Elijah stood as the Lord's faithful witness in a day of national departure from Himself, and having delivered His testimony to the responsible head, the prophet must now retire. To turn our backs on all that dishonours God is an essential duty.

But where was Elijah to go? He had previously dwelt in the presence of the Lord God of Israel. 'Before whom I stand' he could say when pronouncing sentence of judgment unto Ahab, and he should still abide in the secret place of the Most High. The prophet was not left to his own devisings or choice, but directed to a place of God's own appointing – outside the camp, away from the entire religious system. Degenerate Israel was to know him only as a witness *against* themselves: he was to have no place and take no part in either the social or religious life of the nation. He was to turn 'eastward:' the quarter from which the morning light arises, for those who are regulated by the Divine precepts 'shall not walk in darkness, but shall have the light of life,' John 8. 12. 'By the brook Cherith, that is before Jordan.' Jordan marked the very limits of the land. Typically it spoke of death, and spiritual death now rested upon Israel.

But what a message of hope and comfort the 'Jordan' contained for one who was walking with the Lord! How well calculated was it to speak unto the heart of one whose faith was in a healthy condition! Was it not at this very place that Jehovah had shown Himself strong on behalf of His people in the days of Joshua? Was not the Jordan the very scene which had witnessed the miracle-working power of God at the time when Israel left the wilderness behind them? It was there the Lord had said unto Joshua, 'This day will I begin to magnify thee in the sight of all Israel, that they may know that, as I was with Moses, so I will be with thee,' Josh. 3. 7. It was there that 'the living God,' v. 10, made the waters to 'stand upon an heap,' v. 13, so that 'all the Israelites passed over on dry ground,' v. 17. Such are the things which should and no doubt did fill the mind of the Tishbite when his Master ordered him to *this* very place. If his faith was in exercise, his heart would be in perfect peace, knowing that a miracle-working God would not fail him there.

It was also for the prophet's own personal good that the Lord now bade him 'hide thyself.' He was in danger from another quarter than the fury of Ahab. The success of his supplications might prove a snare, tending to fill his heart with pride, and even to harden him against the calamity then desolating the land. Previously he had been engaged in secret prayer, and then for a brief moment he had witnessed a good confession before the king. The future held for him yet more honourable service, for the day was to come when he should witness for God not only in the presence of Ahab, but he should discomfit and utterly rout the assembled hosts of Baal and, in measure at least, turn the wandering nation back again unto the God of their fathers. But the time for that was not ripe; neither was Elijah himself.

The prophet needed further training in secret if he was to be personally fitted to speak again for God in public. Ah, my reader, the man whom the Lord uses has to be kept low: severe discipline has to be experienced by him, if the flesh is to be duly mortified. Three more years must be spent by the prophet in seclusion. How humbling! Alas, how little is man to be trusted: how little is he able to bear being put into the place of honour! How quickly self rises to the surface, and the instrument is ready to believe he is something more than an instrument! How sadly easy it is to make of the very service God entrusts us with a pedestal on which to display ourselves. But God will not share His glory with another, and therefore does He 'hide' those who may be tempted to take some of it unto themselves. It is only by retiring from the public view and getting alone with God that we can learn our own nothingness.

We see this important lesson brought out plainly in Christ's dealings with His beloved apostles. On one occasion they returned to Him flushed with success and full of themselves: they 'told Him all things, both what they had done, and what they had taught,' Mark 6. 30. Most instructive is His quiet response: 'And He said unto them, Come ye yourselves apart into a desert place, and rest a while,' v. 31. This is still His gracious remedy for any of His servants who may be puffed up with their own importance, and imagine that His cause upon earth would suffer a severe loss if *they* were removed from it. God often says to His servants, 'Get thee hence . . . hide thyself': sometimes it is by the dashing of their ministerial hopes, sometimes by a bed of affliction or by a severe bereavement, the Divine purpose is accomplished. Happy the one who can then say from his heart, 'The will of the Lord be done.'

Every servant that God deigns to use must pass through the trying experience of Cherith before he is ready for the triumph of Carmel. This is an unchanging principle in the ways of God. Joseph suffered the indignities of both the pit and the prison before he became governor of all Egypt, second only to the king himself. Moses spent one third of his long life at 'the backside of the desert' before Jehovah gave him the honour of leading His people out of the house of bondage. David had to learn the sufficiency of God's power on the farm before he went forth and slew Goliath in the sight of the assembled armies of Israel and the Philistines. Thus it was, too, with the perfect Servant: thirty years of seclusion and silence before He began His brief public ministry. So too with the chief of His ambassadors: a season in the solitudes of Arabia was his apprenticeship before he became the apostle to the Gentiles.

But is there not yet another angle from which we may contemplate this seemingly strange order, 'Get thee hence . . . hide thyself'? Was it not a very real and severe testing of the prophet's *submissiveness* unto the Divine will? 'Severe' we say, for to a robust man this request was much more exacting than his appearing before Ahab: one with a zealous disposition would find it much harder to spend three years in inactive seclusion than to be engaged in public service. The present writer can testify from long and painful experience that to be removed 'into a corner,' Isa. 30. 20, is a much severer trial than to address large congregations every night month after month. In the case of Elijah this lesson is obvious: he must learn personally to render implicit obedience unto the Lord before he was qualified to command others in His name.

Let us now take a closer look at the particular *place* selected by God as the one where His servant was next to sojourn: 'by the brook Cherith.' Ah, it was a brook and not a river – a brook which might dry up any moment. It is rare that God places His servants, or even His people, in the midst of luxury and abundance: to be surfeited with the things of this world only too often means the drawing away of the affections from the giver Himself. 'How hardly shall they that have riches enter into the kingdom of God!' It is our *hearts* God requires, and often this is put to the proof. The way in which temporal losses are borne generally makes manifest the difference between the real Christian and the worldling. The latter is utterly cast down by financial reverses, and frequently commits suicide. Why? Because his *all* has gone and there is nothing left to live for. In contrast, the genuine believer may be severely shaken and for a time deeply depressed, but he will recover his poise and say, 'God is still my portion and I shall not want.'

Instead of a river, God often gives us a brook, which may be running today and dried up tomorrow. Why? To teach us not to rest in our blessings, but in the blesser Himself. Yet is it not at this very point that we so often fail – our hearts being far more occupied with the gifts than with the giver. Is not this just the reason why the Lord will not trust us with a river? – because it would unconsciously take His place in our hearts. "Jeshurun waxed fat, and kicked: thou art waxen fat, thou art grown thick, thou art covered with fatness; *then* he forsook God which made him, and lightly esteemed the Rock of his salvation,' Deut. 32. 15. And the same evil tendency exists within *us*. We sometimes feel that we are being hardly dealt with because God gives us a brook rather than a river, but this is because we are so little acquainted with our own hearts. God loves His own too well to place dangerous knives in the hands of infants.

And how was the prophet to subsist in such a place? Where was his food to come from? Ah, God will see to that: He will provide for his maintenance: 'And it shall be, that thou shalt drink of the brook,' v. 4. Whatever may be the case with Ahab and his idolators, Elijah shall not perish. In the very worst of times God will show Himself strong on the behalf of His own. Whoever starves they shall be fed: 'Bread shall be given him; his waters shall be sure,' Isa. 33. 16. Yet how absurd it sounds to common sense to bid a man tarry indefinitely by a brook! Yes, but it was *God* who had given this order, and the Divine commands are not to be argued about but obeyed. Thereby Elijah was bidden to trust God contrary to sight, to reason, to all outward appearances, to rest in the Lord Himself and wait patiently for Him.

'I have commanded the ravens to feed thee *there*,' v. 4. Observe the word we have placed in italics. The prophet might have preferred many another hiding-place, but to Cherith he must go if he was to receive the Divine supplies: as long as he tarried there, God was pledged to provide for him. How important, then, is the question, Am I in the place which God has (by His Word or providence) assigned me? If so, He will assuredly supply my every need. But if like the younger son I turn my back upon Him and journey into the far country, then like that prodigal I shall certainly suffer want. How many a servant of God has laboured in some lowly or difficult sphere with the dew of the Spirit on his soul and the blessing of Heaven on his ministry, when there came an invitation from some other field which seemed to offer a wider scope (and a larger salary!), and as he yielded to the temptation, the Spirit was grieved and his usefulness in God's kingdom was at an end.

The same principle applies with equal force to the rank and file of God's people: they must be 'in the way,' Gen. 24. 27, of God's appointing if they are to receive Divine supplies. 'Thy will be done' precedes 'Give us this day our daily bread.' But how many professing Christians have we personally known who resided in a town whither God sent one of His own qualified servants, who fed them with 'the finest of the wheat,' and their souls prospered. Then came a tempting business offer from some distant place, which would improve their position in the world. The offer was accepted, their tent was removed, only to enter a spiritual wilderness where there was no edifying ministry available. In consequence their souls were starved, their testimony for Christ ruined, and a period of fruitless backsliding ensued. As Israel had to follow the cloud of old in order to obtain supplies of manna, so must we be in the place of God's ordering if our souls are to be watered and our spiritual lives prospered.

Let us next view *the instruments* selected by God to minister unto the bodily needs of His servant. 'I have commanded the ravens to feed thee.' Various lines of thought are hereby suggested. First, see here both the high sovereignty and the absolute supremacy of God; His sovereignty in the choice made, His supremacy in His power to make it good. He is a law unto Himself: 'Whatsoever the Lord pleased, that did He in heaven, and in earth, in the seas, and all deep places,' Psa. 135. 6. He prohibited His people from eating ravens, classifying them among the unclean, yea, to be 'an abomination' to them, Lev. 11. 15; Deut. 14. 14. Yet He Himself made use of them to carry food unto His servant. How different are God's ways from ours! He employed Pharaoh's own daughter to succour the infant Moses, and a Balaam to utter one of His most remarkable prophecies. He used the jaw-bone of an ass in the hand of Samson to slay the Philistines, and a sling and stone to vanquish their champion.

'I have commanded the ravens to feed thee.' O what a God is ours! The fowls of the air and the fishes of the sea, the wild beasts of the field, yea, the very winds and waves obey Him. Yes, 'Thus saith the Lord, which maketh a way in the sea, and a path in the mighty waters; which bringeth forth the chariot and horse, the army and the power . . . Behold, I will do a new thing; now it shall spring forth; shall ye not know it? I will even make a way in the wilderness, and rivers in the desert. The beast of the field shall honour me, the dragons and the owls – yes, and the ravens too! – because I give waters in the wilderness, and rivers in the desert, to give drink to my people,' Isa. 43. 16-20. Thus the Lord caused birds of prey, which lived on carrion, to feed the prophet.

But let us also admire here the *wisdom* as well as the power of God. Elijah's fare was provided for partly in a natural and partly in a supernatural way. There was water in the brook, so he could easily go and fetch it. God will work no miracles to spare a man trouble, or that he should be listless and lazy, making no effort to procure his own sustenance. But there was no food in the desert: how is he to get that? God will furnish this in a miraculous manner: 'I have commanded the ravens to feed thee.' Had human beings been used to take him food, they might have divulged his hiding-place. Had a dog or some domestic animal gone each morning and evening, people might have seen this regular journeying to and fro, carrying food, and so been curious, and investigated the same. But *birds* flying with flesh into the desert would arouse no suspicion: it would be concluded they were taking it to their young. See then how careful God is of His people, how judicious in the arrangements He makes for them. He knows what would endanger their safety and provides accordingly.

'Hide thyself by the brook Cherith ... I have commanded the ravens to feed thee there.' Go immediately, without entertaining any doubts, without any hesitation. However contrary to their natural instincts, these birds of prey shall obey the Divine behest. Nor need this appear in the least unlikely. God Himself created them, gave them their peculiar instinct, and He knows how to direct and control the same. He has power to suspend or check it, according to His good pleasure. Nature is exactly what God made it, and entirely dependent upon Him for its continuance. He upholds all things by the word of His power. In Him and by Him the birds and beasts, as well as man, live, move and have their being; and therefore He can, whenever He thinks fit, either suspend or alter the law which He has imposed upon any of His creatures. 'Why should it be thought a thing incredible with you, that God should raise the dead?' Acts 26. 8.

There in his lowly retreat the prophet was called upon to sojourn many days, yet not without a precious promise guaranteeing his sustenance: the supply of needed provision was Divinely assured him. The Lord would take care of His servant while hid from public view, and would daily feed him by His miracle-working power. Nevertheless, it was a real testing of Elijah's *faith*. Whoever heard of such instruments being employed – birds of prey bringing food in a time of famine! Could the ravens be depended upon? Was it not far more likely that they would devour the food themselves than bring it to the prophet? Ah, his trust was not to be in the birds, but in the sure word of Him that cannot lie: '*I* have commanded the ravens.' It was the Creator and not the creature, the Lord Himself and not the instruments, Elijah's heart was to be fixed upon. How blessed to be lifted above 'circumstances' and in the inerrant promise of God have a sure proof of His care.

CHAPTER FIVE

The Drying Brook

'Get thee hence, and turn thee eastward, and hide thyself by the brook Cherith, that is before Jordan. And it shall be, that thou shalt drink of the brook; and I have commanded the ravens to feed thee there,' 1 Kings 17. 3, 4. Notice well the order here: first the Divine command, and then the precious promise: Elijah must comply with the Divine behest if he was to be supernaturally fed. Most of God's promises are conditional ones. And does not this explain why many of us do not extract the good of them, because we fail to comply with their stipulations? God will not put a premium on either unbelief or disobedience. Alas, we are our own worst enemies, and lose much by our perversity. We sought to show in our last chapter that the arrangement here made by God displayed His high sovereignty, His all-sufficient power, and His blessed wisdom; as it also made a demand upon the prophet's submissiveness and faith. We turn now to the sequel.

'So he went and did according unto the word of the Lord: for he went and dwelt by the brook Cherith, that is before Jordan,' v. 5. Not only did God's injunction to Elijah supply a real test of his submission and faith, but it also made a severe demand upon his *humility*. Had pride been in the ascendant he would have said, 'Why should I follow such a course? It would be playing the coward's part to "hide" myself. I am not afraid of Ahab, so I shall not go into seclusion.' Ah, my reader, some of God's commands are quite humiliating to haughty flesh and blood. It may not have struck His disciples as a valorous policy to pursue when Christ bade them 'when they persecute you in this city, *flee ye* into another,' Matt. 10. 23; nevertheless, such were His orders, and He must be obeyed. And why should any servant of His demur at such a command as 'hide thyself,' when of the Master Himself we read that 'Jesus hid Himself,' John 8. 59. Ah, He has left us an example in all things.

Furthermore, compliance with the Divine command would be quite a tax on the *social* side of Elijah's nature. There are few who can endure solitude: to be cut off from their fellows would indeed prove a severe trial to most people. Unconverted men cannot live without company: the conviviality of those like-minded is necessary if they are to silence an uneasy conscience and banish troublesome thoughts. And is it much different with the great majority even of professing Christians? 'Lo, I am with you alway' has little real meaning to most of us. How different the contentment, joy, and usefulness of Bunyan in prison and Madame Guyon in her solitary confinement! Ah, Elijah might be cut off from his fellows, but not from the Lord Himself.

'So he went and did according unto the word of the Lord.' Without hesitation or delay the prophet complied with God's command. Blessed subjection to the Divine will was this: to deliver Jehovah's message unto the king himself, or to be dependent upon ravens, he was equally ready. However unreasonable the precept might appear or however unpleasant the prospect, the Tishbite promptly carried it out. How different was this from the prophet Jonah, who fled from the word of the Lord; yes, and how different the sequel – the one imprisoned for three days and nights in the whale's belly, the other, at the end, taken to Heaven without passing through the portals of death! God's servants are not all alike, either in faith, obedience or fruitfulness. O that all of us may be as prompt in our obedience to the Lord's Word as Elijah was.

'So he went and did according unto the word of the Lord.' The prophet neither delayed in complying with the Divine directions nor did he doubt that God would supply all his need. Happy it is when we can obey Him in difficult circumstances and trust Him in the dark. But why should we not place implicit confidence in God and rely upon His word of promise? Is anything too hard for the Lord? Has His word of promise ever failed? Then let us not entertain any unbelieving suspicions of His future care of us. Heaven and earth shall pass away, but not so His promises. God's dealings with Elijah have been recorded for *our* instruction: O that they may speak loudly to our hearts, rebuking our wicked distrust and moving us to cry in earnest, 'Lord, increase our faith.' The God of Elijah still lives, and fails none who count upon His faithfulness.

'So he went and *did* according unto the word of the Lord.' Elijah not only preached God's Word, but he practised it. This is the crying need of our times. There is a great deal of talking, but little of walking according to the Divine precepts. There is much activity in the religious realm, but only too often it is unauthorized by, and in numerous instances contrary to, the Divine statutes. 'But be ye *doers* of the word, and not hearers only, deceiving your own selves,' James 1. 22, is the unfailing requirement of Him with whom we have to do. To obey is better than sacrifice, and to hearken than the fat of rams. 'Little children, let no man deceive you: he that *doeth* righteousness is righteous,' 1 John 3. 7. Alas, how many are deceived at this very point: they prate about righteousness, but fail to practise it. 'Not every one that saith unto Me, Lord, Lord, shall enter into the kingdom of heaven; but he that *doeth* the will of My Father which is in heaven,' Matt. 7. 21.

'And the ravens brought him bread and flesh in the morning, and bread and flesh in the evening, and he drank of the brook,' v. 6. What proof was this that 'He is faithful that promised,' Heb. 10. 23! All nature shall change her course rather than one of His promises fail. O what comfort is there here for trusting hearts: what God has promised, He will certainly perform. How excuseless is our unbelief, how unspeakably wicked our doubtings. How much of our distrust is the consequence of the Divine promises not being sufficiently real and definite unto our minds. Do we meditate as we ought upon the promises of the Lord? If we were more fully 'acquainted' with Him, Job 22. 21, if we 'set Him' more definitely before our hearts, Psa. 16. 8, would not His promises have far more weight and power with us?

'My God shall supply all your need according to His riches in glory by Christ Jesus,' Phil. 4. 19. It is profitless to ask, *How?* The Lord has ten thousand ways of making good His word. Some reader of this very paragraph may be living from hand to mouth, having no stock of money or store of victuals: yea, not knowing where the next meal will come from. But if you be a child of His, God will not fail you, and if your trust be in Him, it shall not be disappointed. In some way or other 'The Lord will provide.' 'O fear the Lord, ye His saints: for there is no want to them that fear Him. The young lions do lack, and suffer hunger: but they that seek the Lord shall not want any good thing,' Psa. 34. 9, 10; 'Seek ye first the kingdom of God, and His righteousness; and all these things (food and clothing) shall be added unto you,' Matt. 6. 33. These promises are addressed *to us*, to encourage us to cleave unto God and do His will.

'And the ravens brought him bread and flesh in the morning, and bread and flesh in the evening.' Had He so pleased, the Lord could have fed Elijah by angels rather than by ravens. There was then in Israel a hospitable Obadiah, who kept a secret table in a cave for a hundred of God's prophets, 18. 4. Moreover, there were seven thousand faithful Israelites who had not bowed the knee to Baal, any one of whom would have doubtless deemed himself highly honoured to have sustained so eminent a one as Elijah. But God preferred to make use of fowls of the air. Why? Was it not so as to give both the Tishbite and us a signal proof of His absolute command over all creatures, and thereby of His worthiness to be trusted in the greatest extremities? And what is the more striking is this: that Elijah was better fed than the prophets who were sustained by Obadiah, for they had only 'bread and water,' 18. 4, whereas Elijah had meat also.

Though God may not employ literal ravens in ministering unto His needy servants and people today, yet He often works just as definitely and wondrously in disposing the selfish, the covetous, the hard-hearted, and the grossly immoral to render assistance to His own. He can and often does induce them, contrary to their natural dispositions and miserly habits, to deal kindly and liberally in ministering to our necessities. He has the hearts of all in His hand and turneth them whithersoever He will, Prov. 21, 1. What thanks are due unto the Lord for sending His provisions by such instruments! We doubt not that quite a number of our readers could bear similar testimony to that of the present writer when he says: How often in the past did God in the most unlooked-for manner provide for our necessities: we had as soon expected ravens to bring us food as that we should receive from those who actually bestowed it.

'And the ravens brought him bread and flesh in the morning, and bread and flesh in the evening.' Observe, no vegetables, fruit, or sweets are mentioned. There were no luxuries, but simply the bare necessities. 'Having food and raiment let us be therewith content,' 1 Tim. 6. 8. But are we? Alas, how little of this godly contentment is now seen, even among the Lord's people. How many of them set their hearts upon the things which the godless make idols of. Why are our young people dissatisfied with the standard of comfort which sufficed their parents? Self must be denied if we are to show ourselves followers of Him who had not where to lay His head.

'And he drank of the brook,' v. 6. Let us not overlook this clause, for no detail in Scripture is meaningless. Water in the brook was as truly and as definitely a provision of God's as the bread and meat which the ravens brought. Has not the Holy Spirit recorded this detail for the purpose of teaching us that the common mercies of providence (as we term them) are also the gift of God. If we have been supplied with what is needful to sustain our bodies, then gratitude and acknowledgment are due to our God. And yet how many there are, even among professing Christians, who sit down to their meals *without* first asking God's blessing, and rising up therefrom without thanking Him for what they have had. In this matter, too, Christ has left us an example, for on the occasion of His feeding the multitude, we are told that 'Jesus took the loaves; and when He had given thanks, He distributed to the disciples,' John 6. 11. Then let us not fail to do the same.

'And it came to pass after a while, that the brook dried up, because there had been no rain in the land,' v. 7. Weigh attentively these five words: 'And it came to pass.' They mean far more than that it merely happened: they signify that the Divine decree concerning the same was now fulfilled. 'It came to pass' in the good providence of God, who orders all things after the counsel of His own will, and without whose personal permission nothing occurs, not even the falling of a sparrow to the ground, Matt. 10. 29. How this should comfort the children of God and assure them of their security. There is no such thing as chance with reference to God – wherever this term occurs in the Bible it is always in connection with man, referring to something taking place without his design. Everything which occurs in this world is just as God ordained from the beginning, Acts 2. 23. Endeavour to recall that fact, dear reader, the next time you are in difficulty and distress. If you are one of God's people He has provided for every contingency in His 'Everlasting Covenant' and His mercies are *sure,* 2 Sam. 23. 5; Isa. 55. 3.

'And after a while' or (margin) 'at the end of days.' By this expression Lightfoot understood 'after a year,' which is frequently the sense of that phrase in Scripture. However this may be, after an interval of some duration the brook dried up. Krummacher declares that the very name Cherith denotes 'drought,' as though it usually dried up more quickly than any other brook. Most probably it was a mountain stream, which flowed down a narrow ravine. Water was supplied it by the way of nature or ordinary providence, but the course of nature was now altered. The purpose of God was accomplished and the time of the prophet's departure unto another hiding place had arrived. The drying up of the brook was a forceful reminder to Elijah of the transitoriness of everything mundane. 'The fashion of this world passeth away,' 1 Cor. 7. 31, and therefore 'here have we no continuing city,' Heb. 13. 14. Change and decay is stamped upon everything down here: there is nothing stable under the sun. We should therefore be prepared for sudden changes in our circumstances.

The ravens, as heretofore, brought the prophet flesh and bread to eat each morning and evening, but he could not subsist without water. But why should not God supply the water in a miraculous way, as He did the food? Most certainly He could have done so. He could have brought water out of the rock, as He did for Israel, and for Samson out of a jawbone, Judg. 15. 18, 19. Yes, but the Lord is not confined to any one method, but has a variety of ways in bringing the same end to pass. God sometimes works one way and sometimes another, employing this means today and that tomorrow, in accomplishing His counsels. God is sovereign and acts not according to rule and rote. He ever acts according to His own good pleasure, and this He does in order to display His all-sufficiency, to exhibit His manifold wisdom, and to demonstrate the greatness of His power. God is not tied and if He closes one door He can easily open another.

'That the brook dried up.' Cherith would not flow for ever, no, not even for the prophet. Elijah himself must be made to feel the awfulness of that calamity which he had announced. Ah, my reader, it is no uncommon thing for God to suffer His own dear children to become enwrapped in the common calamities of offenders. True, He makes a real difference both in the use and the issue of their stripes, but not so in the infliction of them. We are living in a world which is under the curse of a Holy God, and therefore 'man is born unto trouble as the sparks fly upward.' Nor is there any escape from trouble so long as we are left in this scene. God's own people, though the objects of the everlasting love, are not exempted, for 'many are the afflictions of the righteous.' Why? For various reasons and with various designs: one of them being to wean our hearts from things below and cause us to set our affection on things above.

'The brook dried up.' To outward appearance that would have seemed a real misfortune, to carnal reason an actual calamity. Let us endeavour to visualize Elijah there at Cherith. The drought was everywhere, the famine throughout the whole land: and now his own brook began to dry up. Day by day its waters gradually lessened until soon there was barely a trickle, and then it entirely ceased. Had he grown increasingly anxious and gloomy? Did he say, What shall I do? Must I stay here and perish? Has God forgotten me? Did I take a wrong step, after all, in coming here? It all depended upon how steadily his *faith* remained in exercise. If faith was active, then he admired the goodness of God in causing that supply of water to last so long. How much better for our souls, if instead of mourning over our losses, we praise God for continuing His mercies to us so long – especially when we bear in mind they are only *lent* to us, and that we deserve not the least of them.

Though dwelling in the place of God's appointing, yet Elijah is not exempted from those deep exercises of soul which are ever the necessary discipline of a life of faith. True, the ravens had, in obedience to the Divine command, paid him their daily visits, supplying him with food morning and evening, and the brook had flowed on its tranquil course. But faith must be tested – and developed. The servant of God must not settle down on his lees, but pass from form to form in the school of the Lord; and having learned (through grace) the difficult lessons of one, he must now go forward to grapple with others yet more difficult. Perhaps the reader may now be facing the drying brook of popularity, of failing health, of diminishing business, of decreasing friendships. Ah, a drying brook is a real trouble.

Why does God suffer the brook to dry up? To teach us to trust in Himself, and not in His gifts. As a general rule He does not for long provide for His people in the same way and by the same means, lest they should rest in *them* and expect help from them. Sooner or later God shows us how dependent we are upon *Himself* even for supplies of every-day mercies. But the heart of the prophet must be tested, to show whether his trust was in Cherith or in the living God. So it is in His dealings with us. How often we *think* we are trusting in the Lord, when really we are resting on comfortable circumstances; and when they become uncomfortable, how much faith have we?

CHAPTER SIX

Directed to Zarephath

'He that believeth shall not make haste,' Isa. 28. 16. This is a rule which it is both our wisdom and welfare to heed in all the varied details of our lives – never more needed by God's people than in this mad age of speed and hurry. Most profitably may we apply it to our reading and study of God's Word. It is not so much the amount of time we spend upon the Scriptures, as the measure in which we prayerfully *meditate* upon that which is immediately before us, that so largely determines the degree of benefit the soul receives therefrom. By passing too quickly from one verse to another, by failing to picture vividly before our minds the details before us, and by not taking pains to discover the practical lessons which may be drawn from historical events, we are greatly the losers. It is by putting ourselves in the position of the one we are reading about and thinking what we would most likely have done in such circumstances, that we receive the most help.

An illustration of what we have in view in the above paragraph is supplied by the stage we have now reached in the life of Elijah. At the close of our last chapter we had arrived at the point where, 'It came to pass after a while, that the brook *dried up*': let us not be in too big a hurry to turn unto what follows: rather should we endeavour to visualize the prophet's situation and ponder the trial which confronted him. Picture the Tishbite there in his lowly retreat. Day by day the water in the brook steadily diminished: did his hopes do likewise? Did his songs of worship become feebler and less frequent as the streamlet rolled less noisily over its rocky bed? Was his harp hung upon the willows as he gave himself up to anxious thought and restlessly paced to and fro? There is nothing in Scripture to intimate any such thing. God keeps in perfect peace the one whose mind is stayed upon Himself. Yes, but in order thereto, the heart must steadfastly confide in Him.

Ah, that is the very point: do we *trust the Lord* in trying circumstances, or are we merely 'fair-weather Christians'? It is much to be feared that had *we* been there by the drying brook, our minds had been distracted, and instead of waiting patiently for the Lord, had fretted and schemed, wondering what we had better do next. And then one morning Elijah awoke to find the brook altogether dried up and his supply of sustenance completely cut off! What then should he do? Must he remain there and perish? for he could not expect to live long without something to drink. Must he not now take matters into his own hands and do the best he could for himself? Would it not be better to retract his steps and risk the vengeance of Ahab than remain where he was and die of thirst? Can we doubt that Satan plied him with such temptations in his hour of testing?

The Lord had ordered him, 'hide thyself by the brook Cherith,' adding, 'I have commanded the ravens to feed thee *there*'; and it is striking and blessed to see that he *remained* there even after his supply of water had ceased. The prophet did not move his quarters until he received definite instruction from the Lord to do so. It was thus with Israel of old in the wilderness, as they journeyed to the promised land: 'At the commandment of the Lord the children of Israel journeyed, and at the commandment of the Lord they pitched: as long as the cloud abode upon the tabernacle they rested in their tents. And when the cloud tarried *long* upon the tabernacle many days, then the children of Israel kept the charge of the Lord, and *journeyed not*. And so it was, when the cloud was a few days upon the tabernacle; according to the commandment of the Lord they abode in their tents, and according to the commandment of the Lord they journeyed. And so it was, when the cloud abode from even unto the morning, and that the cloud was taken up in the morning, then they journeyed: whether it was by day or by night . . . two days, or a month, *or a year* . . . the children of Israel abode in their tents and journeyed not,' Num. 9. 18-22. And that is expressly recorded for *our* instruction and comfort, and it is both our wisdom and welfare to heed the same.

'And the word of the Lord came unto him, saying, Arise, get thee to Zarephath,' 1 Kings 17. 8, 9. Did not this show plainly how worthless and needless was any carnal scheming on the part of the prophet, had he indulged in such? God had *not* 'forgotten to be gracious,' nor would He leave His servant without the needed direction or guidance when His time had arrived to grant the same. How loudly ought this to speak unto our hearts – we who are far too full of our *own* plans and devisings. Instead of heeding that injunction, 'My soul, wait thou only upon God,' we contrive some way of getting out of our difficulties and then ask the Lord to prosper the same. If a Samuel does not arrive just when we expect, then we try to force things, 1 Sam. 13. 12.

Let it be duly noted, however, that before God's word came afresh to Elijah both his faith and his patience had been put to the proof. In going to Cherith the prophet had acted under Divine orders, and therefore was he under God's special care. Could he, then, come to any real harm under such guardianship? He must therefore remain where he is until God directs him to leave the place, no matter how unpleasant conditions may become. So with us. When it is clear that God has placed us where we are, there we must 'abide,' 1 Cor. 7. 20, even though our continuance in it be attended with hardships and apparent hazard. If, on the other hand, Elijah had left Cherith of his own accord, how could he count upon the Lord being with him both to provide for his wants and to deliver him from his enemies? The same applies to us with equal force today.

We are now to consider the further provision which the Lord graciously made for His servant in his retirement. 'And the word of the Lord came unto him.' How often has His word come to us: sometimes directly, sometimes through one of His servants, and we have wickedly refused to obey it. If not in actual words, our ways have been like that of the rebellious Jews, who in response to the affectionate remonstrance of Jeremiah replied, 'As for the word that thou hast spoken unto us in the name of the Lord, we will not hearken unto thee,' 44. 16. On other occasions we have been like those spoken of in Ezekiel 33. 21, 32, 'They sit before thee as My people, and they hear thy words, but they will not do them: for with their mouth they shew much love, but their heart goeth after their covetousness. And, lo, thou art unto them as a very lovely song, of one that hath a pleasant voice, and can play well on an instrument: for they hear thy words, but they *do them not.*' And why? Because the Word of God crosses our perverse wills and requires what is contrary to our natural inclinations.

'And the word of the Lord came unto him, saying, Arise, get thee to Zarephath, which belongeth to Zidon, and dwell there,' vv. 8, 9. This meant that Elijah must be disciplined by still further trials and humblings. First of all, the name of the place to which God ordered His servant to go is deeply suggestive, for 'Zarephath' means 'refining,' coming from a root that signifies a crucible – the place where metals are melted. There lay before Elijah not only a further testing of his faith, but also the *refining* of it, for a 'crucible' is for the purpose of separating dross from the fine gold. The experience which now confronted our prophet was a very trying and distasteful one to flesh and blood, for to go from Cherith to Zarephath involved a journey of seventy-five miles across the desert. Ah, the place of refining is not easily reached and involves that from which all of us naturally shrink.

It is also to be carefully noted that Zarephath was 'in Zidon': that is to say, it was in the territory of the Gentiles, outside the land of Palestine. Our Lord threw emphasis on this detail (in His first recorded public address) as being one of the earliest intimations of the favours which God purposed to extend unto the Gentiles, saying, 'there were many widows in Israel' at that time, Luke 4. 25, 26, who might (or might not) have gladly sheltered and succoured the prophet; but unto none of them was he sent – what a severe reflection on the chosen nation, to pass them by! But what is yet more remarkable is the fact that 'Zidon' was the very place from which Jezebel, the wicked corrupter of Israel, had come, 1 Kings 16. 31! How passing strange are the ways of God, yet ever ordered by infinite wisdom! As Matthew Henry says, 'To show Jezebel the impotency of her malice, God will find a hiding-place for His servant even in her country.'

Equally striking is it to observe the particular person whom God selected to entertain Elijah. It was not a rich merchant or one of the chief men of Zidon, but a poor widow – desolate and dependent – who was made both willing and able to minister unto him. It is usually God's way, and to His glory, to make use of and place honour upon 'the weak and foolish things of the world.' In commenting upon the 'ravens' which brought bread and flesh to the prophet while he sojourned by the brook, we called attention to the sovereignty of God and the strangeness of the instruments He is pleased to employ. The same truth is vividly illustrated here: a poor widow! a Gentile! dwelling in Zidon, the original home of Jezebel! Think it not strange then, my reader, if God's dealings with you have been the very opposite of what *you* had expected. The Lord is a law to Himself, and implicit trust and unreserved submission is what He requires from us.

'Behold, I have commanded a widow woman there to sustain thee,' v. 9. Man's extremity is God's opportunity: when Cherith is dried up then shall Zarephath be opened. How this should teach us to refrain from carking care about the future. Remember, dear reader, that tomorrow will bring with it tomorrow's God. 'Fear thou not; for I am with thee; be not dismayed; for I am thy God: I will strengthen thee; yea, I will help thee; yea, I will uphold thee with the right hand of My righteousness,' Isa. 41. 10: make these sure and certain promises – for they are the Word of Him that cannot lie – the stay of your soul; make them your reply to every question of unbelief and every foul aspersion of the Devil. Observe that once more God sent Elijah not to a river but a 'brook' – not to some wealthy person with great resources, but to a poor widow with scanty means. Ah, the Lord would have His servant remain a pensioner upon Himself and as much dependent on *His* power and goodness as before.

This was indeed a severe testing of Elijah, not only to take a long journey through the desert but to enter into an experience

[55]

which was entirely opposed to his natural feelings, his religious training and spiritual inclinations – to be made dependent upon a Gentile in a heathen city. He was required to leave the land of his fathers and sojourn at the headquarters of Baal-worship. Let us duly weigh this truth that God's plan for Elijah demanded from him unquestioning *obedience*. They who would walk with God must not only trust Him implicitly but be prepared to be entirely regulated by His Word. Not only must our faith be trained by a great variety of providences, but our obedience by the Divine commandments. Vain is it to suppose that we can enjoy the smile of Jehovah unless we be in subjection to His precepts. 'Behold, to obey is better than sacrifice, and to hearken than the fat of rams,' 1 Sam. 15. 22. Directly we become disobedient our communion with God is broken and chastisement becomes our portion.

Elijah must go and dwell at Zarephath. But how could he subsist there when he knew no one in that place? Why, the same One who had given him this order had also made arrangements for his reception and maintenance. 'Behold, I have commanded a widow woman there to sustain thee.' This does not necessarily mean that the Lord had acquainted her with His mind – the sequel plainly shows otherwise. Rather do we understand these words to signify that God had appointed it in His counsels and would effect it by His providences – compare His 'I have commanded the ravens to feed thee,' v. 4. When God calls any of His people to go to a place, they may rest assured that He has fully provided for them in His foredetermined purpose. God secretly disposed this widow to receive and sustain His servant. All hearts are in the Lord's hand and He turneth them whithersoever He pleases. He can incline them to show us favour and do us acts of kindness, even though we be entire strangers to them. Many times, in widely different parts of the world, has this been the experience of the writer.

Not only was the faith and obedience of Elijah tested by God's call for him to go to Zarephath, but his *humility* was also put to the proof. He was called to receive charity at the hands of a desolate widow. How humbling to pride to be made dependent upon one of the poorest of the poor. How withering to all self-confidence and self-sufficiency to accept relief from one who did not appear to have sufficient for her own urgent needs! Ah, it takes pressure of circumstances to make us bow to what is repugnant to our natural inclinations. More than once in the past did we feel it acutely to receive gifts and succour from those who had little of this world's goods, but we were comforted by the word, 'And certain women, which had been healed of evil spirits and infirmities . . . and many others which ministered unto *Him* of their substance,' Luke 8. 2, 3. The 'widow' speaks of weakness and desolation: Israel was widowed at this time and therefore Elijah was made to feel it in his own soul.

'So he arose and went to Zarephath,' v. 10. In this Elijah gave proof that he was indeed the servant of God, for the path of a *servant* is the path of obedience: let him forsake that path and he ceases to be a servant. The servant and obedience are as inseparably linked together as the workman and work. Many today talk about their service *for* Christ, as though He needed their assistance, as though His cause would not prosper unless they patronized and furthered it – as though the holy ark must inevitably fall to the ground unless their unholy hands uphold it. This is all wrong, seriously wrong – the product of Satan-fed pride. What is so much needed (by us!) is service *to* Christ, submission to His yoke, surrender to His will, subjection to His commandments. Any 'Christian service' other than walking in His precepts is a human invention, fleshly energy, 'strange fire.'

'So he arose and went to Zarephath.' How can I minister the holy things of God unless I be myself treading the path of obedience? The Jew of Paul's day was very self-important, yet he brought no glory unto God. 'And art confident that thou thyself art a guide of the blind, a light of them which are in darkness, an instructor of the foolish,' Rom. 2. 19, 20. And then the apostle puts him to the test: 'Thou therefore which teachest another, teachest thou not thyself? thou that preachest a man should not steal, dost thou steal?' v. 21. The principle there enunciated is a searching one of wide application. By it each of us who preach the Gospel should diligently measure himself. Thou that preachest that God requireth truth in the inward parts, art thou a man of thy word? Thou that teachest we should provide things honest in the sight of all men, hast thou any unpaid debts? Thou that exhortest believers to be importunate in prayer, spendest thou much time in the secret place? If not, be not surprised if thy sermons meet with little response.

From the pastoral peace of Gilead to the exacting ordeal of confronting the king: from the presence of Ahab to the solitude of Cherith: from the dried-up brook to Zarephath. The disturbances and displacements of Providence are a necessity if our spiritual lives are to prosper. 'Moab hath been at ease from his youth, and he hath settled on his lees, and hath not been emptied from vessel to vessel,' Jer. 48. 11. The figure used here is suggestive. Because Moab had long been at peace she had become lethargic and flabby. Or, like grapejuice unrefined, she had been spoiled. God was emptying Elijah 'from vessel to vessel' so that the scum might rise to the surface and be removed. This stirring of our nest, this constant changing of our circumstances, is not a pleasant experience, but it is essential if we are to be preserved from 'settling on our lees.' But alas, so far from appreciating the gracious designs of the Refiner, how often we are petulant, and murmur when He empties us from vessel to vessel.

'So he arose and went to Zarephath.' He made no demur, but did as he was bid. He made no delay, but set off on his long and unpleasant journey at once. He was as ready to go on foot as though God had provided a chariot. He was as ready to cross a desert as if God had bidden him luxuriate in a shady garden. He was as ready to apply for succour from a Gentile widow as if God had told him to return to his friends in Gilead. It might appear to carnal reason that he was putting his head into the lion's mouth – courting certain disaster by making for the land of Zidon, where the agents of Jezebel would be numerous. But since God had bidden him to go, it was right for him to comply (and wrong not to do so), and therefore he could count upon the Divine protection.

Let it be duly noted that the Lord gave Elijah no more information as to his future residence and maintenance than that it was to be at Zarephath and by a widow. In a time of famine we should be profoundly thankful that the Lord provides for us at all, and be quite content to leave the mode of doing so with Him. If the Lord undertakes to guide us in our life's journey, we must be satisfied with His doing it step by step. It is rarely His way to reveal to us much beforehand. In most cases we know little or nothing in advance. How can it be otherwise if we are to walk by *faith!* We must trust Him implicitly for the full development of His plan concerning us. But if we are really walking with God, taking heed to our ways according to His Word, He will gradually make things plain. His providences will clear up our difficulties, and what we know not now we shall know hereafter. Thus it was with Elijah.

CHAPTER SEVEN

A Widow's Extremity

'And the word of the Lord came unto him, saying, Arise, get thee to Zarephath, which belongeth to Zidon, and dwell there: behold, I have commanded a widow woman there to sustain thee,' 1 Kings 17. 8, 9. Notice carefully the connection between these two verses. The spiritual significance of this may be the more apparent to the reader if we state it thus: our actions must be regulated by the Word of God if our souls are to be nourished and strengthened. That was one of the outstanding lessons taught Israel in the wilderness: their food and refreshment could only be obtained so long as they travelled in the path of obedience, (Num. 9. 18-23 – observe well the seven-fold 'at the commandment of the Lord' in that passage). God's people of old were not allowed to have any plans of their own: the Lord arranged everything for them – when they should journey and when they should encamp. Had they refused to follow the cloud there had been no manna for them.

Thus it was with Elijah, for God has given the same rule unto His ministers as to them unto whom they minister: they must practise what they preach, or woe be unto them. The prophet was not allowed to have any will of his own, and to say how long he should remain at Cherith or whither he should go from there. The Word of Jehovah settled everything for him, and by *obeying* the same he obtained *sustenance*. What searching and important truth is there here for every Christian: the path of obedience is the only one of blessing and enrichment. Ah, may we not discover at this very point the cause of our leanness and the explanation of our unfruitfulness? Is it not because we have been so self-willed that our soul is starved and our faith weak? Is it not because there has been so little denying of self, taking up the cross and following Christ, that we are so sickly and joyless?

Nothing so ministers to the health and joy of our souls as being in subjection to the will of Him with whom we have to do. And the preacher must heed this principle, too, as well as the ordinary Christian. The preacher must himself tread the path of obedience if he would be used by the Holy One. How could Elijah have afterwards said with so much assurance on mount Carmel, 'If the Lord be God, follow Him,' if he had previously followed a course of self-pleasing and insubordination? As we pointed out in our last chapter, the correlative of 'service' is obedience. The two things are indissolubly joined together: as soon as I cease to obey my Master, I am no longer His 'servant.' In this connection let us not forget that one of the noblest titles of our King was '*The Servant* of Jehovah.' None of us can seek to realize a grander aim than that which was the inspiration of His heart: 'I come to do Thy will, O My God.'

But let it be frankly pointed out that the path of obedience to God is far from being an easy one to nature: it calls for the daily denying of self, and therefore it can only be traversed as the eye is fixed steadily on the Lord and the conscience is in subjection to His Word. It is true that in keeping His commandments there is 'great reward,' Psa. 19. 11, for the Lord will be no man's debtor; nevertheless it calls for the setting aside of carnal reason, and to take his place by Cherith and there be fed by ravens – how could a proud intellect understand that? And now he was bidden to journey to a far distant and heathen city, there to be sustained by a desolate widow, who was herself on the point of starvation. Ah, my reader, the path of faith is utterly opposed to what we call 'common sense,' and if you suffer from the same spiritual disease as this writer, then you often find it harder to crucify reason than you do to repudiate the filthy rags of self-righteousness.

'So he arose and went to Zarephath. And when he came to the gate of the city, behold, the widow woman was there gathering of sticks,' v. 10. She was so poor that she was without any fuel, or any servant to go and obtain a few sticks for her. What encouragement could Elijah derive from appearances? None whatever: instead, there was everything which was calculated to fill him with doubts and fears if he was occupied with outward circumstances. 'And he called to her, and said, Fetch me, I pray thee, a little water in a vessel, that I may drink. And as she was going to fetch it, he called to her, and said, Bring me, I pray thee, a morsel of bread in thine hand. And she said, As the Lord thy God liveth, I have not a cake, but a handful of meal in a barrel, and a little oil in a cruse: and, behold, I am gathering two sticks, that I may go in and dress it for me and my son, that we may eat it, and die,' vv. 10-12: *that* was what confronted the prophet when he arrived at his Divinely appointed destination! Put yourself in his place, dear reader, and would you not have felt that such a prospect was a gloomy and disquieting one?

But Elijah 'conferred not with flesh and blood,' and therefore he was not discouraged by what looked so unpromising a situation. Instead, his heart was sustained by the immutable Word of Him that cannot lie. Elijah's confidence rested not in favourable circumstances or 'a goodly outlook,' but in the faithfulness of the living God; and therefore his faith needed no assistance from the things around him. Appearances might be dark and dismal, but the eye of faith could pierce the black clouds and see above them the smiling countenance of his provider. Elijah's God was the Almighty, with whom all things are possible. 'I have commanded a widow woman there to sustain thee': *that* was what his heart was resting on. What is *yours* resting on? Are you being kept in peace in this ever-changing scene? Have you made one of His sure promises your own? 'Trust in the Lord, and do good; so shalt thou dwell in the land, and verily thou *shalt* be fed,' Psa. 37. 3. 'God is our refuge and strength, a very present help in trouble. Therefore will not we fear, though the earth be removed,' Psa. 46. 1, 2.

But let us return to the outward circumstances which confronted Elijah upon his approach to Zarephath. 'When he came to the gate of the city, behold, the widow woman was there gathering of sticks.' God had told His servant to go there and had promised a widow should sustain him, but what her name was, whereabout was her house, and how he was to distinguish her from others, he was not informed. He trusted God to give him further light when he arrived there; nor was he disappointed. He was speedily relieved of any suspense as to the identical person who was to befriend him. Apparently this meeting was quite casual, for there was no appointment between them. 'Behold (ponder and admire) the widow woman *was there*'; see how the Lord in His providence overrules all events, so that this particular woman should be at the gate at the very time the prophet arrived!

Behold! here she comes forth as if on purpose to meet him: yet he did not know her, nor she him. It has all the appearance of being accidental, and yet it was decreed and arranged by God so as to make good His word to the prophet. Ah, my reader, there is no event in this world, however great or however small, which happens by chance. O Lord, I know that the way of man is not in himself: it is not in man that walketh to direct his steps,' Jer. 10. 23. How blessed to be assured that 'the steps of a good man are ordered by the Lord,' Psa. 37. 23. It is sheer unbelief which disconnects the ordinary things of life from God. All our circumstances and experiences are directed by the Lord, for 'of Him, and through Him, and to Him, are all things: to whom be glory for ever. Amen,' Rom. 11. 36. Cultivate the holy habit of seeing the hand of God in everything that happens to you.

'When he came to the gate of the city, behold, the widow woman was there.' How this illustrates once more a principle to which we have frequently called the attention of the reader, namely, that when God works He always works at *both* ends of the line. If Jacob sends his sons down into Egypt seeking food in time of famine, Joseph is moved to give it unto them. If Israel's spies enter Jericho, there is a Rahab raised up to shelter them. If Mordecai is begging the Lord to come to the deliverance of His threatened people, King Ahasuerus is rendered sleepless, made to search the state records and befriend Mordecai and his fellows. If the Ethiopian eunuch is desirous of an understanding of God's Word,

Philip is sent to expound it to him. If Cornelius is praying for an opening up of the Gospel, Peter is charged to preach it to him. Elijah had received no intimation as to where this widow resided, but Divine providence timed her steps so that she encountered him at the entrance to the city. What encouragements to faith are these!

Here, then, was the widow: but how was Elijah to know she was the one whom God had ordained should befriend him? Well he must *try* her, as the servant of Abraham did Rebekah when he was sent to fetch a wife for Isaac: Eliezer prayed that the damsel to whom he should say, 'Let down thy pitcher,' and she should answer, 'Drink, and I will give thy camels drink also; let the same be she whom Thou hast appointed for Isaac,' Gen. 24. Rebekah came forth and fulfilled these conditions. So here: Elijah tests this woman to see if she is kind and benevolent: 'Fetch me, I pray thee, a little water in a vessel, that I may drink.' Just as Eliezer considered that only one possessed of kindness would be a fit companion for his master's son, so Elijah was convinced that only a liberal-minded person would be likely to sustain him in a time of famine and drought.

'He called to her, and said, Fetch me, I pray thee, a little water in a vessel, that I may drink.' Observe the gracious and respectful demeanour of Elijah. The fact that he was a prophet of Jehovah did not warrant him to treat this poor widow in a haughty and overbearing manner. Instead of commanding, he said, 'I pray thee.' What a rebuke does that contain for those who are proud and officious. Civility is due to every one: 'be courteous,' 1 Pet. 3. 8, is one of the Divine precepts given to believers. And what a severe test it was to which Elijah submitted this poor woman: to fetch him a drink of water! Yet she made no demur nor did she demand a high price for what had become a costly luxury; no, not even though Elijah was a complete stranger to her, belonging to another race. Admire here the moving power of God, who can draw out the human heart to acts of kindness unto His servants.

'And as she was going to fetch it.' Yes, she left off gathering sticks for herself, and at the first request of this stranger started for the drink of water. Let us learn to imitate her in this respect, and be always ready to perform an act of kindness toward our fellow creatures. If we do not have the wherewithal to *give* to the distressed, we should be the more ready to *work* for them, Eph. 4. 28. A cup of cold water, though it cost us nothing more than the trouble of fetching it, shall in no wise lose its reward. 'And as she was going to fetch it, he called to her, and said, Bring me, I pray thee, a morsel of bread in thine hand,' v. 11. This the prophet requested in order to test her still further – and what a test: to share her very last meal with him – and also to pave the way for a further discourse with her.

'Bring me, I pray thee, a morsel of bread in thine hand.' What a selfish request this seemed! How likely it was that human nature would resent such a demand upon her slender resources. Yet in reality it was *God* that was meeting with her in the hour of her deepest need. 'Therefore will the Lord *wait*, that He may be gracious unto you, and therefore will He be exalted, that He may have mercy upon you: for the Lord is a God of judgment: blessed are all they that *wait for Him*,' Isa. 30. 18. But this widow must first be proved, as later another Gentile woman was proved by the Lord incarnate, Matt. 15. God would indeed supply all her need, but would she trust Him? So often He allows things to get worse before there is any improvement. He 'waits to be gracious.' Why? To bring us to the end of ourselves and of our resources, till all seems lost and we are in despair: that we may more clearly discern His delivering hand.

'And she said, As the Lord thy God liveth, I have not a cake, but a handful of meal in a barrel, and a little oil in a cruse: and, behold, I am gathering two sticks, that I may go in and dress it for me and my son, that we may eat it, and die,' v. 12. The effects of the terrible famine and drought in Palestine were also felt in the adjacent countries. In connection with 'oil' being found in this widow's possession at Zarephath in Zidon, J. J. Blunt in his admirable work, 'Undesigned Coincidences in the Old and New Testament,' has a helpful chapter. He points out that on the division of Canaan the district of *Zidon* fell to the lot of *Asher*, Josh. 19. 28.

Then he turns the reader back to Deuteronomy 33, reminding him that when Moses blessed the twelve tribes he said, 'Let Asher be blessed with children; let him be acceptable to his brethren, and let him dip his foot *in oil*,' v. 24 – indicating the fertility of that district and the character of its principal product. Thus, after a long spell of famine, oil was most likely to be found *there*. Hence by comparing Scripture with Scripture we see their perfect harmony.

'Behold, I am gathering two sticks that I may go in and dress it for me and my son, that we may eat it, and *die*.' Poor soul: reduced to the last extremity, with nothing but a most painful death staring her in the face! Hers was the language of carnal reason and not of faith, of unbelief and not of confidence in the living God; yes, and quite natural in the circumstances. As yet she knew nothing of that word to Elijah, 'Behold, *I* have commanded a widow woman there to sustain thee,' v. 9. No, she thought the end had come. Ah, my reader, how much better is God than our fears. The unbelieving Hebrews imagined they would starve in the wilderness, but they did not. David once said in his heart, 'I shall now perish one day by the hand of Saul,' 1 Sam. 27. 1, but he did not. The apostles thought they would drown in the stormy sea, but they did not.

> 'Were half the breath in sorrow spent
> To Heaven in supplication sent,
> Our cheerful song would oftener be
> Hear what the Lord hath done for me.'

'And she said, As the Lord thy God liveth, I have not a cake, but an handful of meal in a barrel, and a little oil in a cruse; and, behold, I am gathering two sticks, that I may go in and dress it for me and my son, that we may eat it, and die,' v. 12. To natural sight, to human reason, it seemed impossible that she could sustain anyone. In abject poverty, the end of her provisions was now in sight. And her eyes were not on God (any more than ours are till the Spirit works within us!) but upon the barrel, and *it* was now failing her; consequently there was nothing before her mind except *death*. Unbelief and death are inseparably joined together. This widow's confidence lay in the barrel and the cruse, and beyond them she saw no hope. As yet her soul knew nothing of the blessedness of communion with Him to whom alone belong the issues from death, Psa. 68. 20. She was not yet able 'against hope to believe in hope,' Rom. 4. 18. Alas, what a poor tottering thing is that hope which rests on nothing better than a barrel of meal.

How prone we all are to lean on something just as paltry as a barrel of meal! And just so long as we do so our expectations can only be scanty and evanescent. Yet, on the other hand, let us remember that the smallest measure of meal in the hand of God is to faith as sufficient and effectual as 'the cattle upon a thousand hills.' But alas, how rarely is faith in healthy exercise. Only too often we are like the disciples when, in the presence of the hungry multitude, they exclaimed, 'There is a lad here, which hath five barley loaves, and two small fishes: but what are *they* among so many?' John 6. 9 – that is the language of unbelief, of carnal reason. Faith is not occupied with difficulties, but with Him with whom all things are possible. Faith is not occupied with circumstances, but with the God of circumstances. Thus it was with Elijah, as we shall see when we contemplate the immediate sequel.

And what a test of Elijah's faith was now supplied by those doleful words of the poor widow. Consider the situation which now confronted his eyes. A widow and her son starving: a few sticks, a handful of meal, and a little oil between them and death. Nevertheless God had said to him, 'I have commanded a widow woman there *to sustain thee*.' How many would exclaim, How deeply mysterious, what a trying experience for the prophet! Why, he needed to help her rather than become a burden upon her. Ah, but like Abraham before him, 'He staggered not at the promise of God through unbelief, but was strong in faith.' He knew that the Possessor of heaven and earth had decreed she *should* sustain him, and even though there had been no meal or oil at all, that had in no wise dampened his spirits or deterred him. O my reader, if you know anything experimentally of the goodness, the power and faithfulness of God, let your confidence in Him remain unshaken, no matter what appearances may be.

> 'He who hath helped thee hitherto,
> Will help thee all thy journey through;
> And give thee daily cause to raise
> New Ebenezers to His praise.'

'Behold, I am gathering two sticks that I may go in and dress it for me and my son, that we may eat it, and die.' Let it be duly noted that this woman did not fail to discharge her responsibility. Up to the very end she was industrious, making use of the means to hand. Instead of giving way to utter despair, sitting down and wringing her hands, she was busily occupied, gathering sticks for what she fully believed would be her last meal. This is not an unimportant detail, but one which we need to take to heart. Idleness is never justified, least of all in an emergency: nay, the more desperate the situation the greater the need for us to bestir ourselves. To give way to dejection never accomplishes any good. Discharge your responsibility to the very end, even though it be in preparing for your final meal. Richly was the widow repaid for her industry. It was while she was *in the path of duty* (household duty!), that God, through His servant, met with and blessed her.

CHAPTER EIGHT

The Lord Will Provide

In that which is now to be before us we are to behold how the prophet conducted himself in quite different surroundings and circumstances from those which have previously engaged our attention. Hitherto we have seen something of how he acquitted himself in public: his courage and spiritual dignity before Ahab; and also how he acted in private: his life in secret before God by the brook – obedient unto the word of the Lord, patiently waiting His next marching orders. But here the Spirit grants us a view of how Elijah conducted himself in the home of the widow at Zarephath, revealing as it does most blessedly the sufficiency of Divine grace for God's servants and people in every situation in which they may find themselves. Alas, how often the servant of God who is uncompromising in public and faithful in his secret devotions, fails lamentably in the domestic sphere, the family circle. This should not be; nor was it so with Elijah.

That to which we have just alluded calls perhaps for a few remarks, which we offer not by way of extenuation but of explanation. Why is it that the servant of God is often seen to far less advantage in the home than he is in the pulpit or the closet? In the first place, as he goes forth to discharge his public duties, he is keyed up to do battle against the enemy; but he returns home with his nervous energy spent, to relax and recuperate. Then it is that he is more easily upset and irritated by comparative trifles. In the second place, in his public ministry he is conscious that he is opposing the powers of evil, but in the family circle he is surrounded by those who love him, and is more off his guard, failing to realize that Satan may use his friends to gain an advantage over him. Third, conscious faithfulness in public may have stimulated his pride, and a thorn in the flesh – the painful realization of sad failure in the home – may be necessary to humble him. Yet there is no more justification for God-dishonouring conduct in the domestic circle than in the pulpit.

In our last chapter we reached the point where Elijah – in response to Jehovah's orders – had left his retirement at Cherith, had crossed the desert and had duly arrived at the gates of Zarephath, where the Lord had (secretly) commanded a widow woman to sustain him. He encountered her at the entrance of the town, though in circumstances which presented a most unpromising appearance to carnal sight. Instead of this woman joyfully welcoming the prophet, she dolefully spoke of the impending death of herself and her son. Instead of being amply furnished to minister unto Elijah, she tells him that 'a handful of meal and a little oil in a cruse' was all she had left. What a testing of faith! How unreasonable it seemed that the man of God should expect sustenance under *her* roof. No more unreasonable than that Noah should be required to build an ark before there was any rain, still less any signs of a flood; no more unreasonable than that Israel should be required simply to walk round and round the walls of Jericho. The path of obedience can only be trodden as faith is in exercise.

'And Elijah said, Fear not: go and do as thou hast said,' 1 Kings 17. 13. What a gracious word was this to quiet the poor widow's heart! Be not afraid of the consequences, either to yourself or to your son, in making use of the means to hand, scant though they be. 'But make me thereof a little cake first, and bring it unto me, and after make for thee and for thy son, v. 13. What a severe testing was this! Was ever a poor widow so sorely tried, before or since? To make him a cake 'first' was surely in her extreme circumstances one of the hardest commands ever given. Did it not appear to issue from the very essence of selfishness? Did either the laws of God or of man require a sacrifice like this? God has never bidden us do more than love our neighbour *as* ourselves, nowhere has He bidden us to love him *better*. But here 'make *me* a cake *first*'!

'For thus saith the Lord God of Israel, The barrel of meal shall not waste, neither shall the cruse of oil fail, until the day that the Lord sendeth rain upon the earth,' v. 14. Ah, *that* made all the difference: that removed the sting from the request, showing there was no selfishness inspiring the same. She was asked for a portion of that little which she had remaining, but Elijah tells her she need not hesitate to bestow it, for although the case seemed desperate God would take care of her and of her son. Observe with what implicit confidence the prophet spoke: there was no uncertainty, but positive and unwavering assurance that their supply should not diminish. Ah, Elijah had learned a valuable lesson at Cherith – learned it experimentally: he had *proved* the faithfulness of Jehovah by the brook, and therefore was he now qualified to quiet the fears and comfort the heart of this poor widow – compare 2 Corinthians 1. 3, 4, which reveals the secret of all effective ministry.

Observe the particular title here accorded Deity. The woman had said, 'As the Lord thy God liveth,' v. 12, but this was not sufficient. Elijah declared, 'Thus saith the Lord God of *Israel*': this Gentile must be made to realize the humbling truth that 'salvation is of the Jews,' John 4. 22. 'The Lord God of Israel': of whose wondrous works you must have heard so much: the One who made a footstool of the haughty Pharaoh, who brought His people through the Red Sea dry-shod, who miraculously sustained them for forty years in the wilderness, and who subdued the Canaanites for them. Such a One may surely be trusted for our daily bread. The 'Lord God of Israel' is He whose promise never fails, for 'the Strength of Israel will not lie nor repent: for He is not a man, that He should repent' or change His mind, 1 Sam. 15. 29. Such a One may be safely relied upon.

'For thus saith the Lord God of Israel, The barrel of meal shall not waste, neither shall the cruse of oil fail, until the day that the Lord sendeth rain upon the earth,' v. 14. God gave her His word of promise to rest upon: could she rely upon it? Would she really trust Him? Note how definite was the promise: it was not barely, God will not suffer thee to starve, or will surely supply all your need; rather was it as though the prophet had said, The meal in *thy* barrel shall not diminish nor the oil in *thy* cruse dry up. And if *our* faith be a Divinely-sustained one it will cause us to trust in God's promise, to commit ourselves unreservedly to His care, and to do good unto our fellow-creatures. But observe how faith must *continue* in exercise: no new barrel of meal was promised or furnished: just an undiminished 'handful' – seemingly an inadequate quantity for the family, but quite sufficient with God. 'Until the day that the Lord sendeth rain upon the earth' evidenced the firm faith of the prophet himself.

'And she went and did according to the saying of Elijah: and she, and he, and her house, did eat many days,' v. 15. Who can forbear exclaiming, O woman, great is thy faith! She might have advanced many excuses to the prophet's request, especially as he was a stranger to her, but great as the test was, her faith in the Lord was equal to it. Her simple trust that God would take care of them overcame all the objections of carnal reason. Does she not remind us of another Gentile woman, the Syro-Phoenician, a descendant of the idolatrous Canaanites, who long afterwards welcomed the appearance of Christ to the borders of Tyre, and who sought His aid on behalf of her demon-distressed daughter? With astonishing faith she overcame every obstacle, and obtained a portion of the children's bread in the healing of her daughter, Matt. 15. Would that such cases moved us to cry from our hearts, 'Lord, increase our faith,' for none but He who bestows faith can increase it.

'And she, and he, and her house, did eat many days. And the barrel of meal wasted not, neither did the cruse of oil fail, according to the word of the Lord which He spake by Elijah,' vv. 15, 16. She was no loser by her generosity. Her little supply of meal and oil was but sufficient for a single meal and then she and her son must die. But her willingness to minister unto God's servant brought her sufficient, not only for many days, but until the famine ended. She gave Elijah of the best she had, and for her kindness to him God kept her household supplied throughout the famine. How true it is that 'He that receiveth a prophet in the name of a prophet shall receive a prophet's reward,' Matt. 10. 41. But all of God's people are not granted the privilege of succouring a *prophet*, yet they may succour God's *poor*. Is it not written, 'He that hath pity upon the poor lendeth unto the Lord; and that which he hath given will He pay again,' Prov. 19. 17? And again, 'Blessed is he that considereth the poor: the Lord will deliver him in time of trouble,' Psa. 41. 1. God will be no man's debtor.

'And she went and did according to the saying of Elijah: and she, and he, and her house, did eat many days. And the barrel of meal wasted not, neither did the cruse of oil fail.' Here again we have exemplified the fact that the receiving of God's blessing and obtaining of food (in figure, spiritual food) is the result of *obedience*. This woman complied with the request of God's servant and great was her reward. Are you, my reader, fearful of the future? Afraid that when strength fails and old age comes you may be left without the necessities of life? Then suffer us to remind you that there is no need whatever for such fears. 'Seek ye first the kingdom of God, and His righteousness; and all these things (temporal necessities) shall be added unto you,' Matt. 6. 33. 'O fear the Lord, ye His saints: for there is no want to them that fear Him,' Psa. 34. 9. 'No good thing will He withhold from them that walk uprightly,' Psa. 84. 11. But note well that each of these promises is *conditional*: your business is to give God the first place in your life, to fear, obey and honour Him in all things, and in return He guarantees your bread and water shall be sure.

Is there a reader inclined to reply, 'Such wholesome counsel is easier to receive than to act on. It is simpler to be reminded of God's promises than to rely upon the same'? Someone else may be disposed to say, 'Ah, you know not how distressing are my circumstances, how dark the outlook, how sorely Satan is injecting doubts into my mind.' True, yet however desperate your case may be, we would earnestly beg you to think upon the widow of Zarephath: it is most unlikely that your situation is as extreme as hers, yet she perished not of starvation. He who puts God first will always find Him with him at the last. Things which seem to be acting against us, work together for our good in His wondrous hands. Whatever be your need, dear friend, forget not Elijah's God.

'And she, and he, and her house, did eat many days.' Here we see Elijah dwelling safely in the humble abode of this poor widow. Though the fare was frugal, yet it was sufficient to preserve life in the body. There is no hint that God provided any variation of diet during those 'many days,' nor any intimation that the prophet became dissatisfied with being required to eat the same kind of food over so long a period. This is where we obtain our first glimpse of how he conducted himself within the family circle. Blessedly did he exemplify that Divine precept, 'Having food and raiment let us be therewith content,' 1 Tim. 6. 8. And from whence does such contentment proceed? From a submissive and peaceful heart which rests in God: subjection to His sovereign pleasure, satisfaction with the portion He is pleased to allot us, seeing *His* hand both in providing and in withholding.

'And the barrel of meal wasted not, neither did the cruse of oil fail.' Certainly the widow had no cause to complain of the severe testing to which her faith had been put. God, who sent His prophet to board with her, paid well for his table – by providing her family with food while her neighbours were starving, and by granting her the company and instruction of His servant. Who can tell what blessing came to her soul under the edifying conversation of Elijah and from the efficacy of his prayers? She was of a humane and generous disposition, ready to relieve the misery of others and minister to the needs of God's servants; and her liberality was returned to her a hundredfold. Unto the merciful God shows mercy. 'For God is not unrighteous to forget your work and labour of love, which ye have shewed toward His name, in that ye have ministered to the saints, and do minister,' Heb. 6. 10.

'And the barrel of meal wasted not, neither did the cruse of oil fail.' Let us now endeavour to look higher, lest we miss the lovely type which is to be found here. The 'meal' is certainly a Divinely-selected figure of Christ, the 'corn of wheat' that died, John 12. 24, being ground between the upper and nether millstones of Divine judgment that He might be unto us the 'Bread of life.' This is clear from the first few chapters of Leviticus, where we have the five great offerings appointed for Israel, which set forth the person and work of the Redeemer; the Meal offering of 'fine flour,' Lev. 2, portraying the perfections of His humanity. It is equally clear that the 'oil' is an emblem of the Holy Spirit in His anointing, enlightening and sustaining operations. It is a most blessed line of study to trace through the Scriptures the typical references to the 'oil.'

As the little family of Zarephath was not sustained by meal or oil alone, but the two in conjunction, so the believer is not sustained spiritually without both Christ and the Holy Spirit. We could not feed upon Christ, yea, we would never feel our need of so doing, were it not for the gracious influence of the Spirit of God. The one is as indispensable to us as the other: Christ for us, the Spirit in us; the One maintaining our cause on high, the Other ministering to us down here. The Spirit is here to 'testify' of Christ, John 15. 26, yea to 'glorify' Him, John 16. 14, and therefore did the Saviour add, 'He shall receive of Mine, and shall shew it unto you.' Is not this why the 'meal' (three times over) is mentioned first in the type? Nor is this the only passage where we see the two types combined: again and again in the beautiful prefigurations of the Old Testament we read of the 'oil' being placed upon the blood, Ex. 29. 21; Lev. 14. 14, etc.

"And the barrel of meal wasted not, neither did the cruse of oil fail.' There was a steady increase and supply of both according to the mighty power of God working a continuous miracle: is there not a close parallel between this and the Saviour's supernatural increasing of the five barley loaves and the two small fishes, while the disciples were distributing and the multitude eating, Matt. 14. 19, 20? But again we would look from the type to the Antitype. The meal continued undiminished, the supply unabated, and the meal pointed to Christ as the nourisher of our souls. The provision which God has made for His people in the Lord Jesus remains the same throughout the centuries: we may come to Him again and again, and though we receive from Him 'grace for grace' yet His 'fulness,' John 1. 16, continues the same 'yesterday, and today, and for ever.' 'Neither did the cruse of oil fail' foreshadowed the grand truth that the Holy Spirit is with us to the very end of our pilgrimage, Eph. 4. 30.

But let us point out again that God did not give a new barrel of meal and cruse of oil unto this family at Zarephath, nor did He fill to the brim the old one. There is another important lesson for us in this. God gave them sufficient for their daily use, but not a whole year's supply in advance or even a week's provision all at once. In like manner, there is no such thing as our laying up for ourselves a stock of grace for future use. We have to go constantly to Christ for fresh supplies of grace. The Israelites were expressly forbidden to hoard up the manna: they had to go out and gather it anew each morning. We cannot procure sufficient sustenance for our souls on the Sabbath to last us throughout the week, but must feed on God's Word each morning. So too, though we have been regenerated by the Spirit once and for all, yet He renews us in the inner man 'day by day,' 11 Cor. 4. 16.

'According to the word of the Lord, which He spake by Elijah, v. 16. This was illustrative and demonstrative of a vital principle: no word of His shall fall to the ground, but all things 'which God hath spoken by the mouth of all His holy prophets since the world began,' Acts 3. 21, shall surely be accomplished. This is both solemn and blessed. Solemn, because the threatenings of Holy Writ are not idle ones, but the faithful warnings of Him that cannot lie. Just as surely as Elijah's declaration, 'There shall not be dew nor rain these years, but according to my word,' v. 1, was fulfilled to the letter, so will the Most High make good every judgment He has denounced against the wicked. Blessed, because as truly as the widow's meal and oil failed not according to His word through Elijah, so shall every promise made to His saints yet receive its perfect accomplishment. The unimpeachable veracity, unchanging faithfulness and almighty power of God to make good His Word, is the impregnable foundation on which faith may securely rest.

CHAPTER NINE

A Dark Providence

'Change and decay in all around I see.' We live in a mutable world where nothing is stable, and where life is full of strange vicissitudes. We cannot, and we should not, expect things to go on smoothly for us for any length of time while we are sojourning in this land of sin and mortality. It would be contrary to the present constitution of our lot as fallen creatures, for 'man is born unto trouble as the sparks fly upward'; neither would it be for our good if we were altogether exempted from affliction. Though we be the children of God, the objects of His special favour, yet this does not free us from the ordinary calamities of life. Sickness and death may enter our dwellings at any time: they may attack us personally, or those who are nearest and dearest to us, and we are obliged to bow to the sovereign dispensations of Him who ruleth over all. These are commonplace remarks, we know, nevertheless they contain a truth of which – unpalatable though it be – we need constant reminding.

Though we are quite familiar with the fact mentioned above, and see it illustrated daily on every side, yet we are reluctant and slow to acknowledge its application *to ourselves*. Such is human nature: we wish to ignore the unpleasant, and persuade ourselves that if our present lot be a happy one it will remain so for some time to come. But no matter how healthy we be, how vigorous our constitution, how well provided for financially, we must not think that our mountain is so strong it cannot be moved, Psa. 30. 6, 7. Rather must we train ourselves to hold temporal mercies with a light hand, and use the relations and comforts of this life as though we had them not, 1 Cor. 7. 30, remembering that 'the fashion of this world passeth away.' Our rest is not here, and if we build our nest in any earthly tree it should be with the realization that sooner or later the whole forest will be cut down.

Like many a one both before and since, the widow of Zarephath might have been tempted to think that all her troubles were now over. She might reasonably expect a blessing from entertaining the servant of God in her home, and a real and liberal blessing she received. In consequence of sheltering him, she and her son were supplied by a Divine miracle in a time of famine for 'many days'; and from this she might draw the conclusion that she had nothing further to fear. Yet the next thing recorded in our narrative is, 'And it came to pass after these things, that the son of the woman, the mistress of the house, fell sick; and his sickness was so sore, that there was no breath left in him,' 1 Kings 17. 17. The language in which this pathetic incident is couched seems to denote that her son was stricken suddenly, and so sorely that he expired quickly, before there was opportunity for Elijah to pray for his recovery.

How deeply mysterious are the ways of God! The strangeness of the incident now before us is the more evident if we link it with the verse immediately preceding: 'The barrel of meal wasted not, neither did the cruse of oil fail, according to the word of the Lord which He spake by Elijah. And it came to pass after *these* things that the son of the woman . . . fell sick,' etc. Both she and her son had been miraculously fed for a considerable interval of time, and now he is drastically cut off from the land of the living, reminding us of those words of Christ concerning the sequel to an earlier miracle: 'Your fathers did eat manna in the wilderness and are dead,' John 6. 49. Even though the smile of the Lord be upon us and He is showing Himself strong on our behalf, this does not grant us an immunity from the afflictions to which flesh and blood is the heir. As long as we are left in this vale of tears we must seek grace to 'rejoice with trembling,' Psa. 2. 11.

On the other hand, this widow had most certainly erred if she concluded from the snatching away of her son that she had forfeited the favour of God and that this dark dispensation was a sure mark of His wrath. Is it not written, 'For whom the Lord loveth

He chasteneth, and scourgeth every son whom He receiveth,' Heb. 12. 6? Even when we have the clearest manifestations of God's good will – as this woman had in the presence of Elijah under her roof and the daily miracle of sustenance – we must be prepared for the frowns of Providence. We ought not to be staggered if we meet with sharp afflictions while we are treading the path of duty. Did not Joseph do so again and again? Did not Daniel? Above all, did not the Redeemer Himself? – so too with His apostles. 'Beloved, think it not strange concerning the fiery trial which is to try you, as though some strange thing happened unto you,' 1 Pet. 4. 12.

Let it be duly noted that this poor soul had received particular marks of God's favour before she was cast into the furnace of affliction. It often happens that God exercises His people with the heaviest trials when they have been the recipients of His richest blessings. Yet here the anointed eye may discern His tender mercies. Does that remark surprise you, dear reader? Do you ask, How so? Why, the Lord, in His infinite grace, often *prepares* His children for suffering by previously granting them great spiritual enjoyments: giving them unmistakable tokens of His kindness, filling their hearts with His love, and diffusing an indescribable peace over their minds. Having tasted experimentally of the Lord's goodness, they are better fitted to meet adversity. Moreover, patience, hope, meekness and the other spiritual graces, can only be developed in the fire: the faith of this widow then, must needs be tried yet more severely.

The loss of her child was a heavy affliction for this poor woman. It would be so to any mother, but it was more especially severe on her, because she had previously been reduced to widowhood, and there would now be none left to support and comfort her declining years. In him all her affections were centred, and with his death all her hopes were destroyed: her coal was now indeed quenched, 2 Sam. 14. 7, for none remained to preserve the name of her husband on the earth. Nevertheless, as in the case of Lazarus and his sisters, this heavy blow was 'for the glory of God,' John 11. 4, and was to afford her a still more distinguishing mark of the Lord's favour. Thus it was, too, with Joseph and Daniel to whom we have alluded above: Severe and painful were their trials, yet subsequently God conferred yet greater honour upon them. O for faith to lay hold of the 'afterward' of Hebrews 12. 11!

'And she said unto Elijah, What have I to do with thee, O thou man of God? art thou come unto me to call my sin to remembrance, and to slay my son?' v. 18. Alas, what poor, failing, sinful creatures we are! How wretchedly we requite God for His abundant mercies! When His chastening hand is laid upon us, how often we rebel instead of meekly submitting thereto. Instead of humbling ourselves beneath God's mighty hand and begging Him to show wherefore He is contending with us, Job 10. 2, we are far readier to blame some other person as being the cause of our trouble. Thus it was with this woman. Instead of entreating Elijah to pray with and for her – that God would enable her to understand wherein she had 'erred,' Job 6. 24, that He would be pleased to sanctify this affliction unto the good of her soul, and enable her to glorify Him 'in the fires,' Isa. 24. 15 – she reproached him. How sadly we fail to use our privileges.

'And she said unto Elijah, What have I to do with thee, O thou man of God? art thou come unto me to call my sin to remembrance, and to slay my son?' This is in striking contrast with the calmness she had displayed when Elijah first encountered her. The swift calamity which had befallen her had come as a sore surprise, and in such circumstances, when trouble overtakes us unexpectedly, it is hard to keep our spirits composed. Under sudden and severe trials much grace is needed if we are to be preserved from impatience, petulant outbursts, and to exercise unshaken confidence in and complete submission to God. Not all of the saints are enabled to say with Job, 'Shall we receive good at the hand of God, and shall we not receive evil? . . . the Lord gave, and the Lord hath taken away; blessed be the name of the Lord,' Job 2. 10; 1. 21. But so far from such failure excusing us, we must judge ourselves unsparingly and contritely confess such sins unto God.

The poor widow was deeply distressed over her loss, and her language to Elijah is a strange mixture of faith and unbelief, pride and humility. It was the inconsistent outburst of an agitated mind as the disconnected and jerky nature of it intimates. First, she asks him, 'What have I to do with thee?' – what have I done to displease thee? wherein have I injured thee? She wished that she had never set eyes on him if he was responsible for the death of her child. Yet second, she owns him as 'thou man of God' – one who was separated unto the Divine service. She must have known by this time that the terrible drought had come upon Israel in answer to the prophet's prayers, and she probably concluded her own affliction had come in a similar way. Third, she humbled herself, asking, 'Art thou come to me to call *my sin* to remembrance? – possibly a reference to her former worship of Baal.

It is often God's way to employ afflictions in bringing former sins to our remembrance. In the ordinary routine of life it is so easy to go on from day to day without any deep exercise of conscience before the Lord, especially so when we are in the enjoyment of a replenished barrel. It is only as we are really walking closely with Him, or when we are smitten with some special chastisement of His hand that our conscience is sensitive before Him. But when death entered her family the question of sin came up, for death is the wages of sin, Rom. 6. 23. It is always the safest attitude for us to assume when we regard our losses as the voice of God speaking to our sinful hearts, and diligently to examine ourselves, repent of our iniquities, and duly confess them unto the Lord, that we may obtain His forgiveness and cleansing, 1 John 1. 9.

It is at this very point that the difference between an unbeliever and a believer so often appears. When the former is visited with some sore trouble or loss, the pride and selfrighteousness of his heart is quickly manifested by his, 'I know not what I have done to deserve this: I always sought to do what is right; I am no worse than my neighbours who are spared such sorrow – why should I be made the subject of such a calamity?' But how different is it with a person truly humbled. He is distrustful of himself, aware of his many shortcomings, and ready to fear that he has displeased the Lord. Such a one will diligently consider his ways, Hag. 1. 5, reviewing his former manner of life and carefully scrutinizing his present behaviour, so as to discover what has been or still is amiss, that it may be set right. Only thus can the fears of our minds be relieved and the peace of God confirmed in our souls.

It is this calling to mind our manifold sins and judging ourselves for them which will make us meek and submissive, patient and resigned. It was thus with Aaron who, when the judgment of God fell so heavily upon his family, 'held his peace,' Lev. 10. 3. It was thus with poor old Eli who had failed to admonish and discipline his sons, for when they were summarily slain, he exclaimed, 'It is the Lord: let Him do what seemeth Him good,' 1 Sam. 3. 18. The loss of a child may sometimes remind parents of sins committed with respect to it long previously. So it was with David when he lost his child by the hand of God smiting it for his wickedness, 2 Sam. 12. No matter how heavy the loss, how deep his grief, when in his right mind the language of the saint will ever be, 'I know, O Lord, that Thy judgments are *right*, and that Thou in faithfulness hast afflicted me,' Psa. 119. 75.

Though the widow and her son had been kept alive for many days, miraculously sustained by the power of God, whilst the rest of the people had suffered, yet she was less impressed by the Divine beneficence than by His taking away her child: 'What have I to do with thee, O thou man of God? Art thou come unto me to call my sin to remembrance, and to slay my son?' While she seems to acknowledge God in the death of her son, she cannot shake off the thought that the prophet's presence was responsible for it. She attributes her loss to Elijah: as though he had been commissioned to go to her for the purpose of inflicting punishment upon her for her sin. As he had been sent to Ahab to denounce the drought upon Israel for their sin, so now she was afraid of his presence, alarmed at the very sight of him. Alas, how ready we are to mistake the grounds of our afflictions and ascribe them to false causes.

'And he said unto her, Give me thy son,' v. 19. In the opening paragraph of our last chapter we pointed out how the second half of 1 Kings 17 presents to us a picture of the domestic life of Elijah, his deportment in the widow's home at Zarephath. First, he evidenced his contentment with the humble fare, expressing no dissatisfaction with the unvarying menu day after day. And here we behold how he conducted himself under great provocation. The petulant outburst of this agitated woman was a cruel one to make unto the very man who had brought deliverance to her house. Her 'Art thou come to call my sin to remembrance, and to slay my son?' was uncalled for and unjust, and might well have prompted a bitter reply. It had undoubtedly done so had not the subduing grace of God been working with him, for Elijah was naturally of a warm temper.

The wrong construction which the widow placed upon Elijah's presence in her home was enough to shake any person. Blessed is it to observe there was no angry reply made to her inconsiderate judgment, but instead a 'soft answer' to turn away her wrath. If one speaks to us unadvisedly with his lips that is no reason why we should descend to his level. The prophet took no notice of her passionate inquiry and thereby evidenced that he was a follower of Him who is 'meek and lowly in heart,' of whom we read 'Who, when He was reviled, reviled not again,' 1 Pet. 2. 23. 'Elijah saw that she was in extreme distress and that she spoke as one in great anguish of spirit; and therefore, taking no notice of her words, he calmly said to her 'Give me thy son'; leading her at the same time to expect the restoration of her child through his intercession' (J. Simpson).

It may be thought that the last words cited above are entirely speculative: personally we believe that they are fully warranted by Scripture. In Hebrews 11. 35 we read, 'Women received their dead raised to life again.' It will be remembered that this statement is found in the great faith chapter, where the Spirit has set forth some of the wondrous achievements and exploits of those who trust the living God. One individual case after another is mentioned, and then there is a grouping together and generalizing: 'who *through faith* subdued kingdoms . . . women received their dead raised to life again.' There can be no room for doubt that the reference here is to the case now before us and the companion one in that of the Shunammite, 2 Kings 4. 17-37. Here, then, is where the New Testament again throws its light upon the earlier Scriptures, enabling us to obtain a more complete conception of that which we are now considering.

The widow of Zarephath, though a Gentile, was a daughter of Sarah, to whom had been committed the faith of God's elect. Such a faith is a supernatural one, its author and object being supernatural. When this faith was first born within her we are not told – very likely while Elijah was sojourning in her home, for 'faith cometh by hearing, and hearing by the word of God,' Rom. 10 .17. The supernatural character of her faith was evidenced by its supernatural fruits, for it was in response to her faith (as well as to Elijah's intercession) that her child was restored to her. What is the more remarkable is that, so far as the Word informs us, there had been no previous case of the dead being brought back again to life. Nevertheless, He who had caused a handful of meal to waste not and a little oil in a cruse to fail not while it sustained three people for 'many days,' surely *He* could also quicken the dead. Thus does faith reason: nothing is impossible to the Almighty.

It may be objected that there is no hint in the historical narrative of the widow's faith as to the restoring of her son to life, but rather a hint to the contrary. True, yet this in no wise makes against what has been pointed out above. Nothing is said in Genesis about Sarah's faith to conceive seed, but instead her scepticism is mentioned. What is there in Exodus to suggest that the parents of Moses were exercising faith in God when they placed their son in the ark of bulrushes? – yet see Hebrews 11. 23. One would be hard put to it to find anything in the book of Judges which suggests that Samson was a man of faith, yet it is clear from Hebrews 11. 32 that he was. But if nothing is said in the Old Testament of her *faith*, we may also note that the unkind words of the widow to Elijah are not recorded in the New Testament – any more than the unbelief of Sarah or the impatience of Job – because they are blotted out by the blood of the Lamb.

CHAPTER TEN

'Women Received Their Dead Raised To Life Again'

———

We are now to consider one of the most remarkable incidents recorded in the Old Testament, namely, the restoring to life of the widow's son at Zarephath. It is an incident staggering to unbelief, yet he who has any experimental acquaintance with the Lord finds no difficulty therein. When Paul was making his defence before Agrippa the apostle asked him, 'Why should it be thought a thing incredible (not simply that a deceased person should be restored to life, but) that *God* should raise the dead?' Acts 26. 8. Ah, there is where the believer throws all the emphasis: upon the absolute sufficiency of the One with whom he has to do. Bring into the scene the living God, and no matter how drastic and desperate be the situation, all difficulties at once disappear, for nothing is impossible to Him. He who first implanted life, He who now holdeth our souls in life, Psa. 66. 9, can re-vivify the dead.

The modern infidel (like the Sadducees of old) may scoff at the Divinely-revealed truth of resurrection, but not so the Christian. And why? Because he has experienced in his own soul the quickening power of God: he has been brought from death unto life spiritually. Even though Satan should inject vile doubts into his mind, and for a while shake his confidence in the resurrection of the Lord Jesus, yet he will soon recover his poise; he knows the blessedness of that grand verity, and when grace has again delivered him from the power of darkness, he will joyfully exclaim with the apostle 'Christ liveth in me.' Moreover, when he was born again, a supernatural principle was planted within his heart – the principle of faith – and that principle causes him to receive the Holy Scriptures with full assurance that they are indeed the Word of Him that cannot lie, and therefore does he believe *all* that the prophets have spoken.

Here is the reason why that which staggers and stumbles the wise of this world is plain and simple to the Christian. The preservation of Noah and his family in the ark, Israel's passing through the Red Sea dryshod, the survival of Jonah in the whale's belly, present no difficulty to him at all. He knows that the Word of God is inerrant, for the truth thereof has been verified in his own experience. Having proved for himself that the Gospel of Christ is 'the power of God unto salvation,' he has no reason to doubt anything recorded in Holy Writ concerning the prodigies of His might in the material realm. The believer is fully assured that nothing is too hard for the Maker of heaven and earth. It is not that he is an intellectual simpleton, credulously accepting what is altogether contrary to reason, but that, in the Christian, reason is restored to its normal functioning: predicate a God who is almighty, and the supernatural working of His hand necessarily follows.

The entire subject of miracles is hereby reduced to its simplest factor. A great deal of learned jargon has been written on this theme: the laws of nature, their suspension, God's acting contrary thereto, and the precise nature of a miracle. Personally we would define a miracle as something which none but God Himself can perform. In so doing we are not under-estimating the powers possessed by Satan, or overlooking such passages as Revelation 16. 14 and 19. 20. It is sufficient for the writer that Holy Writ affirms the Lord to be 'He *who alone* doeth great wonders,' Psa. 136. 4. As for the 'great signs and wonders' shown by false christs and false prophets, *their* nature and design is to 'deceive,' Matt. 24. 24, for they are '*lying* wonders,' 2 Thess. 2. 9, just as their predictions are false ones. Here we rest: God alone doeth great wonders, and being *God* this is just what faith expects from Him.

In our last chapter we were occupied with the sore affliction which came upon the Zarephath widow in the sudden death of her son, and the immediate effect which it had upon her. Stirred to the depths, she turned to Elijah and accused him of being the occasion of her heavy loss. The prophet made no harsh reply to the unkind and unjust charge, but instead, quietly said, 'Give me thy son.' Observe that he did not autocratically lay hands upon the corpse, but courteously requested that the body should be turned over to him. We believe that Elijah's design therein was to still her passion and cause her 'against hope to believe in hope,' Rom. 4. 18, as long before Abraham had done, when he 'believed God who quickeneth the dead,' for it was (in part) in response to *her* faith that she 'received her dead restored to life again,' Heb. 11. 35.

'And he took him out of her bosom, and carried him up into a loft, where he abode, and laid him upon his own bed,' 1 Kings 17. 19. This was evidently an upper room reserved for the prophet's personal use, as Elisha had his in another place 2 Kings 4. 10. Thither he now retired for privacy, as Peter to the house-top and Christ into the garden. The prophet himself must have been quite oppressed and disconcerted by the sad event which had overtaken his hostess. Stern as Elijah might be in the discharge of duty, yet he possessed a tender spirit underneath (as such stern men usually do), full of benignity and sensitive to the misery of others. It is quite evident from the sequel, Elijah grieved that one who had been so kind to him should be so heavily afflicted since he had come to her hospitable abode, and it would add to his distress that she should think he was responsible for her loss.

It must not be lost sight of that this dark dispensation occasioned a real testing of Elijah's faith. Jehovah is the God of the widow and the rewarder of those who befriend His people, especially of those who show kindness to His servants. Why, then, should such evil now come upon the one who was affording him shelter? Had he not come by the Lord's own appointment as a messenger of mercy to her house? True, he had proved himself to be such; but this was forgotten by her under the stress of the present trial, for he is now regarded as the emissary of wrath, an avenger of her sin, the slayer of her only child. Worst of all, would he not feel that the honour of his Master was also involved? that the name of the Lord would be scandalized! Might the widow not ask, Is *this* how God repays those who befriend His servants?

Blessed is it to observe how Elijah reacted to this trial. When the widow asked if the death of her son was due to his presence, he indulged in no carnal speculations, making no attempt to solve the deep mystery which now confronted himself as well as her. Instead, he retires to his chamber that he may get alone with God and spread his perplexity before Him. This is ever the course we should follow, for not only is the Lord 'a very present help in trouble,' but His Word requires that we should seek Him *first*, Matt. 6. 33. 'My soul, wait thou only upon God,' applies with double force in times of perplexity and distress. Vain is the help of man; worthless are carnal conjectures. In the hour of His acutest trial the Saviour Himself withdrew from His own disciples and poured out His heart unto the Father in secret. The widow was not allowed to witness the deepest exercises of the prophet's soul before his Master.

'And he cried unto the Lord,' v. 20. As yet Elijah apprehended not the meaning of this mystery, but he well understood what to do in his difficulty. He betook himself unto his God and spread his complaint before Him. He sought relief with great earnestness and importunity, humbly reasoning with Him regarding the death of the child. But note well his reverent language: he did not ask, *Why* hast Thou inflicted this dismal dispensation upon us? But instead, 'O Lord my God, hast Thou also brought evil upon the widow with whom I sojourn, by slaying her son?' v. 20. The *why* of it was none of his business. It is not for us to call into question the ways of the Most High nor to inquire curiously into His secret counsels. Sufficient for us to know that the Lord makes no mistakes, that He has a good and sufficient reason for all He does, and therefore should we meekly submit to His sovereign pleasure. Man's 'Why doth He?' and 'Why hast Thou?' is designated a 'replying *against God*,' Rom. 9. 19, 20.

In Elijah's address unto God we may note, first, how that he fell back upon the special relation which He sustained to him: 'O Lord, *my* God,' he cried. This was a pleading of his personal interest in God, for these words are always expressive of covenant relationship. To be able to say 'O Lord, *my* God' is worth more than gold or rubies. Second, he traced the calamity back to its original source: 'Hast *Thou* also brought evil upon the widow?' v. 20 – he saw death striking by Divine commission: 'Shall there be evil in a city, and the Lord hath not done it?' Amos 3. 6. What a comfort when we are enabled to realize that no evil can befall God's children but such as He brings upon them. Third, he pleaded the severity of the affliction: this evil has come upon, not simply the woman nor even the mother, but 'the *widow*' – whom Thou dost specially succour. Moreover, she it is 'with whom I sojourn': my kind benefactor.

'And he stretched himself upon the child three times, and cried unto the Lord,' v. 21. Was this proof of the prophet's humility? How remarkable that so great a man should spend so much time and thought on that slender form, and bring himself into immediate contact with that which ceremonially defiled! Was this act indicative of his own affection for the child, and to show how deeply he was stirred by his death? Was it a token of the fervency of his appeal unto God, as though he would, if he could, put life into his body from the life and warmth of his own? Does not his doing this three times over so intimate? Was it a sign of what God would do by His power and accomplish by His grace in the bringing of sinners from death unto life, the Holy Spirit overshadowing them and imparting His own life to them? If so, is there not more than a hint here that those whom He employs as instruments in conversion must themselves become as little children, bringing themselves to the level of those to whom they minister, and not standing on a pedestal as though they were superior beings.

'Cried unto the Lord, and said, O Lord my God, I pray Thee, let this child's soul come into him again,' v. 21. What a proof is this that Elijah was accustomed to expect wondrous blessings from God in response to his supplications, accounting that nothing was too hard for Him to do, nothing too great for Him to bestow in answer to prayer. Undoubtedly this petition was prompted by the Holy Spirit, yet it was a marvellous effect of the prophet's faith to anticipate the restoration of the child to life, for there is no record in Scripture that anyone had been raised from the dead before this time. And remember, Christian reader, that this is recorded for *our* instruction and encouragement: the effectual fervent prayer of a righteous man availeth much. At the throne of grace we approach unto a great King, so let us bring large petitions with us. The more faith counts upon the infinite power and sufficiency of the Lord, the more is He honoured.

'And the Lord heard the voice of Elijah; and the soul of the child came into him again, and he revived,' v. 22. What a proof was this that 'the eyes of the Lord are over the righteous, and His ears are open unto their prayer,' 1 Pet. 3. 12. What a demonstration of the potency and efficacy of prayer! Ours is a prayer-hearing and a prayer-answering God: to Him therefore let us have recourse whatever be our distress. Hopeless as our case may be to all human help, yet nothing is too hard for the Lord. He is able to do far more exceeding abundantly above all that we ask or think. But let us 'ask *in faith*, nothing wavering. For he that wavereth is like a wave of the sea driven with the wind and tossed. For let not that man think that he shall receive anything of the Lord,' James 1. 6, 7. 'This is the confidence that we have in Him, that, if we ask anything according to His will, He heareth us,' 1 John 5. 14. Surely we have need, all of us, to cry more earnestly, 'Lord, teach us to pray.' Unless this be one of the effects produced by pondering the incident now before us, our study of the same has availed us little.

It is not sufficient for us to cry, 'Lord, teach us to pray!', however, we must also carefully ponder those portions of His Word which chronicle cases of prevailing intercession, that we may learn the secrets of successful prayer. In this instance we may note the following points. First, Elijah's retiring to his own private chamber, that he might be alone with God. Second, his fervency: he 'cried unto the Lord' – no mere lip-service was this. Third, his reliance upon his own personal interest in the Lord, avowing his covenant relationship: 'O Lord, my God.' Fourth, his encouraging himself in God's attributes: here, the Divine sovereignty and supremacy – 'hast Thou also brought evil upon the widow.' Fifth, his earnestness and importunity: evidenced by his 'stretching himself upon the child' no less than three times. Sixth, his appeal to God's tender mercy: 'the *widow* with whom I sojourn.' Finally, the definiteness of his petition: 'Let this child's soul come into him again.'

'And the soul of the child came into him again, and he revived,' v. 22. These words are important for clearly establishing the definite distinction which there is between the soul and the body, a distinction as real as that which exists between the house and its inhabitant. Scripture tells us that, in the day of his creation, the Lord God first formed man's body out of 'the dust of the ground,' and, second, that He 'breathed into his nostrils the breath of life,' and only then did he become 'a living soul,' Gen. 2. 7. The language employed on this occasion affords clear proof that the soul is distinct from the body, that it does not die with the body, that it exists in a separate state after the death of the body, and that none but God can restore it to its original habitat, compare Luke 8. 55. Incidentally we may observe that this request of Elijah's and the Lord's response make it quite clear that the child was actually dead.

Relatively speaking, though in a very real sense nevertheless, the age of miracles has ceased, so that we cannot expect to have our dead supernaturally restored to us in this life. Yet the Christian may and ought to look forward with certain assurance to meeting again with those beloved relatives and friends who departed hence in Christ. Their spirits are not dead, nor even sleeping as some erroneously assert, but have returned to God who gave them, Eccl. 12. 7, and are now in a state that is 'far better,' Phil. 1. 23, which could not be were they deprived of all conscious communion with their Beloved. Being absent from the body they are 'present with the Lord,' 2 Cor. 5. 8, and in His presence is 'fulness of joy,' Psa. 16. 11. As to their bodies they await that great Day when they shall be fashioned like unto Christ's glorious body.

'And Elijah took the child, and brought him down out of the chamber into the house, and delivered him unto his mother: and Elijah said, See, thy son liveth,' v. 23. What joy must have filled the prophet's heart as he witnessed the miraculous answer to his intercession! What fervent ejaculations of praise must have issued from his lips unto God for this additional manifestation of His goodness in delivering him from his grief. But it was no time for delay: the sorrow and suspense of the poor widow must now be allayed. Elijah therefore promptly took the child downstairs and gave him to his mother. Who can imagine her delight as she saw her child restored to life again? How the prophet's procedure on this occasion reminds us of our Lord's action following upon the miracle of restoring to life the only son of the widow of Nain, for no sooner did he sit up and speak than we are told that the Saviour 'delivered him to his mother,' Luke 7. 15.

'And the woman said to Elijah, Now by this I know that thou art a man of God, and that the word of the Lord in thy mouth is truth,' v. 24. Very blessed is this. Instead of giving vent to her natural emotions she appears to have been entirely absorbed with the power of God which rested upon His servant, which now firmly established her conviction of his Divine mission and assurance in the truth which he proclaimed. Full demonstration had been given her that Elijah was indeed a prophet of the Lord and that his witness was true. It must not be forgotten that he had first presented himself to her as a 'man of God' (note her words in v. 18), and therefore it was essential he should establish his claim to that character. And this was done by the restoration of her child to life. Ah, my reader, *we* avow ourselves to be the children of the living God, but how are we making good our profession? There is only one conclusive way of so doing, and that is by walking in 'newness of life,' evidencing that we are new creatures in Christ.

Now, let us observe how that which has been before us supplies yet another feature of Elijah's domestic life. In considering how he conducted himself in the widow's home, we noted first his *contentment*, murmuring not at the humble fare which was placed before him. Second, his *gentleness*, in refusing to reply to her unkind words with an angry retort. And now we behold the blessed effect upon his hostess of the miracle wrought in answer to his prayers. Her confession, 'By this I know thou art a man of God,' was a personal testimony to the reality and power of *a holy life*. O to live in the energy of the Holy Spirit so that those who come into contact with us may perceive the power of God working in and through us! Thus did the Lord overrule the widow's grief unto her spiritual good, by establishing her faith in the veracity of His word.

CHAPTER ELEVEN

Facing Danger

━━━━

To one filled with such zeal for the Lord and love for His people the prolonged inactivity to which he was forced to submit must have proved a severe trial to Elijah. So energetic and courageous a prophet would naturally be anxious to take advantage of the present distress of his countrymen: he would desire to awaken them to a sense of their grievous sins and urge them to return unto the Lord. Instead – so different are God's ways from ours – he was required to remain in complete seclusion month after month and year after year. Nevertheless, his Master had a wise and gracious design in this trying discipline of His servant. Throughout his long stay by the brook Cherith, Elijah proved the faithfulness and sufficiency of the Lord, and he gained not a little from his protracted sojourn at Zarephath. As the apostle reveals, both in 2 Corinthians 6. 4 and 12. 12, the first mark of an approved servant of Christ is the grace of spiritual 'patience,' and this is developed by the trials of faith, James 1. 3.

The years spent by Elijah at Zarephath, were far from being wasted, for during his stay in the widow's home he obtained confirmation of his Divine call, by the remarkable seal which was there given to his ministry. Thereby he approved himself to the conscience of his hostess: 'Now by this I know that thou art a man of God, and that the word of the Lord in thy mouth is truth,' 17. 24. It was highly important that the prophet should have such a testimony to the Divine source of his mission before entering upon the more difficult and dangerous part of it which yet lay before him. His own heart was blessedly confirmed and he was enabled to start afresh upon his public career with the assurance that he was a servant of Jehovah and that the Word of the Lord was indeed in his mouth. Such a seal to his ministry (the quickening of the dead child) and the approving of himself in the conscience of the mother was a grand encouragement for him as he set out to face the great crisis and conflict at Carmel.

What a message is there here for any ardent ministers of Christ whom Providence may for a season have laid by from public service! They are so desirous of doing good and promoting the glory of their Master in the salvation of sinners and the building up of His saints, that they feel their enforced inactivity to be a severe trial. But let them rest assured that the Lord has some good reason for laying this restraint upon them, and therefore they should earnestly seek grace that they may not be fretful under it, nor take matters into their own hands in seeking to force a way out of it. Ponder the case of Elijah! He uttered no complaints nor did he venture out of the retirement into which God had sent him. He waited patiently for the Lord to direct him, to set him at liberty, and to enlarge his sphere of usefulness. Meanwhile, by fervent intercession, he was made a great blessing unto those in the home.

'And it came to pass after many days,' 1 Kings 18. 1. Let us attend to this expression of the blessed Spirit's. It is not 'after three years' (as was indeed the case), but 'after many *days*.' There is here an important lesson for our hearts if we will heed it: we should live a day at a time, and count our lives by days. 'Man that is born of a woman is of few *days*, and full of trouble. He cometh forth like a flower, and is cut down,' Job. 14. 1, 2. Such was the view of life taken by the aged Jacob: for when Pharaoh asked the patriarch, 'How old are thou?' he answered 'the *days* of the years of my pilgrimage are a hundred and thirty years,' Gen. 47. 9. Happy are they whose constant prayer is 'So teach us to number our *days*, that we may apply our hearts unto wisdom,' Psa. 90. 12. Yet how prone we are to count by *years*. Let us endeavour to live each day as though we knew it were our last.

'And it came to pass': that is, the predetermined counsel of Jehovah was now actualized. The fulfilment of the Divine purpose can neither be retarded nor forced by us. God will not be hurried

[95]

either by our petulance or our prayers. We have to wait His appointed hour, and when it strikes, He acts – it 'comes to pass' just as He had foreordained. The precise length of time His servant is to remain in a certain place was predestined by Him from all eternity. 'It came to pass after many days': that is, over a thousand since the drought had commenced, 'that the word of the Lord came to Elijah.' God had not forgotten His servant. The Lord never forgets any of His people, for has He not said, 'Behold, I have graven thee upon the palms of My hands; thy walls are continually before Me,' Isa. 49. 16? O that we might never forget Him, but 'set the Lord always before us,' Psa. 16. 8!

'The word of the Lord came to Elijah in the third year, saying, Go, shew thyself unto Ahab; and I will send rain upon the earth,' 1 Kings 18. 1. So that we may better understand the tremendous test of the prophet's courage which this command involved, let us seek to obtain some idea of what must now have been the state of that wicked king's mind. We commenced this study of the life of Elijah by pondering the words, 'And Elijah the Tishbite, who was of the inhabitants of Gilead, said unto Ahab, As the Lord God of Israel liveth, before whom I stand, there shall not be dew nor rain these years, but according to my word,' 17. 1. Now we are to consider the sequel to this. We have seen how it fared with Elijah during the lengthy interval, we must now ascertain how things were going with Ahab, his court, and his subjects. Dreadful indeed must be the state of things on earth when the heavens are shut up and no moisture is given for three years. 'There was a *sore famine* in Samaria,' 18. 2.

'And Ahab said unto Obadiah, Go into the land, unto all fountains of water and unto all brooks: peradventure we may find grass to save the horses and mules alive, that we lose not all the beasts,' v. 5. The barest possible outline is here presented, but it is not difficult to fill in the details. Israel had sinned grievously against the Lord, and so they were made to feel the weight of the rod of His righteous anger. What a humbling picture of God's favoured people, to behold their king going forth to seek grass, if perchance he could find a little somewhere so that the lives of those beasts which remained might be saved. What a contrast with the abundance and glory of Solomon's days! But Jehovah had been grossly dishonoured, His truth had been rejected. The vile Jezebel had defiled the land by the pestilential influence of her false prophets and priests. The altars of Baal had supplanted that of the Lord, and therefore, as Israel had sown the wind, they must now be made to reap the whirlwind.

And what effect had the severe judgment of Heaven produced upon Ahab and his subjects? 'And Ahab said unto Obadiah, Go into the land unto all fountains of water and unto all brooks: peradventure we may find grass to save the horses and mules alive, that we lose not all the beasts.' There is not a single syllable here about *God!* not a word about the awful *sins* which had called down His displeasure upon the land! Fountains, brooks and grass were all that occupied Ahab's thoughts – *relief* from the Divine affliction was all he cared about. It is ever thus with the reprobate. It was so with Pharaoh: as each fresh plague descended upon Egypt he sent for Moses and begged him to pray for its removal, and as soon as it was removed he hardened his heart and continued to defy the Most High. Unless God is pleased to sanctify directly to our souls His chastisements, they profit us not. No matter how severe His judgments or how long they be protracted, man is never softened thereby unless God performs a work of grace *within* him. 'And they gnawed their tongues for pain, and blasphemed the God of heaven because of their pains and their sores, and *repented not* of their deeds,' Rev. 16. 10, 11.

Nowhere is the awful depravity of human nature more grievously displayed than at this very point. First, men look upon a prolonged dry season as a freak of nature which must be endured, refusing to see the hand of *God* in it. Later, if it be borne in upon them that they are under a Divine judgment, they assume a spirit of defiance, and brazen things out. A later prophet in Israel complained of the people in his day for manifesting this vile temper: 'O Lord, are not Thine eyes upon the truth? Thou hast stricken them, but they have not grieved; Thou has consumed them, but they have refused to receive correction: they have made their faces harder than a rock,' Jer. 5. 3. From this we may see how utterly absurd and erroneous are the teachings of Romanists on purgatory and of Universalists on Hell. 'The imagined fire of purgatory or the real torments of Hell possess no purifying effect, and the sinner under the anguish of his sufferings will continually increase in wickedness and accumulate wrath to all eternity' (Thomas Scott).

'And Ahab said unto Obadiah, Go into the land, unto all fountains of water, and unto all brooks: peradventure we may find grass to save the horses and mules alive, that we lose not all the beasts. So they divided the land between them to pass throughout it: Ahab went one way by himself, and Obadiah went another way by himself,' vv. 5, 6. What a picture do these words present! Not only had the Lord no place in his thoughts, but Ahab says nothing about his people, who next to God should have been his chief concern. His evil heart seemed incapable of rising higher than horses and mules: such was what concerned him in the day of Israel's dire calamity. What a contrast between the low grovelling selfishness of this wretch and the noble spirit of the man after God's own heart. 'And David spake unto the Lord when he saw the angel that smote the people, and said, Lo, I have sinned, and I have done wickedly: but these sheep, what have they done? let Thine hand, I pray Thee, be against me, and against my father's house,' 2 Sam. 24. 17: that was the language of a regenerate king when his land was trembling beneath God's chastening rod because of *his* sin.

As the drought continued and the distressing effects thereof became more and more acute we can well imagine the bitter resentment and hot indignation borne by Ahab and his vile consort against the one who had pronounced the terrible interdict of no dew nor rain. So incensed was Jezebel that she had 'cut off (slain) the prophets of the Lord,' v. 4, and so infuriated was the king that he had sought diligently for Elijah in all the surrounding nations, requiring an oath from their rulers that they were not providing asylum for the man whom he regarded as his worst enemy, and cause of all his trouble. And now the Word of the Lord came to

Elijah saying, 'Go, show thyself unto Ahab!' If much boldness had been required when he was called upon to announce the awful drought, what intrepidation was needed for him now to face the one who sought him with merciless rage.

'It came to pass after many days that the word of the Lord came to Elijah in the third year, saying, Go, show thyself to Ahab.' The movements of Elijah were all ordered of God: he was 'not his own' but the servant of another. When the Lord bade him 'hide thyself,' 17. 3, he must retire at His orders, and when He said 'Go, show thyself' he must comply with the Divine will. Elijah's courage did not fail him, for 'the righteous are bold as a lion,' Prov. 28. 1. He declined not the present commission but went forth without murmur or delay. Humanly speaking, it was highly dangerous for the prophet to return unto Samaria, for he could not expect any welcome from the people who were in such sore straits nor any mercy from the king. But with the same unhesitating obedience as had previously characterized him, so now he complied with his Master's orders. Like the Apostle Paul he counted not his life dear unto himself, but was ready to be tortured and slain if that was the Lord's will for him.

'And as Obadiah was in the way, behold, Elijah met him,' v. 7. A few extremists ('Separatists') have grossly traduced the character of Obadiah, denouncing him as an unfaithful compromiser, as one who sought to serve two masters. But the Holy Spirit has not stated he did wrong in remaining in Ahab's employ, nor intimated that his spiritual life suffered in consequence: instead, He has expressly told us that 'Obadiah feared the Lord greatly,' v. 3, which is one of the highest encomiums which could be paid him. God has often given His people favour in the sight of heathen masters (as Joseph and Daniel), and has magnified the sufficiency of His grace by preserving their souls in the midst of the most unpromising environments. His saints are found in very unlikely places – as in 'Caesar's household,' Phil. 4. 22.

There is nothing wrong in a child of God holding a position of influence if he can do so without the sacrifice of principle. And indeed, it may enable him to render valuable service to the cause of God. Where would Luther and the Reformation have been, humanly speaking, had it not been for the Elector of Saxony? And what would have been the fate of our own Wycliffe if John of Gaunt had not constituted him his ward? As the governor of Ahab's household Obadiah was undoubtedly in a most difficult and dangerous position, yet so far from bowing his knee to Baal he was instrumental in saving the lives of many of God's servants. Though surrounded by so many temptations he preserved his integrity. It is also to be carefully noted that when Elijah met him he uttered no word of reproach unto Obadiah. Let us not be too hasty in changing our situation, for the Devil can assail us in one place just as easily as in another.

As Elijah was on his way to confront Ahab, he met the pious governor of the king's household, 'And as Obadiah was in the way, behold, Elijah met him: and he knew him, and fell on his face, and said, Art thou that my lord Elijah?' v. 7. Obadiah recognized Elijah, yet he could scarcely believe his eyes. It was remarkable that the prophet had survived the merciless onslaught of Jezebel on the servants of Jehovah: it was still more incredible to see him here, alone, journeying into Samaria. Most diligent search had long been made for him, but in vain, and now he comes unexpectedly upon him. Who can conceive the mixed feelings of awe and delight as Obadiah gazed upon the man of God, by whose word the awful drought and sore famine had almost completely desolated the land? Obadiah at once showed the greatest respect for him and did obeisance to him. 'As he had shown the tenderness of a father to the sons of the prophets, so he showed the reverence of a son to the father of the prophets, and by this made it appear he did indeed fear the Lord greatly' (Matthew Henry).

'And he answered him, I am: go, tell thy lord, Behold, Elijah is here,' v. 8. The prophet's courage did not fail him. He had received orders from God to 'show himself unto Ahab,' and therefore he made no attempt to conceal his identity when interrogated by the governor: let us shrink not boldly to declare our Christian discipleship when challenged by those who meet us. It is also to be duly noted that Elijah honoured Ahab, wicked though he was, by speaking of him to Obadiah as 'thy lord.' It is the duty of inferiors to show respect to their superiors: of subjects concerning their sovereign, of servants concerning their master. We must render to all, that to which their office or station entitles them. It is no mark of spirituality to be vulgar in our conduct or brusque in our speech. God commands us to 'Honour the king,' 1 Pet. 2. 17 – because of his *office* – even if he be an Ahab or a Nero.

'And he answered him, I am: go, tell thy lord, Behold, Elijah is here. And he said, What have I sinned, that thou wouldest deliver thy servant into the hand of Ahab, to slay me?' vv. 8, 9. It was only natural that Obadiah should wish to be excused from so perilous an errand. First, he asks *wherein* he had offended either the Lord or His prophet that he should be asked to be the messenger of such distasteful tidings to the king – sure proof that his own conscience was clear! Second, he lets Elijah know of the great pains which his royal master had taken in endeavouring to track down the prophet and discover his hiding place: 'As the Lord thy God liveth, there is no nation or kingdom, whither my lord hath not sent to seek thee,' v. 10. Yet in spite of all their diligence they were not able to discover him: so effectually did God secure him from their malice. Utterly futile is it for man to attempt to hide when the Lord seeks him out: equally useless is it for him to seek when God hides anything from him.

'And now thou sayest, Go, tell thy lord, Behold, Elijah is here,' v. 11. Surely you are not serious in making such a request. Do you not know the consequences will be fatal to me if I am unable to make good such a declaration! 'And it shall come to pass, as soon as I am gone from thee, that the Spirit of the Lord shall carry thee whither I know not; and so when I come and tell Ahab, and he cannot find thee, he shall slay me: but I thy servant fear the Lord from my youth,' v. 12. He was afraid that Elijah would again mysteriously disappear, and then his master would likely be enraged because he had not arrested the prophet, and certainly he would be furious if he found himself imposed upon by discovering no trace of him when he duly arrived at this spot. Finally, he asks, 'Was it not told my lord what I did when Jezebel slew the prophets of the Lord, how I hid a hundred men of the Lord's prophets by fifty in a cave, and fed them with bread and water?' v. 13. Obadiah made reference to these noble and daring deeds of his, not in any boastful spirit, but for the purpose of attesting his sincerity. Elijah reassured him in God's name, and Obadiah obediently complied with his request: 'And Elijah said, As the Lord of hosts liveth, before whom I stand, I will surely shew myself unto him today. So Obadiah went to meet Ahab, and told him: and Ahab went to meet Elijah,' vv. 15, 16.

CHAPTER TWELVE

Confronting Ahab

In previous chapters we have seen Elijah called suddenly out of obscurity to appear before the wicked king of Israel and deliver unto him a fearful sentence of judgment, namely, that 'there shall not be dew nor rain these years but according to my word,' 1 Kings 17. 1. Following the pronouncement of this solemn ultimatum the prophet, in obedience to his Master, retired from the stage of public action and went into seclusion, spending part of the time by the brook Cherith and part in the humble home of the widow at Zarephath, where in each place his needs were miraculously supplied by God, who suffers none to be the loser by complying with His orders. But now the hour had arrived when this intrepid servant of the Lord must issue forth and once more face Israel's idolatrous monarch: 'the word of the Lord came to Elijah in the third year, saying, Go, shew thyself unto Ahab,' 1 Kings 18. 1.

In our last chapter we contemplated the effect which the protracted drought had upon Ahab and his subjects, an effect which made sadly evident the depravity of the human heart. It is written, 'The goodness of God leadeth thee to repentance,' Rom. 2. 4; and again, 'when Thy judgments are in the earth, the inhabitants of the world will learn righteousness,' Isa. 26. 9. How often do we find these sentences cited as though they are absolute and unqualified statements, and how rarely are the words quoted which immediately follow them: in the one case 'But after thy hardness and impenitent heart treasurest up unto thyself wrath against the day of wrath, and in the other 'Let favour be showed to the wicked, yet will he not learn righteousness: in the land of uprightness will he deal unjustly, and will not behold the majesty of the Lord.' How are we going to understand these passages, for to the natural man they appear to cancel themselves, the second part of the Isaiah reference seeming flatly to contradict the former.

If Scripture be compared with Scripture it will be found that each of the above declarations receives clear and definite exemplification. For example, was it not a sense of the Lord's goodness – His 'lovingkindness' and 'the multitude of His tender mercies' – which led David to repentance and made him to cry, 'Wash me thoroughly from mine iniquity, and cleanse me from my sin,' Psa. 51. 1, 2? and again, was it not his realization of the Father's goodness – the fact that there was 'bread enough and to spare' in His house – which led the prodigal son to repentance and confession of his sins? So also when God's judgments were in the earth, to such an extent that we are told, 'In those times there was no peace to him that went out, nor to him that came in, but great vexations were upon all the inhabitants of the countries. And nation was destroyed of nation, and city of city: for God did vex them with all adversity,' 2 Chron. 15. 5, 6, did Asa and his subjects (in response to the preaching of Azariah) 'put away the abominable idols out of all the land, and renewed the altar of the Lord . . . and they entered into a covenant to seek the Lord God of their fathers with all their heart,' vv. 8-12. See also Revelation 11. 15.

On the other hand, how many instances are recorded in Holy Writ of individuals and of peoples who were the subjects of God's goodness to a marked degree, who enjoyed both His temporal and spiritual blessings in unstinted measure, yet so far were those privileged persons from being suitably affected thereby and led to repentance, their hearts were hardened and God's mercies were abused: 'Jeshurun waxed fat, and kicked,' Deut. 32.15 and cf. Hos. 13. 6. So, too, how often we read in Scripture of God's judgments being visited upon both individuals and nations, only for them to illustrate the truth of that word, 'Lord, when Thy hand is lifted up, they will not see,' Isa. 26. 11. A conspicuous example is Pharaoh, who after each plague hardened his heart afresh and continued in his defiance of Jehovah. Perhaps even more notable is the case of the Jews, who century after century have been inflicted with the sorest judgments from the Lord, yet have not learned righteousness thereby.

Ah, have we not witnessed striking demonstrations of these truths in our own lifetime, both on the one side and on the other? Divine favours were received as a matter of course, yea, were regarded far more as the fruits of our own industry than of Divine bounty. The more the nations were prospered the more God faded from view.

How, then, are we to understand these Divine declarations: 'The goodness of God leadeth thee to repentance'; 'When Thy judgments are in the earth, the inhabitants of the world will learn righteousness'? Obviously they are not to be taken absolutely and without modification. They are to be understood with this proviso: if a sovereign God is pleased to *sanctify them* unto our souls. It is God's ostensible (we say not, His secret and invincible) design that displays of His goodness should lead men into the paths of righteousness: such is their natural tendency, and such ought to be their effect upon us. Yet the fact remains that neither prosperity nor adversity *by themselves* will produce these beneficent results, for where the Divine dispensations are not expressly sanctified unto us, neither His mercies nor His chastisements avail to work any improvement in us.

Hardened sinners 'despise the Lord's goodness and long-suffering,' prosperity rendering them the less disposed to receive the instructions of righteousness, and where the means of grace (the faithful preaching of God's Word) are freely afforded among them, they continue profane and close their eyes to all the discoveries of Divine grace and holiness. When God's hand is lifted up to administer gentle rebukes, it is despised; and when more terrible vengeance is inflicted, they steel their hearts against the same. It has always been thus. Only as God is pleased to work in our hearts, as well as before our eyes, only as He deigns to bless unto our souls His providential dealings, is a teachable disposition wrought in us, and we are brought to acknowledge His justice in punishing us and to reform our evil ways. Whenever Divine judgments are not definitely sanctified to the soul, sinners continue to stifle conviction and rush forward in defiance, until they are finally swallowed up by the wrath of a holy God.

Does someone ask, What has all the above to do with the subject in hand? The answer is, much every way. It goes to show that the terrible perversity of Ahab was no exceptional thing, while it also serves to explain *why* he was quite unaffected by the sore visitation of God's judgment on his dominions. A total drought which had continued for upwards of three years was upon the land, so that 'there was a sore famine in Samaria,' 1 Kings 18. 2. This was indeed a Divine judgment: did, then, the king and his subjects learn righteousness thereby? Did their ruler set them an example by humbling himself beneath the mighty hand of God, by acknowledging his vile transgressions, by removing the altars of Baal and restoring the worship of Jehovah? No! So far from it, during the interval he suffered his wicked consort to 'cut off the prophets of the Lord,' 18. 4, thus adding iniquity to iniquity and exhibiting the fearful depths of evil into which the sinner will plunge unless deterred by God's restraining power.

'And Ahab said unto Obadiah, Go into the land, unto all fountains of water, and unto all brooks: peradventure we may find grass to save the horses and mules alive, that we lose not all the beasts,' 1 Kings 18. 5. As a straw in the air reveals the direction of the wind so these words of Ahab indicate the state of his heart. The living God had no place in his thoughts, nor was he exercised over the sins which had called down His displeasure on the land. Nor does he seem to have been the least concerned about his subjects, whose welfare – next to the glory of God – should have been his chief concern. No, his aspirations do not appear to have risen any higher than fountains and brooks, horses and mules, that the beasts which yet remained might be saved. This is not evolution but devolution, for when the heart is estranged from its Maker its direction is ever lower and lower.

In the hour of his deep need Ahab turned not in humility unto God, for he was a stranger to Him. Grass was now his all-absorbing object – provided *that* could be found, he cared nothing about anything else. If food and drink were obtainable then he could have enjoyed himself in the palace and been at ease among Jezebel's idolatrous prophets, but the horrors of famine drove him out. Yet instead of dwelling upon and rectifying the causes thereof, he seeks only a temporary relief. Alas, he had sold himself to work wickedness and had become the slave of a woman who hated Jehovah. And, my reader, Ahab was not a Gentile, a heathen, but a favoured Israelite; but he had married a heathen and become enamoured with her false gods. He had made shipwreck of the faith and was being driven to destruction. What a terrible thing it is to depart from the living God and forsake the Refuge of our fathers!

'So they divided the land between them to pass throughout it: Ahab went one way by himself, and Obadiah went another way by himself,' v. 6. The reason for this procedure is obvious: by the king going in one direction and the governor of his household in another, twice as much ground would be covered as if they had remained together. But may we not also perceive a mystical meaning in these words: 'Can two walk together, except they be agreed?' Amos 3. 3. And what agreement was there between these two men? No more than there is between light and darkness, Christ and Belial, for whereas the one was an apostate, the other feared the Lord from his youth, v. 12. It was meet, then, they should separate and take opposite courses, for they were journeying unto entirely different destinies eternally. Let not this suggestion be regarded as 'far fetched,' but rather let us cultivate the habit of looking for the spiritual meaning and application beneath the literal sense of Scripture.

'And as Obadiah was *in the way*, behold, Elijah met him,' v. 7. This certainly appears to confirm the mystical application made of the previous verse, for there is surely a spiritual meaning in what we have just quoted. What was 'the way' which Obadiah was treading? It was the path of duty, the way of obedience to his master's orders. True, it was a humble task he was performing: that of seeking grass for horses and mules, yet this was the work Ahab had assigned him, and *while complying* with the king's word he was rewarded by meeting Elijah! A parallel case is found in

Genesis 24. 27, where Eliezer in compliance with Abraham's instructions encountered the damsel whom the Lord had selected as a wife for Isaac: 'I being *in the way*, the Lord led me to the house of my master's brethren.' So also it was while she was in the path of duty (when gathering of sticks) that the widow of Zarephath met with the prophet.

We considered in our last chapter the conversation which took place between Obadiah and Elijah, but would just mention here that mixed feelings must have filled the heart of the former as his gaze encountered such an unexpected but welcome sight. Awe and delight would predominate as he beheld the one by whose word the fearful drought and famine had almost completely desolated the land: here was the prophet of Gilead, alive and well, calmly making his way, alone, back into Samaria. It seemed too good to be true and Obadiah could scarcely believe his eyes. Greeting him with becoming deference, he asks, 'Art thou that my lord Elijah?' Assuring him of his identity, Elijah bids him go and inform Ahab of his presence. This was an unwelcome commission, yet it was obediently discharged: 'So Obadiah went to meet Ahab, and told him,' v. 16.

And what of Elijah while he awaited the approach of the apostate king: was his mind uneasy, picturing the angry monarch gathering around him his officers ere he accepted the prophet's challenge, and then advancing with bitter hatred and murder in his heart? No, my reader, we cannot suppose so for a moment. The prophet knew full well that the One who had watched over him so faithfully, and supplied his needs so graciously during the long drought, would not fail him now. Had he not good reason to recall how Jehovah had appeared to Laban when he was hotly pursuing Jacob: 'And God came to Laban the Syrian in a dream by night, and said unto him, Take heed that thou speak not to Jacob from good to bad,' Gen. 31. 24 (marg.). It was a simple matter for the Lord to over-awe the heart of Ahab and keep him from murdering Elijah, no matter how much he desired to do so. Let the servants of God fortify themselves with the reflection that He has their enemies completely under His control, He has His bridle in their mouths and turns them about just as He pleases, so that they cannot touch a hair of their heads without His knowledge and permission.

Elijah then waited with dauntless spirit and calmness of heart for the approach of Ahab, as one who was conscious of his own integrity and of his security in the Divine protection. Well might he appropriate to himself those words: 'In God have I put my trust: I will not fear what flesh can do unto me.' Different far must have been the state of the king's mind as 'Ahab went to meet Elijah,' v. 16. Though incensed against the man whose fearful announcement had been so accurately fulfilled, yet he must have been half afraid to meet him. Ahab had already witnessed his uncompromising firmness and amazing courage, and knowing that Elijah would not now be intimidated by his displeasure, had good reason to fear that this meeting would not be honourable unto himself.

The very fact that the prophet was seeking *him* out, yea had sent Obadiah before him to say, 'Behold, Elijah is here,' must have rendered the king uneasy. Wicked men are generally great cowards: their own consciences are their accusers, and often cause them many misgivings when in the presence of God's faithful servants, even though these occupy an inferior position in life to themselves. Thus it was with King Herod in connection with Christ's forerunner, for we are told, 'Herod feared John, knowing that he was a just man and an holy,' Mark 6. 20. In like manner, Felix, the Roman governor, trembled before Paul (though he was his prisoner) when the apostle 'reasoned of righteousness, temperance, and judgment to come,' Acts 24. 25. Let not the ministers of Christ hesitate boldly to deliver their message, nor be afraid of the displeasure of the most influential in their congregations.

'And Ahab went to meet Elijah.' We might have hoped that, after proving from painful experience that the Tishbite was no deceiver, but a true servant of Jehovah whose word had accurately come to pass, Ahab had now relented, been convinced of his sin and folly, and become ready to turn to the Lord in humble repentance. But not so: instead of advancing toward the prophet with a desire to receive spiritual instruction from him or to request his prayers for him, he fondly hoped that he might now avenge himself for all that he and his subjects had suffered. His opening salutation at once revealed the state of his heart: 'Ahab said unto him, Art thou he that troubleth Israel?' v. 17 – what a contrast from the greeting given Elijah by the pious Obadiah! No word of contrition fell from Ahab's lips. Hardened by sin, his conscience 'seared as with a hot iron,' he gave vent to his obduracy and fury.

'Ahab said unto him, Art thou he that troubleth Israel?' This is not to be regarded as an unmeasured outburst, the petulant expression of a sudden surprisal, but rather as indicating the wretched state of his soul, for 'out of the abundance of the heart the mouth speaketh.' It was the avowed antagonism between evil and good: it was the hissing of the Serpent's seed against one of the members of Christ: it was the vented spite of one who felt condemned by the very presence of the righteous. Years later, speaking of another devoted servant of God, whose counsel was demanded by Jehoshaphat, this same Ahab said, 'I hate him; for he doth not prophesy good concerning me, but evil,' 22. 8. So far, then, from this charge of Ahab's making against the character and mission of Elijah, it was a tribute to his integrity, for there is no higher testimony to the fidelity of God's servants than their evoking of the hearty hatred of the Ahabs around them.

CHAPTER THIRTEEN

The Troubler of Israel

'And it came to pass, when Ahab saw Elijah, that Ahab said unto him, Art thou he that troubleth Israel?' 1 Kings 18. 17. How the words of our lips betray the state of our hearts! Such language from the king after the sore judgment which God had sent upon his dominion revealed the hardness and impenitency of his heart. Consider the opportunities which had been given him. He was warned by the prophet of the certain consequences that would follow his continuance in sin. He had seen that what the prophet had announced surely came to pass. It had been demonstrated before his eyes that the idols which he and Jezebel worshipped could not avert the calamity nor give the rain which was so urgently needed. There was everything to convince him that 'the Lord God of Elijah' was the sovereign Ruler of heaven and earth, whose decree none can disannul and whose almighty arm no power can withstand.

Such is the sinner who is left to himself. Let Divine restraint be removed from him and the madness which possesses his heart will burst forth like a broken dam. He is determined to have his own way at all costs. No matter how serious and solemn be the times in which his lot is cast, he is unsobered thereby. No matter how gravely his country be imperilled, nor how many of his fellows be maimed and killed, he must continue to take his fill of the pleasures of sin. Though the judgments of God thunder in his ears louder and louder, he deliberately closes them and seeks to forget un-pleasantries in a whirl of gaiety. Though the country be at war, fighting for its very existence, 'night life' with its 'bottle parties' goes on unabated. If air raids compel munition workers to seek refuge in underground shelters, then their eyes (in one shelter at least) are greeted with notices on its walls, 'Cards and gambling encouraged.' What is this but a strengthening themselves 'against the Almighty,' a flinging of themselves 'upon the thick bosses of His bucklers,' Job. 15. 25, 26?

Yet, while writing the above lines, we are reminded of those searching words, 'Who maketh *thee* to differ from another?' 1 Cor. 4. 7. There is but one answer: a sovereign God, in the plenitude of His amazing grace. And how the realization of this should humble us into the dust, for by nature and by practice there was no difference between us and them: 'Wherein in time past *ye* walked according to the course of this world, according to the prince of the power of the air, the spirit that now worketh in the children of disobedience: among whom also we all had our conversation (manner of life) in times past in the lusts of our flesh, fulfilling the desires of the flesh and of the mind,' Eph. 2. 2, 3. It was distinguishing mercy which sought us out when we were 'without Christ.' It was distinguishing love which quickened us into newness of life when we were 'dead in trespasses and sins.' Thus we have no cause for boasting and no ground for self-complacency. Rather must we walk softly and penitently before Him who has saved us from ourselves.

'And it came to pass, when Ahab saw Elijah, that Ahab said unto him, Art thou he that troubleth Israel?' Elijah was the one who above all others stood out against Ahab's desire for uniting Israel in the worship of Baal: and thus, as he supposed from effecting a peaceful settlement of the religion of the nation. Elijah was the one who in his view had been responsible for all the distress and suffering which filled the land. There was no discernment of *God's* hand in the drought, nor any compunction for his own sinful conduct: instead, Ahab seeks to transfer the onus to another and charges the prophet with being the author of the calamities which had befallen the nation. It is always the mark of an unhumbled and unjudged heart for one who is smarting beneath the righteous rod of God to throw the blame upon someone else, just as a sin-blinded nation which is being scourged for its iniquities will attribute its troubles to the blunders of its political rulers.

It is no unusual thing for God's upright ministers to be spoken of as troublers of peoples and nations. Faithful Amos was charged with conspiring against Jeroboam the second, and told that the land was not able to bear all his words, Amos 7. 10. The Saviour Himself was accused of 'stirring up the people,' Luke 23. 5. It was said of Paul and Silas at Philippi that they did 'exceedingly trouble the city,' Acts 16. 20, and when at Thessalonica they were spoken of as having 'turned the world upside down,' Acts 17. 6. There is therefore no higher testimony to their fidelity than for the servants of God to evoke the rancour and hostility of the reprobate. One of the most scathing condemnations that could be pronounced on men is contained in those terrible words of our Lord to His unbelieving brethren: 'The world *cannot hate you*; but Me it hateth, because I testify of it, that the works thereof are evil,' John 7. 7. But who would not rather receive all the charges which the Ahabs can heap upon us than incur that sentence from the lips of Christ!

It is the duty of God's servants to warn men of their danger, to point out that the way of rebellion against God leads to certain destruction and to call upon them to throw down the weapons of their revolt and flee from the wrath to come. It is their duty to teach men that they must turn from their idols and serve the living God, otherwise they will eternally perish. It is their duty to rebuke wickedness wherever it be found and to declare that the wages of sin is death. This will not make for their popularity, for it will condemn and irritate the wicked, and such plain speaking will seriously annoy them. Those who expose hypocrites, resist tyrants, oppose the wicked, are ever viewed by them as trouble-makers. But as Christ declared, 'Blessed are ye, when men shall revile you, and persecute you, and shall say all manner of evil against you falsely, for My sake. Rejoice, and be exceeding glad: for great is your reward in heaven: for so persecuted they the prophets which were before you,' Matthew 5. 11, 12.

'And he answered, I have not troubled Israel; but thou, and thy father's house, in that ye have forsaken the commandments of the

Lord, and thou hast followed Baalim,' 18. 18. Had Elijah been one of those cringing sycophants which are usually found in attendance upon kings, he had thrown himself at Ahab's feet, suing for mercy, or rendering mean submission. Instead, he was the ambassador of a greater King, even the Lord of hosts: conscious of this, he preserved the dignity of his office and character by acting as one who represented a superior power. It was because Elijah realized the presence of Him by whom kings reign, who can restrain the wrath of man and make the remainder thereof to praise Him, that the prophet feared not the face of Israel's apostate monarch. Ah, my reader, did we but realize more of the presence and sufficiency of our God, we should not fear what anyone might do unto us. Unbelief is the cause of our fears. O to be able to say 'Behold, God is my salvation; I will trust, and not be afraid,' Isa. 12. 2.

Elijah was not to be intimidated by the wicked aspersion which had just been cast upon him. With undaunted courage, he first denies the foul charge: 'I have not troubled Israel.' Happy for us if we can truthfully make the same claim: that the chastisements which Zion is now receiving at the hands of a holy God have not been caused in any measure by *my* sins. Alas, who among us could affirm this? Second, Elijah boldly returns the charge upon the king himself, placing the blame where it duly belonged: 'I have not troubled Israel, but thou and thy father's house.' See here the fidelity of God's servant: as Nathan said to David, so Elijah unto Ahab, 'Thou art the man.' A truly solemn and heavy charge: that Ahab and his father's house were the cause of all the sore evils and sad calamities which had befallen the land. The Divine authority with which he was invested warranted Elijah thus to indict the king himself.

Third, the prophet proceeded to supply proof of the charge which he had made against Ahab: 'in that ye have forsaken the commandments of the Lord, and thou hast followed Baalim.' So far from the prophet being the enemy of his country he sought only its good. True, he had prayed for and called down God's judgment for the wickedness and apostasy of the king and nation, but this was because he desired they should repent of their sins and reform their ways. It was the evil doings of Ahab and his house which had called down the drought and famine. Elijah's intercession had never prevailed against a holy people: 'the curse causeless shall not come,' Prov. 26. 2. The king and his family were the leaders in rebellion against God, and the people had blindly followed: here then was the cause of the distress: *they* were the reckless 'troublers' of the nation, the disturbers of its peace, the displeasers of God.

Those who by their sins provoke God's wrath are the real troublers, and not those who warn them of the dangers to which their wickedness exposes them. 'Thou and thy father's house, in that ye have forsaken the commandments of the Lord, and thou hast followed Baalim.' It is quite plain even from the comparatively brief record of Scripture that Omri, the father of Ahab, was one of the worst kings that Israel ever had, and Ahab had followed in the wicked steps of his father. The statutes of those kings were the grossest idolatry. Jezebel, Ahab's wife, had no equal for her hatred of God and His people and her zeal for the worship of debased idols. So powerful and persistent was their evil influence that it prevailed some two hundred years later, Micah 6. 16, and drew down the vengeance of Heaven upon the apostate nation.

'In that ye have forsaken the commandments of the Lord.' Therein lies the very essence and heinousness of sin. It is a throwing off of the Divine yoke, a refusing to be in subjection to our Maker and Governor. It is a wilful disregard of the Lawgiver and rebellion against His authority. The law of the Lord is definite and emphatic. Its first statute expressly forbids our having any other gods than the true God; and the second prohibits our making of any graven image and bowing down ourselves before it in worship. These were the awful crimes which Ahab had committed, and they are *in substance* those which our own evil generation is guilty of, and that is why the frown of Heaven now lies so heavily upon us. 'Know therefore and see that it is an evil thing and bitter, that thou hast forsaken the Lord thy God, and that My fear is not in thee, saith the Lord God of hosts,' Jer. 2. 19. 'And thou hast followed Baalim': when the true God is departed from, false ones take His place – 'Baalim' is in the plural number, for Ahab and his wife worshipped a variety of false deities.

'Now therefore send, and gather to me all Israel unto mount Carmel, and the prophets of Baal four hundred and fifty, and the prophets of the groves four hundred, which eat at Jezebel's table,' v. 19. Very remarkable is this: to behold Elijah alone, hated by Ahab, not only charging the king with his crimes, but giving him instructions, telling him what he must do. Needless to say, his conduct on this occasion did not furnish a precedent or set an example for all God's servants to follow under similar circumstances. The Tishbite was endowed with extraordinary authority from the Lord, as is intimated by that New Testament expression, 'the spirit and power of Elijah,' Luke 1. 17. Exercising that authority Elijah demanded there should be a convening of all Israel at Carmel, and that thither should also be summoned the prophets of Baal and Ashtaroth, who were dispersed over the country at large. More strange still was the peremptory language used by the prophet: he simply issued his orders without offering any reason or explanation as to what was his real object in summoning all the people and prophets together.

In the light of what follows, the prophet's design is clear: what he was about to do must be done openly and publicly before impartial witnesses. The time had now arrived when things must be brought to a head: Jehovah and Baal come face to face as it were, before the whole nation. The venue selected for the test was a mountain in the tribe of Asher, which was well situated for the people to gather there from all parts – it was, be it noted, *outside* the land of Samaria. It was on Carmel that an altar had been built and sacrifices offered on it unto the Lord (see v. 30), but the worship of Baal had supplanted even this irregular service of the true God – irregular, for the Law prohibited any altars outside those in the temple at Jerusalem. There was only one way in which the dreadful drought and its resultant famine could be brought to an end and the blessing of Jehovah restored to the nation, and that was by the sin which had caused the calamity being dealt with in judgment, and for that Ahab must gather all Israel together on Carmel.

'As Elijah designed to put the worship of Jehovah on a firm foundation, and to restore the people to their allegiance to the God of Israel, he would have the two religions to be fairly tested, and by such a splendid miracle as none could question: and as the whole nation was deeply interested in the issue, it should take place most publicly, and on an elevated spot, on the summit of lofty Carmel, and in the presence of all Israel. He would have them all to be convened on this occasion, that they might witness with their own eyes both the absolute power and sovereignty of Jehovah, whose service they had renounced, and also the entire vanity of those idolatrous systems which had been substituted for it' (John Simpson). Such ever marks the difference between truth and error: the one courts the light, fearing no investigation; whereas error, the author of which is the prince of darkness, hates the light, and thrives most under cover of secrecy.

There is nothing to indicate that the prophet made known unto Ahab his intention: rather does he appear to have summarily ordered the king to summon together the people and the prophets: all concerned in the terrible sin – leaders and led – must be present. 'So Ahab sent unto all the children of Israel, and gathered the prophets together unto mount Carmel.' And *why* did Ahab comply so meekly and promptly with Elijah's demand? The general idea among the commentators is that the king was now desperate, and as beggars cannot be choosers he really had no other alternative than to consent. After three and a half years' famine the suffering must have been so acute that if the sorely-needed rain could be obtained in no other way except by being beholden to the prayers of Elijah, then so be it. Personally, we prefer to regard Ahab's acquiescence as a striking demonstration of the power of God over the hearts of men, yea, even over the king's, so that 'He turneth it whithersoever He will,' Prov. 21. 1.

This is a truth – a grand and basic one – which needs to be strongly emphasized in this day of scepticism and infidelity, when attention is confined to secondary causes and the prime mover is lost to view. Whether it be in the realm of creation or providence, it is the creature rather than the Creator who is regarded. Let our fields and gardens bear good crops, and the industry of the farmer and the skill of the gardener are praised; let them yield poorly, and the weather or something else is blamed: neither God's smile nor His frown is owned. So too in political affairs. How few, how very few acknowledge the hand of *God* in the present conflict of the nations. And let it be affirmed that the Lord is dealing with us in judgment for our sins, and even the majority of professing Christians are angered by such a declaration. But read through the Scriptures and observe how frequently it is there said, *the Lord* 'stirred' up the spirit of a certain king to do this, 'moved' him to do that, or 'withheld' him from doing the other.

As this is so rarely recognized and so feebly apprehended today we will cite a number of passages in proof. 'I also withheld thee from sinning against me,' Gen. 20. 6. 'I will harden his (Pharaoh's) heart, that he shall not let the people go,' Ex. 4. 21. 'The Lord shall cause thee to be smitten before thine enemies,' Deut. 28. 25. 'And the Spirit of the Lord began to move him,' Judges 13. 25. 'And the Lord stirred up an adversary unto Solomon,' 1 Kings 11. 14. 'And the God of Israel stirred up the spirit of Pul king of Assyria,' 1 Chron. 5. 26. 'The Lord stirred up against Jehoram the spirit of the Philistines,' 2 Chron. 21. 16. 'The Lord stirred up the spirit of Cyrus king of Persia, that he made a proclamation,' Ezra 1. 1. 'Behold, I will stir up the Medes against them,' Isa. 13. 17. 'I have caused thee to multiply as the bud of the field,' Ezek. 16. 7. 'Behold, I *will bring* upon Tyrus Nebuchadrezzar, king of Babylon, a king of kings, from the north, with horses, and with chariots,' Ezek. 26. 7.

'So Ahab sent unto all the children of Israel and gathered the prophets together unto mount Carmel.' In the light of the above scriptures, what believing heart will doubt for a moment that it was the Lord who made Ahab willing in the day of His power, willing to obey the one whom he hated above all others! And when God works, He works at *both* ends of the line: He who inclined the wicked king to carry out Elijah's instructions, moved not only the people of Israel but also the prophets of Baal to comply with Ahab's proclamation, for He controls His foes as truly as He does His friends. Possibly the people in general assembled together under the hope of beholding the rain fall at the call of Elijah, while the false prophets probably looked with contempt upon their being required to journey unto Carmel at the demand of Elijah through Ahab.

Because the Divine judgment had been inflicted on account of the apostasy of the nation and especially as a testimony against its idolatry, the nation must be (outwardly and avowedly at least) reclaimed before the judgment could be removed. The lengthy drought had wrought no change, and the consequent famine had not brought the people back to God. So far as we can gather from the inspired narrative, the people were, with few exceptions, as much wedded to their idols as ever; and whatever may have been either the convictions or the practices of the remnant who bowed not their knee to Baal, they were so afraid publicly to express themselves (lest they be put to death) that Elijah was unaware of their very existence. Nevertheless, till the people were brought back unto their allegiance to God, no favour could be expected from Him.

'They must repent and turn themselves from their idols, or nothing could avail to avert God's judgment. Though Noah and Samuel and Job had made intercession, it would not have induced the Lord to withdraw from the conflict. They must forsake their idols and return to Jehovah.' Those words were written almost a century ago, yet they are as true and pertinent now as they were then, for they enunciate an abiding principle. God will not wink at sin or gloss over evil doing. Whether He be dealing in judgment with an individual or with a nation, that which has displeased Him must be rectified before there can be a return of His favour. It is useless to pray for His blessing while we refuse to put away that which has called down His curse. It is vain to talk about exercising faith in God's promises until we have exercised repentance for our sins. Our idols must be destroyed ere God will again accept of our worship.

CHAPTER FOURTEEN

The Call to Carmel

'So Ahab sent unto all the children of Israel, and gathered the prophets together unto mount Carmel,' 1 Kings 18. 20. Let us endeavour to picture the scene. It is early morning. From all sides the eager crowds are making their way toward this spot, which from remotest times has been associated with worship. No work is being done anywhere: a single thought possesses the minds of young and old alike as they respond to their king's summons to gather together for this mighty concourse. Behold the many thousands of Israel occupying every foot of vantage ground from which they could obtain a view of the proceedings! Were they to witness a miracle? Was an end now to be put unto their sufferings? Was the long hoped-for rain about to fall? A hush descends upon the multitude as they hear the tread of marshalled men: conspicuous with the sun-symbols flashing on their turbaned heads, sure of court favour and insolently defiant, come the four hundred and fifty prophets of Baal. Then, through the crowds, is carried the litter of the king, on the shoulders of his guard of honour, surrounded by his officers of state. Something like that must have been the scene presented on this auspicious occasion.

'And Elijah came unto all the people,' v. 21. Behold the sea of upturned faces as every eye is focused on this strange and stern figure, at whose word the heavens had been as brass for the last three years. With what intense interest and awe must they have gazed upon this lone man of sinewy build, with flashing eyes and compressed lips. What a solemn hush must have fallen upon that vast assembly as they beheld one man pitted against the whole company. With what malignant glances would his every movement be watched by the jealous priests and prophets. As one commentator puts it, 'No tiger ever watched its victim more fiercely! If they may have *their* way, he will never touch yonder plain again.' As Ahab himself watched this servant of the Most High, fear and hatred must have alternated in his heart, for the king regarded Elijah as the cause of all his troubles, yet he felt that somehow the coming of rain depended upon him.

The stage was now set. The huge audience was assembled, the leading characters were about to play their parts, and one of the most dramatic acts in the whole history of Israel was about to be staged. There was to be a public contest between the forces of good and evil. On the one side was Baal with his hundreds of prophets, on the other Jehovah and His lone servant. How great was the courage of Elijah, how strong his faith, as he dared to stand alone in the cause of God against such powers and numbers. But we need not fear for the intrepid Tishbite: he needs no sympathy of ours. He was consciously standing in the presence of One to whom the nations are but as a drop in a bucket. All Heaven was behind him. Legions of angels filled that mountain, though they were invisible to the eye of sense. Though he was but a frail creature like ourselves, yet Elijah was full of faith and spiritual power, and by that faith he subdued kingdoms, wrought righteousness, escaped the edge of the sword, waxed valiant in fight and turned to flight the armies of the aliens.

'Elijah stands forth before them all with a confident and majestic mien, as the ambassador of Heaven. His manly spirit, emboldened by the consciousness of the Divine protection, inspired with courage, and awed all opposition. But what an awful and loathsome sight presented itself to the man of God, to see such a gathering of Satan's agents, who had withdrawn the people of Jehovah from His holy and honourable service, and had seduced them into the abominable and debasing superstitions of the Devil! Elijah was not of a kindred spirit with those who can see with composure their God insulted, their fellow-countrymen degrading themselves at the instigation of wily men, and destroying their immortal souls through the gross impositions practised upon them. He could not look with a placid eye upon the four hundred and fifty vile impostors, who made it their business, for filthy lucre or for courtly favour, to delude the ignorant multitude to their eternal destruction. He looked upon idolatry as a crying shame: as nothing better than evil personified, the Devil deified, and Hell formed into a religious establishment; and he would regard the abettors of the diabolical system with abhorrence' (John Simpson).

It seems reasonable to conclude that Ahab and his assembled subjects would expect Elijah on this occasion to pray for rain, and that they would now witness the sudden end of the long drought and its attendant famine. Had not the three years of which he had prophesied, 1 Kings 17. 1, run their weary course? Was mourning and suffering now to give place to joy and plenty again? Ah, but there was something else besides praying that the windows of Heaven might be opened, something of much greater importance which must first be attended to. Neither Ahab nor his subjects were yet in any fit state of soul to be made the recipients of His blessings and mercies. God had been dealing with them in judgment for their awful sins, and thus far His rod had not been acknowledged, nor had the occasion of His displeasure been removed. As Matthew Henry pointed out, 'God will first prepare our hearts, and then cause His ear to hear: will first turn us to Him, and then turn to us (see Psa. 10. 17). Deserters must not look for God's favours till they return to their allegiance.'

'And Elijah came unto all the people, and said.' The servant of God at once took the initiative, being in complete command of the situation. It is unspeakably solemn to note that he said not a single word to the false prophets, making no attempt to convert *them*. They were devoted to destruction, v. 40. No, instead he addressed himself to the people, of whom there was some hope, saying, 'How long halt ye between two opinions?' v. 21. The word for 'halt' is *totter*: they were not walking uprightly. Sometimes they tottered over to the side of the God of Israel, and then they lurched like an intoxicated person over on the side of the false gods. They were not fully decided which to follow. They dreaded Jehovah, and therefore would not totally abandon Him; they desired to curry favour with the king and queen, and so felt they must embrace the religion of the state. Their conscience forbade them to do the former, their fear of man persuaded them to do the latter; but in neither were they heartily engaged. Thus Elijah upbraided them with their inconstancy and fickleness.

Elijah made a demand *for definite decision.* It is to be borne in mind that *Jehovah* was the name by which the God of the Israelites had always been distinguished since their coming out of Egypt. Indeed, the Jehovah-God of their fathers was the God of Abraham, of Isaac, and of Jacob, Ex. 3. 15, 16. 'Jehovah' signifies the self-existent, omnipotent, immutable, and Eternal Being, the only God, beside whom there is none else. 'If Jehovah be God, follow Him: but if Baal, then follow him.' There was no 'if' in the mind of the prophet: he knew full well that Jehovah *was* the one true and living God, but the people must be shown the untenability and absurdity of their vacillation. Religions which are diametrically opposed cannot both be right: one must be wrong, and as soon as the true is discovered, the false must be cast to the winds. The present-day application of Elijah's demand would be this: if the Christ of Scripture be the true Saviour, then surrender to Him; if the christ of modern Christendom, then follow him. One who demands the *denying* of self, and another who allows the *gratifying* of self, cannot both be right. One who insists on separation from the world, and another who permits you to enjoy its friendship, cannot both be right. One who requires the uncompromising mortification of sin, and another who suffers you to trifle with it, cannot both be the Christ of God.

There were times when those Israelites attempted to serve both God and Baal. They had some knowledge of Jehovah, but Jezebel with her host of false prophets had unsettled their minds. The example of the king misled them and his influence corrupted them. The worship of Baal was popular and his prophets fêted; the worship of Jehovah was discountenanced and His servants put to death. This caused the people in general to conceal any regard they had for the Lord. It induced them to join in the idolatrous worship in order to escape ill-will and persecution. Consequently they halted between the two parties. They were like lame persons: unsteady, limping up and down. They vacillated in their sentiments and conduct. They thought so to accommodate themselves to both parties as to please and secure the favour of both. There was no evenness in their walk, no steadiness in their principles, no consistency in their conduct. Thus they both dishonoured God and debased themselves by this mongrel kind of religion, wherein they 'feared the Lord, and served other gods,' 2 Kings 17. 33. But God will not accept a divided heart: He will have all or none.

The Lord is a jealous God, demanding our whole affection, and will not accept a divided empire with Baal. You must be for Him or against Him. He will permit of no compromise. You must *declare yourself*. When Moses saw the people of Israel dancing around the golden calf, after destroying the idol and rebuking Aaron, he stood in the gate of the camp and said, 'Who is on the Lord's side? let him come unto me,' Ex. 32. 26. O my reader, if you have not already done so, resolve with godly Joshua, 'But as for me and my house, we will serve the Lord,' Josh. 24. 15. Ponder these solemn words of Christ: 'He that is not with Me is against Me; and he that gathereth not with Me scattereth abroad,' Matt. 12. 30. Nothing is so repulsive to Him as the lukewarm professor: 'I would thou wert cold or hot,' Rev. 3. 15 – one thing or the other. He has plainly warned us that 'no man can serve two masters.' Then 'How long halt *ye* between two opinions?' Come to some decision one way or the other, for there can be no compromise between Christ and Belial.

There are some who have been brought up under the protection and sanctifying influence of a godly home. Later, they go out into the world, and are apt to be dazzled by its glittering tinsel and carried away by its apparent happiness. Their foolish hearts hanker after its attractions and pleasures. They are invited to participate, and are sneered at if they hesitate. And only too often, because they have not grace in their hearts, nor strength of mind to withstand the temptations, they are drawn aside, heeding the counsel of the ungodly and standing in the way of sinners. True, they cannot altogether forget their early training, and at times an uneasy conscience will move them to read a chapter out of the Bible and to say their prayers; and so they halt between two alternatives and vainly attempt to serve two masters. They will not cleave to God alone, relinquish all for Him, and follow Him with undivided hearts. They are halters, borderers, who love and follow the world, and yet retain something of the form of godliness.

There are others who cling to an orthodox creed, yet enter into the gaieties of the world and freely indulge the lusts of the flesh. 'They profess that they know God; but in works they deny Him,' Titus 1. 16. They attend religious services regularly, posing as worshippers of God through the one Mediator and claiming to be indwelt by that Spirit through whose gracious operations the people of God are enabled to turn from sin and to walk in the paths of righteousness and true holiness. But if you entered their homes, you would soon have reason to doubt their pretensions. You would find no worship of God in their family circle, perhaps none, or at best a mere formal worship in private; you would hear nothing about God or His claims in their daily conversation, and see nothing in their conduct to distinguish them from respectable worldlings; yea, you would behold some things which the more decent non-professors would be ashamed of. There is such a lack of integrity and consistency in their characters as renders them offensive to God and contemptible in the eyes of men of understanding.

There are yet others who must also be classed among those who halt and hesitate, being inconstant in their position and practice. This is a less numerous class, who have been brought up in the world, amid its follies and vanities. But by affliction, the preaching of God's Word, or some other means, they have been made sensible that they must turn to the Lord and serve *Him* if they are to escape the wrath to come and lay hold on eternal life. They have become dissatisfied with their worldly life, yet, being surrounded with worldly friends and relatives, they are afraid of altering their line of conduct, lest they should give offence to their godless companions and bring down upon them their scoffs and opposition. Hence they make sinful compromises, trying to conceal their better convictions but neglecting many of God's claims upon them. Thus they halt between two opinions: what God will think of them, and what the world will think of them. They have not that firm reliance on the Lord which will lead them to break from His enemies and be out and out for Him.

There is one other class which we must mention, who, though they differ radically from those which we have described above, yet must be regarded as proper subjects to ask, 'How long halt ye between two opinions?' While they are certainly to be pitied, yet they must be reproved. We refer to those who know that the Lord is to be loved and served with all the heart and in all that He commands, but for some reason or other they fail to avow themselves openly on His side. They are outwardly separated from the world, taking no part in its empty pleasures, and none can point to anything in their conduct which is contrary to the Scriptures. They honour the Sabbath day, attend regularly the means of grace, and like to be in the company of God's people. Yet they do not publicly take their place among the followers of Christ and sit down at His table. Either they feel too unworthy to do so, or fear they might bring some reproach on His cause. But such weakness and inconsistency is wrong. If the Lord be God, follow Him as He bids, and trust Him for all needed grace.

'If Jehovah be God, follow Him; but if Baal, then follow him.' The 'double minded man is unstable in all his ways,' James 1. 8. We must be as decided in our practice as in our opinion or belief, otherwise – no matter how orthodox our creed – our profession is worthless. It was evident there could not be two supreme Gods, and therefore Elijah called upon the people to make up their minds which was really God; and as they could not possibly serve two masters, let them give their whole hearts and undivided energies to that Being whom they concluded to be the true and living God. And this is what the Holy Spirit is saying to you, my unsaved reader: weigh the one against the other – the idol you have been giving your affections unto and Him whom you have slighted; and if you are assured that the Lord Jesus Christ be 'the true God,' 1 John 5. 20, then choose Him as your portion, surrender to Him as your Lord, cleave to Him as your all in all. The Redeemer will not be served by halves or with reserves.

'And the people answered him not a word,' v. 21: either because they were unwilling to acknowledge their guilt, and thereby offend Ahab; or because they were unable to refute Elijah, and so were ashamed of themselves. They did not know what to say. Whether convicted or confused, we know not; but certainly they were confounded – incapable of finding an error in the prophet's reasoning. They seem to have been stunned that such alternatives should be presented to their choice, but they were neither honest enough to own their folly nor bold enough to say they had acted in compliance with the king's command, following a multitude to do evil. They therefore sought refuge in silence, which is to be much preferred to the frivolous excuses proffered by most of such people today when they are rebuked for their evil ways. There can be little doubt but what they were awed by the searching questions of the prophet.

'And the people answered him not a word.' O for that plain and faithful preaching which would so reveal to men the unreasonableness of their position, which would so expose their hypocrisy, so sweep away the cobwebs of their sophistry, which would so arraign them at the bar of their own consciences that their every objection would be silenced, and they would stand self-condemned. Alas, on every side we behold those who are seeking to serve both God and mammon, attempting to win the smile of the world and to earn the 'well done' of Christ. Like Jonathan of old, they wish to retain their standing in Saul's palace and yet keep in with David. And how many professing Christians there are in these days who can hear Christ and His people reviled, and never open their mouths in reprimand – afraid to stand up boldly for God, ashamed of Christ and His cause, though their consciences approve of the very things for which they hear the Lord's people criticized. O guilty silence, which is likely to meet with a silent Heaven when they are pleased to cry for mercy.

'Then said Elijah unto the people, I, even I only, remain a prophet of the Lord; but Baal's prophets are four hundred and fifty men. Let them therefore give us two bullocks; and let them choose one bullock for themselves, and cut it in pieces, and lay it on wood, and put no fire under: and I will dress the other bullock, and lay it on wood, and put no fire under. And call ye on the name of your gods, and I will call on the name of the Lord: and the God that answereth by fire, let Him be God. And all the people answered and said, It is well spoken,' vv. 22-24. This was an eminently fair challenge, because Baal was supposed to be the fire god, or lord of the sun. Elijah gave the false prophets the preference, so that the outcome of the contest might be the more conspicuous to the glory of God. The proposal was so reasonable that the people at once assented to it, which forced their seducers out into the open: they must either comply with the challenge or acknowledge that Baal was an impostor.

CHAPTER FIFTEEN

Elijah's Challenge

——

'Then said Elijah unto the people, I, even I only, remain a prophet of the Lord; but Baal's prophets are four hundred and fifty men,' 1 Kings 18. 22. The righteous are bold as a lion: undeterred by difficulties, undismayed by the numbers which are arrayed against them. If God be for them, Rom. 8. 31, it matters not who be against them, for the battle is His and not theirs. True, there were 'a hundred men of the Lord's prophets' hidden away in a cave, v. 13, but what were they worth to His cause? Apparently they were afraid to show their faces in public, for there is no hint that they were present here on Carmel. Out of the four hundred and fifty-one prophets assembled on the mount that day, Elijah only was on the side of Jehovah. Ah, my readers, truth cannot be judged by the numbers who avow and support it: the Devil has ever had the vast majority on his side. And is it any otherwise today? What percentage of present-day preachers are uncompromisingly proclaiming the truth, and among them how many practise what they preach?

'Let them therefore give us two bullocks, and let them choose one bullock for themselves, and cut it in pieces, and lay it on wood, and put no fire under: and I will dress the other bullock, and lay it on wood, and put no fire under: and call ye on the name of your gods, and I will call on the name of the Lord: and the God that answereth by fire, let him be God,' vv. 23, 24. The time had now arrived when things must be brought to a head: Jehovah and Baal brought face to face as it were before the whole nation. It was of the utmost importance that the people of Israel should be roused from their ungodly indifference and that it should be incontrovertibly settled who was the true God, entitled to their obedience and worship. Elijah therefore proposed to put the matter beyond dispute. It had already been demonstrated by the three years' drought, at the word of the prophet, that Jehovah could withhold rain at His pleasure, and that the prophets of Baal could not reverse it or produce either rain or dew. Now a further test shall be made, a trial *by fire*, which came more immediately within their own province, since Baal was worshipped as the lord of the sun, and his devotees consecrated to him by 'passing through the fire,' 2 Kings 16. 3. It was therefore a challenge which his prophets could not refuse without acknowledging they were but impostors.

Not only was this trial by fire one which forced the prophets of Baal out into the open and therefore made manifest the emptiness of their pretensions, but it was one eminently calculated to appeal to the minds of the people of Israel. On how many a glorious occasion in the past had Jehovah 'answered *by fire!*' That was the sign given to Moses at Horeb, when 'the Angel of the Lord appeared unto him in a flame of fire out of the midst of a bush: and he looked, and, behold, the bush burned with fire, and the bush was not consumed,' Ex. 3. 2. This was the symbol of His presence with His people in their wilderness wanderings: 'The Lord went before them by day in a pillar of a cloud, to lead them the way; and by night in a pillar of fire, to give them light,' Ex. 13. 21. Thus it was when the Covenant was made and the Law was given, for 'mount Sinai was altogether on a smoke, because the Lord descended upon it in fire: and the smoke thereof ascended as the smoke of a furnace,' Ex. 19. 18. This too was the token He gave of His acceptance of the sacrifices which His people offered upon His altar: 'there came a fire out from before the Lord, and consumed upon the altar the burnt offering and the fat: which when all the people saw, they shouted, and fell on their faces,' Lev. 9. 24. So it was in the days of David: see 1 Chronicles 21. 26. Hence the descent of supernatural fire from Heaven on this occasion would make it manifest to the people that the Lord God of Elijah was the God of their fathers.

'The God that answereth by fire.' How strange! Why not 'The God that answereth *by water?*' That was what the land was in such urgent need of. True, but before the rain could be given, something else had to intervene. The drought was a Divine judgment upon the idolatrous country and God's wrath must be appeased before His judgment could be averted. And this leads us to the deeper meaning of this remarkable drama. There can be no reconciliation between a holy God and sinners save on the ground of atonement, and there can be no atonement or remission of sins except by the shedding of blood. Divine justice must be satisfied: the penalty of the broken law must be inflicted – either on the guilty culprit or upon an innocent substitute. And this grand and basic truth was unmistakably set before the eyes of that assembled host on Mount Carmel. A bullock was slain, cut in pieces, and laid upon wood, and He who caused fire to descend and consume that sacrifice avouched Himself to be the true and only God of Israel. The fire of God's wrath must fall either on the guilty people or on a sacrificial substitute.

As we have pointed out above, the descent of fire from Heaven on the vicarious victim, 1 Chron. 21. 26, was not only the manifestation of God's holy wrath, consuming that upon which sin was laid, but it was also the public attestation of His acceptance of the sacrifice, as it ascended to Him in the smoke as a sweet-smelling savour. It was therefore an evident proof that sin had been dealt with, atoned for, put away, Divine holiness now being vindicated and satisfied. Therefore it was that on the day of Pentecost the Holy Spirit descended, appearing as 'cloven tongues like as *of fire,*' Acts 2. 3. In his explanation of the phenomena of that day, Peter said, 'This Jesus hath God raised up, whereof we all are witnesses. Therefore being by the right hand of God exalted, and having received of the Father the promise of the Holy Ghost, He hath shed forth *this*, which ye now see and hear,' and again, 'Therefore let all the house of Israel know assuredly, that God hath made that same Jesus, whom ye have crucified, both Lord and Christ,' Acts 2. 32, 33, 36. The gift of the Spirit as 'tongues like as of fire' evidenced God's acceptance of Christ's atoning sacrifice, testified to His resurrection from the dead, and affirmed His exaltation to the Father's throne.

'The God that answereth by fire.' Fire, then, is the evidence of the Divine presence, Ex. 3. 2: it is the symbol of His sin-hating wrath, Mark 9. 43-49: it is the sign of His acceptance of an appointed and substitutionary sacrifice, Lev. 9. 24: it is the emblem of the Holy Spirit, Acts 2. 3, who enlightens, inflames and cleanses the believer. And it is by fire that He shall yet deal with the unbeliever, for when the despised and rejected Redeemer returns, it will be '*in flaming fire* taking vengeance on them that know not God and that obey not the Gospel of our Lord Jesus Christ: who shall be punished with everlasting destruction from the presence of the Lord,' 2 Thess. 1. 8, 9. And again it is written, 'The Son of man shall send forth His angels, and they shall gather out of His kingdom all things that offend, and them which do iniquity; and shall cast them into a furnace of fire: there shall be wailing and gnashing of teeth,' Matt. 13. 41, 42. Unspeakably solemn is this: alas that the unfaithful pulpit now conceals the fact that 'our God is a consuming fire,' Heb. 12. 29. O what a fearful awaking there will yet be, for in the last day it shall appear that 'whosoever was not found written in the book of life was cast into the lake of fire,' Rev. 20. 15.

'Let them therefore give us two bullocks; and let them choose one bullock for themselves, and cut it in pieces, and lay it on the wood, and put no fire under: and I will dress the other bullock, and lay it on wood, and put no fire under. And call ye on the name of your gods, and I will call on the name of the Lord: and the God that answereth by fire, let Him be God.' It will thus be seen that the test submitted by Elijah was a threefold one: it was to centre around a slain sacrifice; it was to evidence the efficacy of prayer; it was to make manifest the true God by the descent of fire from Heaven, which in its ultimate significance pointed to the gift of the Spirit as the fruit of an ascended Christ. And it is at these same three points, my reader, that every religion – *our* religion – must be tested today. Does the ministry you sit under focus your mind upon, draw out your heart unto, and demand your faith in, the atoning death of the Lord Jesus Christ? If it fails to do so, you may know it is *not* the Gospel of God. Is the One you worship a prayer-answering God? If not, either you worship a false god, or you are not in communion with the true God. Have you received the Holy Spirit as a sanctifier? If not, your state is no better than that of the heathen.

It must of course be borne in mind that this was an extraordinary occasion, and that Elijah's procedure supplies no example for Christ's ministers to follow today. Had not the prophet done according to Divine commission, he had acted in mad presumption, tempting God, by demanding such a miracle at His hands, placing the truth at such hazard. But it is quite clear from his own statement that he acted on instructions from Heaven: 'I have done all these things at Thy Word,' v. 36. That, and nothing else but *that*, is to regulate the servants of God in all their undertakings: they must not go one iota beyond what their Divine commission calls for. There must be no experimenting, no acting in self-will, no following of human traditions; but a doing of all things according to God's Word. Nor was Elijah afraid to trust the Lord as to the outcome. He had received his orders, and in simple faith had carried them out, fully assured that Jehovah would not fail him, and put him to confusion before that great assembly. He knew that God would not place him at the front of the battle, and then desert him. True, a wondrous miracle would have to be wrought, but *that* occasioned no difficulty to one who dwelt in the secret place of the Most High.

'And the God that answereth by fire, *let Him be God*,' let Him be accounted and owned as the true God: followed, served and worshipped as such. Since He has given such proofs of His existence, such demonstrations of His mighty power, such manifestations of His character, such a revelation of His will, all unbelief, indecision and refusal to give Him His rightful place in our hearts and lives is utterly inexcusable. Then let Him be your God, by surrendering yourself to Him. He does not force Himself upon you, but condescends to present Himself to you: deigns to offer Himself to your acceptance, bids you choose Him by an act of your own will. His claims upon thee are beyond dispute. It is for thine own good that thou shouldest make Him thy God – thy supreme good, thy portion, thy King. It is thine irreparable loss and eternal destruction if thou failest to do so. Heed, then, that affectionate invitation of His servant: 'I beseech you therefore, brethren, by the mercies of God, that ye present your bodies a living sacrifice, holy, acceptable unto God, which is *your reasonable service*,' Rom. 12. 1.

'And all the people answered and said, It is well spoken,' v. 24. They were agreed that such a proposal should be made, for it struck them as an excellent method of determining the controversy and arriving at the truth as to who was the true God and who was not. This would be a demonstration to their senses, the witnessing of a miracle. The word which Elijah had addressed to their conscience had left them silent, but an appeal to their reason was at once approved. Such a supernatural sign would make it evident that the sacrifice had been accepted of God, and they were eagerly anxious to witness the unique experiment. Their curiosity was all alive, and they were keen to ascertain whether Elijah or the prophets of Baal should obtain the victory. Alas, such is poor human nature; ready to witness the miracles of Christ, but deaf to His call to repentance; pleased with any outward show that appeals to the senses, but displeased with any word that convicts and condemns. Is it thus *with us?*

It is to be noted that Elijah not only gave his opponents choice of the two bullocks, but also conceded them the stage for the first trial, that they might, if they could, establish the claims of Baal and their own power, and thus settle the dispute without any further action: yet knowing full well they would be foiled and confused. In due course the prophet would do, in every respect, what they had done, so that there should be no difference between them. Only one restriction was placed upon them (as also on himself) namely, 'put no fire under,' v. 23, the wood – so as to prevent any fraud. But there was a deeper principle involved, one which was to be unmistakably demonstrated that day on Carmel – man's extremity is God's opportunity. The utter impotency of the creature must be felt and seen before the power of God could be displayed. Man has first to be brought to the end of himself ere the sufficiency of Divine grace is appreciated. It is only those who know themselves to be undone and lost sinners who can welcome One who is mighty to save.

'And Elijah said unto the prophets of Baal, Choose you one bullock for yourselves, and dress it first; for ye are many; and call on the name of your gods, but put no fire under. And they took the bullock which was given them, and they dressed it, and called on the name of Baal from morning even until noon, saying, O Baal, hear us. But there was no voice, nor any that answered. And they leaped upon the altar which was made,' vv. 25, 26. For the first time in their history these false priests were unable to insert the secret spark of fire among the faggots which lay upon their altar. They were compelled, therefore, to rely on a direct appeal to their patron deity. And this they did with might and main. Round and round the altar they went in their wild and mystic dance, breaking rank now and again to leap up and down on the altar, all the while repeating their monotonous chant, 'O Baal, hear us, O Baal hear us' – send down fire on the sacrifice. They wearied themselves with going through the various exercises of their idolatrous worship, keeping it up three whole hours.

But notwithstanding all their zeal and all their importunity with Baal, 'There was no voice nor any that answered.' What a proof that idols are but 'the work of *men's* hands.' 'They have mouths, but they speak not: eyes have they, but they see not: . . . they have hands, but they handle not: feet have they, but they walk not . . . they that make them are like unto them; so is everyone that trusteth in them,' Psa. 115. 4-8. 'No doubt Satan could have sent fire, Job 1. 9-12, and would, if he might have done it; but he could do nothing except what is permitted him' (Thomas Scott). Yes, we read of the second beast of Revelation 13 that 'he doeth great wonders, so that he maketh fire come down from heaven on the earth in the sight of men,' v. 13. But on this occasion the Lord would not suffer the Devil to use his power, because there was an open trial between Himself and Baal.

'But there was no voice nor any that answered.' The altar stood cold and smokeless, the bullock unconsumed. The powerlessness of Baal and the folly of his worshippers was made fully apparent. The vanity and absurdity of idolatry stood completely exposed. No false religion, my reader, is able to send down fire upon a vicarious sacrifice. No false religion can put away sin, bestow the Holy Spirit, or grant supernatural answers to prayer. Tested at these three vital points they one and all fail, as Baal's worship did that memorable day on Carmel.

CHAPTER SIXTEEN

Ears That Hear Not

———

'And it came to pass at noon, that Elijah mocked them, and said, Cry aloud: for he is a god; either he is talking, or he is pursuing, or he is in a journey, or peradventure he sleepeth, and must be awaked,' 1 Kings 18. 27. Hour after hour the prophets of Baal had called upon their god to make public demonstration of his existence by causing fire to come down from heaven and consume the sacrifice which they had placed upon his altar; but all to no purpose: 'there was no voice, nor any that answered.' And now the silence was broken by the voice of the Lord's servant, speaking in derision. The absurdity and fruitlessness of their efforts richly merited this biting sarcasm. Sarcasm is a dangerous weapon to employ, but its use is fully warranted in exposing the ridiculous pretensions of error, and is often quite effective in convincing men of the folly and unreasonableness of their ways. It was due unto the people of Israel that Elijah should hold up to contempt those who were seeking to deceive them.

'And it came to pass at noon, that Elijah mocked them.' It was at midday, when the sun was highest and the false priests had the best opportunity of success, that Elijah went near them and in ironical terms bade them increase their efforts. He was so sure that nothing could avert their utter discomfiture that he could afford to ridicule them by suggesting a cause for the indifference of their god: 'Peradventure he sleepeth, and must be awaked.' The case is so urgent, your credit and his honour are so much at stake, that you must arouse him: therefore shout louder, for your present cries are too feeble, they are not heard, your voice does not reach his remote dwellingplace: you must redouble your efforts in order to gain his attention. Thus did the faithful and intrepid Tishbite pour ridicule on their impotency and hold up to contempt their defeat. He knew it would be so, and that no zeal on their part could change things.

Is the reader shocked at these sarcastic utterances of Elijah on this occasion? Then let us remind him that it is written in the Word of Truth, 'He that sitteth in the heavens shall laugh: the Lord shall have them in derision,' Psa. 2. 4. Unspeakably solemn is this, yet unmistakably just: *they* had laughed at God and derided *His* warnings and threatenings, and now He answers such fools according to their folly. The Most High is indeed long-suffering, yet there is a limit to His patience. He calls unto men, but they refuse; He stretches out His hand unto them, but they will not regard. He counsels them, but they set it all at nought; He reproves, but they will have none of it. Shall, then, He be mocked with impunity? No, He declares, 'I also will laugh at your calamity; I will mock when your fear cometh; when your fear cometh as desolation, and your destruction cometh as a whirlwind; when distress and anguish cometh upon you. Then shall they call upon Me, but I will not answer; they shall seek Me early, but they shall not find Me,' Prov. 1. 24-28.

The derision of Elijah upon Mount Carmel was but a shadowing forth of the derision of the Almighty in the day when He deals in judgment. Is our own lot now cast in such a day? 'For that they hated knowledge, and did not choose the fear of the Lord: they would none of My counsel: they despised all My reproof.' Who, with any spiritual discernment, can deny that those fearful words accurately describe the conduct of our own generation? Is then the awful sentence now going forth, 'Therefore shall they eat of the fruit of their own way, and be filled with their own devices. For the ease of the simple shall slay them, and the prosperity of fools shall destroy them,' Prov. 1. 29-32 (marg.)? If so, who can question the righteousness of it? How blessed to note that this unspeakably solemn passage ends with – 'But whoso hearkeneth unto me shall dwell safely, and shall be quiet from fear of evil.' That is a precious promise for faith to lay hold of, to plead before God, and to expect an answer thereto, for our God is not a deaf or impotent one like Baal.

One would have thought those priests of Baal had perceived that Elijah was only mocking them while he lashed them with such cutting irony, for what sort of a god must he be which answered to the prophet's description! Yet so infatuated and stupid were those devotees of Baal that they do not appear to have discerned the drift of his words, but rather to have regarded them as containing good advice. Accordingly, they roused themselves to yet greater earnestness, and by the most barbarous measures strove to move their god by the sight of the blood which they shed out of love to him and zeal in his service, and in which they supposed he delighted. What poor, miserable slaves are idolaters, whose objects of worship can be gratified with human gore and with the self-inflicted torments of their worshippers! It has ever been true, and still is today, that 'the dark places of the earth are full of the habitations of cruelty,' Psa. 74. 20. How thankful we should be if a sovereign God has mercifully delivered us from such superstitions.

'And they cried aloud, and cut themselves after their manner with knives and lancets, till the blood gushed out upon them,' v. 28. What a concept they must have held of their deity who required such cruel lacerations at their hands! Similar sights may be witnessed today in heathendom. The service of Satan, whether in the observance of idolatrous worship or in the practice of immoralities, whilst it promises indulgence to men's lusts is cruel to their persons and tends to torment them in this world. Jehovah expressly forbade *His* worshippers to 'cut themselves,' Deut. 14. 1. He indeed requires us to mortify our corruptions, but bodily severities are no pleasure to Him. He desires only our happiness, and never requires one thing which has not a direct tendency to make us more holy that we may be more happy, for there cannot be any real *happiness* apart from *holiness*.

'And it came to pass, when midday was past, and they prophesied until the time of the offering of the evening sacrifice, that there was neither voice, nor any to answer, nor any that regarded,' v. 29. Thus they continued praying and prophesying, singing and dancing, cutting themselves and bleeding, until the time when the evening sacrifice was offered in the temple at Jerusalem, which was at 3 p.m. For six hours without intermission had they importuned their god. But all the exertions and implorings of Baal's prophets were unavailing: no fire came down to consume their sacrifice. Surely the lengths to which they had gone was enough to move the compassion of any deity! And since the heavens remained completely silent, did it not prove to the people that the religion of Baal and his worship was a delusion and a sham?

'There was neither voice, nor any to answer, nor any that regarded.' How this exposed *the powerlessness* of false gods. They are impotent creatures, unable to help their votaries in the hour of need. They are useless for this life; how much more so for the life to come! Nowhere does the imbecility which sin produces more plainly evidence itself than in idolatry. It makes utter fools of its victims, as was manifest there on Carmel. The prophets of Baal reared their altar and placed upon it the sacrifice, and then called upon their god for the space of six hours to evidence his acceptance of their offering. But in vain. Their importunity met with no response: the heavens were as brass. No tongue of fire leaped from the sky to lick up the flesh of the slain bullock. The only sound heard was the cries of anguish from the lips of the frantic priests as they maltreated themselves till their blood gushed forth.

And my reader, if *you* be a worshipper of idols, and continue so, you shall yet discover that your god is just as impotent and disappointing as was Baal. Is your *belly* your god? Do you set your heart upon enjoying the fat of the land, eating and drinking not to live, but living to eat and drink? Does your table groan beneath the luxuries of the earth, while many today are lacking its necessities? Then know you that, if you persist in this wickedness and folly, the hour is coming when you shall discover the madness of such a course.

Is *pleasure* your god? Do you set your heart upon a ceaseless whirl of gaiety – rushing from one form of entertainment to another, spending all your available time and money in visiting the garish shows of 'Vanity Fair?' Are your hours of recreation made up of a continual round of excitement and merriment? Then know you that, if you persist in this folly and wickedness, the hour is coming when you shall taste of the bitter dregs which lie at the bottom of such a cup.

Is *mammon* your god? Do you set your heart upon material riches, bending all your energies to the obtaining of that which you imagine will give you power over men, a place of prominence in the social world, and enable you to procure those things which are supposed to make for comfort and satisfaction? Is it the acquisition of property, a large bank-balance, the possession of stocks and shares, for which you are bartering your soul? Then know you that, if you persist in such a senseless and evil course, the time is coming when you shall discover the worthlessness of such things, and their powerlessness to mitigate your remorse.

O the folly, the consummate madness of serving false gods! From the highest viewpoint it is madness, for it is an affront unto the true God, a giving unto some other object that which is due unto Him alone, an insult which He will not tolerate or pass by. But even on the lowest ground it is crass folly, for no false god, no idol, is capable of furnishing real help at the time man needs help most of all. No form of idolatry, no system of false religion, no god but the true One, can send miraculous answers to prayer, can supply satisfactory evidence that sin is put away, can give the Holy Spirit, who, like fire, illumines the understanding, warms the heart and cleanses the soul. A false god could not send down fire on Mount Carmel, and he cannot do so today. Then turn to the true God, my reader, while there is yet time.

Ere passing on, there is one other point which should be noted in what has been before us, a point which contains an important lesson for this superficial age. Let us state it thus: the expenditure of great earnestness and enthusiasm is no proof of a true and good cause. There is a large class of shallow-minded people today who conclude that a display of religious zeal and fervour is a real sign of spirituality, and that such virtues fully compensate for whatever lack of knowledge and sound doctrine there may be. 'Give me a place,' say they, 'where there is plenty of life and warmth even though there be no depth to the preaching, rather than a sound ministry which is cold and unattractive.' Ah, my reader, all is not gold that glitters. Those prophets of Baal were full of earnest zeal and fervour, but it was in a false cause, and brought down nothing from Heaven! Then take warning therefrom, and be guided by God's Word and not by what appeals to your emotions or love of excitement.

'And Elijah said unto all the people, Come near unto me. And all the people came near unto him,' v. 30. Clearly evident was it that nothing could be gained by waiting any longer. The test which had been proposed by Elijah, which had been approved by the people, and which had been accepted by the false prophets, had convincingly demonstrated that Baal could have no claim to be the (true) God. The time had thus arrived for the servant of Jehovah to act. Remarkable restraint had he exercised all through those six hours while he had allowed his opponents to occupy the stage of action, breaking the silence only once to goad them on to increased endeavour. But now he addressed the people, bidding them to come near unto himself, that they might the better observe his actions. They responded at once, no doubt curious to see what he would do and wondering whether his appeal to Heaven would be more successful than had been that of the prophets of Baal.

'And he repaired the altar of the Lord that was broken down,' v. 30. Mark well his first action, which was designed to speak unto the hearts of those Israelites. Another has pointed out that here on Carmel Elijah made a threefold appeal unto the people. First, he had appealed to their *conscience*, when he asked and then exhorted them: 'How long halt ye between two opinions? if the Lord be God, follow Him: but if Baal, then follow him,' v. 21. Second, he had appealed to their *reason*, when he had proposed that trial should be made between the prophets of Baal and himself that 'the God that answereth by fire, let Him be God,' v. 24. And now, by 'repairing the altar of the Lord,' he appealed to their *hearts*. Therein he has left an admirable example for the servants of God in every age to follow. The ministers of Christ should address themselves unto the consciences, the understandings and the affections of their hearers, for only thus can the truth be adequately presented, the principal faculties of men's souls be reached, and a definite decision for the Lord be expected from them. A balance must be preserved between the Law and the Gospel. Conscience must be searched, the mind convinced, the affections warmed, if the will is to be moved unto action. Thus it was with Elijah on Carmel.

'And Elijah said unto all the people, Come near unto me. And all the people came near unto him.' How strong and unwavering was the prophet's confidence in his God. He knew full well what his faith and prayer had obtained from the Lord, and he had not the slightest fear that he would now be disappointed and put to confusion. The God of Elijah *never* fails any who trust in Him with all their hearts. But the prophet was determined that this answer by fire should be put beyond dispute. He therefore invited the closest scrutiny of the people as he repaired the broken altar of Jehovah. They should be in the nearest proximity so that they might see for themselves there was no trickery, no insertion of any secret spark beneath the wood on which the slain bullock was laid. Truth does not fear the closest investigation. It does not shun the light, but courts it. It is the evil one and his emissaries who love darkness and secrecy, and act under the cloak of mysticism.

'And he repaired the altar of the Lord that was broken down,' v. 30. There is far more here than meets the eye at first glance. Light is cast thereon by comparing the language of Elijah in 19. 10 – 'The children of Israel have forsaken Thy covenant, thrown down Thine altars.' According to the Mosaic law there was only one altar upon which sacrifices might be offered, and that was where the Lord had fixed His peculiar residence – from the days of Solomon, in Jerusalem. But before the tabernacle was erected, sacrifices might be offered in any place, and in the previous dispensation altars were built wherever the patriarchs sojourned for any length of time, and it is probably unto *them* that Elijah alluded in 19. 10. This broken altar, then, was a solemn witness that the people had departed from God. The prophet's repairing of the same was a rebuking of the people for their sin, a confession of it on their behalf, and, at the same time, bringing them back to *the place of beginning*.

And reader, this is recorded for our instruction: Elijah began by repairing the broken altar. And that is where *we* must begin if the blessing of Heaven is to come again on the churches and on our land. In many a professing Christian home there is a *neglected* altar of God. There was a time when the family gathered together and owned God in the authority of His Law, in the goodness of His daily providence, in the love of His redemption and continuing grace, but the sound of united worship no longer is heard ascending from that home. Prosperity, worldliness, pleasure, has silenced the accents of devotion. The altar has fallen down: the dark shadow of sin rests on that house. And there can be no approach to God while sin is unconfessed. They who hide sin cannot prosper, Prov. 28. 13. Sin must be confessed before God will respond with holy fire. And sin must be confessed in deed as well as in word: the altar must be *set up again*. The Christian must go back to the place of *beginning*. See Genesis 13. 1-4; Revelation 2. 4, 5.

CHAPTER SEVENTEEN

The Confidence of Faith

———

'And Elijah took twelve stones, according to the number of the tribes of the sons of Jacob, unto whom the word of the Lord came, saying, Israel shall be thy name,' 1 Kings 18. 31. This was striking and blessed, for it was taking the place of faith against the evidence of sight. There were present in that assembly only the subjects of Ahab, and consequently, members of none but the ten tribes. But Elijah took *twelve* stones to build the altar with, intimating that he was about to offer sacrifice in the name of the whole nation, cf. Josh. 4. 20; Ezra 6. 17. Thereby he testified to *their unity*, the union existing between Judah and the ten tribes. The Object of their worship had originally been one and the same and must be so now. Thus Elijah viewed Israel from the Divine standpoint. In the mind of God the nation had appeared before Him as one from all eternity. Outwardly they were now two. But the prophet ignored that division: he walked not by sight, but by faith, 2 Cor. 5. 7. This is what God delights in. Faith is that which honours Him, and therefore does He ever own and honour faith wherever it is found. He did so here on Carmel, and He does so today. 'Lord, *increase* our faith.'

And what is the grand truth that was symbolized by this incident? Is it not obvious? Must we not look beyond the typical and natural Israel unto the antitypical and spiritual Israel, the Church which is the Body of Christ? Surely! Then what? This: amid the widespread dispersion which now obtains – the 'children of God' which are 'scattered abroad,' John 11. 52 – amid the various denominations, we must not lose sight of the mystical and essential oneness of all the people of God. Here too we must walk by faith and not by sight. We should view things from the Divine standpoint: we should contemplate that Church which Christ loved and for which He gave Himself as it exists in the eternal purpose and everlasting counsels of the blessed Trinity. We shall never see the unity of the Bride, the Lamb's wife, visibly manifested before our outward eyes until we behold her descending out of Heaven 'having the glory of God.' But meanwhile it is both our duty and privilege to enter into God's ideal, to perceive the spiritual unity of His saints, and to *own* that unity by receiving into our affections *all* who manifest something of the image of Christ. Such is the truth inculcated by the 'twelve stones' used by Elijah.

'And Elijah took twelve stones, according to the number of the tribes of the sons of Jacob.' Let us also take notice how Elijah was regulated here by the Law of the Lord. God had given express directions about His altar: "If thou wilt make Me an altar of stone, thou shalt not build it of hewn stone: for if thou lift up thy tool upon it, thou hast polluted it. Neither shalt thou go up by steps unto Mine altar, that thy nakedness be not discovered thereon,' Ex. 20. 25, 26. In strict accordance with that Divine statute, Elijah did not send for stones that had been quarried and polished by human art, but used rough and unhewn stones which lay upon the mountain side. He took what God had provided and not what man had made. He acted according to the Divine pattern furnished him in the Holy Scriptures, for God's work must be done in the manner and method appointed by God.

This too is written for our learning. Each several act on this occasion, every detail of Elijah's procedure, needs to be noted and pondered if we would discover what is required from us if the Lord is to show Himself strong on our behalf. In connection with His service God has not left things to *our* discretion nor to the dictates of either human wisdom or expediency. He has supplied us with a 'pattern,' compare Heb. 8. 5, and He is very jealous of that pattern and requires us to be ordered by the same. Everything must be done as God has appointed. The moment we depart from God's pattern, that is, the moment we fail to act in strict conformity to a 'thus saith the Lord,' we are acting in self-will, and can no longer count upon His blessing. We must not expect 'the fire of God' until we have fully met His requirements.

In view of what has just been pointed out, need we have any difficulty in discovering why the blessing of God has departed from the churches, why His miracle-working power is no longer seen working in their midst? It is because there has been such woeful departure from His 'pattern,' because so many innovations have come in, because they have employed carnal weapons in their spiritual warfare, because they have wickedly brought in worldly means and methods. In consequence, the Holy Spirit is grieved and quenched. Not only must the occupant of the pulpit heed the Divine injunction and preach 'the preaching that I bid thee,' Jonah 3. 2, but the whole service, discipline and life of the church must be regulated by the directions God has given. The path of obedience is the path of spiritual prosperity and blessing, but the way of self-will and self-seeking is one of impotency and disaster.

'And with the stones he built an altar in the name of the Lord: and he made a trench about the altar, as great as would contain two measures of seed,' v. 32. Ah, take note of that: 'He built an altar *in the name of the Lord*': that is, by His authority, for His glory. And thus should it ever be with us: 'Whatsoever ye do in word or deed, do all in the name of the Lord Jesus,' Col. 3. 17. This is one of the basic rules for the governance of all our actions. O what a difference it would make if professing Christians were regulated thereby. How many difficulties would be removed and how many problems solved. The young believer often wonders whether this or that practice is right or wrong. Let it be brought to this touchstone: Can I ask God's blessing upon it? Can I do it in the name of the Lord? If not, then it is sinful. Alas, how much in Christendom is now being done under the holy Name of Christ which He has never authorized, which is grievously dishonouring to Him, which is a stench in His nostrils. 'Let everyone that nameth the name of Christ depart from iniquity,' 2 Tim. 2. 19.

'And he put the wood in order, and cut the bullock in pieces, and laid him on the wood,' v. 33. And here again observe how strictly Elijah kept to the 'pattern' furnished him in the Scriptures. Through Moses the Lord had given orders in connection with the burnt offering that, 'he shall flay the burnt offering, and *cut it into his pieces*. And the sons of Aaron the priest shall put fire upon the altar, and *lay the wood in order* upon the fire: and the priests, Aaron's sons, shall lay the parts, the head, and the fat, in order upon the wood,' Lev. 1. 6-8. Those details in the conduct of Elijah are the more noteworthy because of what is recorded of the prophets of Baal on this occasion: nothing is said of *their* 'putting the wood in order' or of 'cutting the bullock in pieces and laying him on the wood,' but merely that they 'dressed it and called on the name of Baal,' v. 26. Ah, it is in these 'little things,' as men term them, that we see the difference between the true and false servants of God.

'And he put the wood in order, and cut the bullock in pieces, and laid him on the wood.' And is there not here also important instruction *for us*? The work of the Lord is not to be performed carelessly and hurriedly, but with great precision and reverence. Think of *whose* service we are engaged in if we be the ministers of Christ. Is He not richly entitled to our best? How we need to 'study to show ourselves approved unto God' if we are to be 'workmen that needeth not to be ashamed,' 2 Tim. 2. 15. What a fearful word is that in Jeremiah 48. 10 (marg.): 'Cursed be he that doeth the work of the Lord negligently': then let us seek grace to heed this malediction in the preparing of our sermons (or articles) or whatsoever we undertake in the name of our Master. Searching indeed is that declaration of Christ's, 'He that is faithful in that which is least is faithful also in much: and he that is unjust in the least is unjust also in much,' Luke 16. 10. Not only is the glory of God immediately concerned, but the everlasting weal or woe of immortal souls is involved when we engage in the work of the Lord.

'And he made a trench . . . and said, Fill four barrels with water, and pour it on the burnt sacrifice, and on the wood. And he said, Do it the second time. And they did it the second time. And he said, Do it the third time. And they did it the third time. And the water ran round about the altar; and he filled the trench also with water,' vv. 32-35. How calm and dignified was his manner! There was no haste, no confusion: everything was done 'decently and in order.' He did not labour under the fear of failure, but was certain of the outcome. Some have wondered where so much water could be obtained after three years' drought, but it must be remembered that the sea was near by, and doubtless it was from it the water was brought – *twelve* barrels in all, again corresponding to the number of Israel's tribes!

Ere passing on, let us pause and behold here the strength of the prophet's faith in the power and goodness of his God. The pouring of so much water upon the altar, the flooding of the offering and the wood beneath it, would make it appear utterly impracticable and unlikely for any fire to consume it. Elijah was determined that the Divine interposition should be the more convincing and illustrious. He was so sure of God that he feared not to heap difficulties in His way, knowing that there can be no difficulty unto One who is omniscient and omnipotent. The more unlikely the answer was, the more glorified therein would be his Master. O wondrous faith which can laugh at impossibilities, which can even increase them so as to have the joy of seeing God vanquish them! It is the bold and venturesome faith which He delights to honour. Alas, how little of this we now behold. Truly this is a day of 'small things.' Yea, it is a day when unbelief abounds. Unbelief is appalled by difficulties, and schemes to remove them, as though God needed any help from us!

'And it came to pass at the time of the offering of the evening sacrifice, that Elijah the prophet came near,' v. 36. By waiting until the hour when 'the evening sacrifice' was offered (in the temple), Elijah acknowledged *his fellowship with* the worshippers at Jerusalem. And is there not a lesson in this for many of the Lord's people in this dark day? Living in isolated places, cut off from the means of grace, yet they should recall the hour of the weekly preaching-service, and the prayer-meeting, and at the same hour draw near unto the Throne of Grace and mingle *their* peti-

[149]

tions with those of their brethren away yonder in the church of their youth. It is our holy privilege to have and maintain *spiritual communion* with saints when bodily contact with them is no longer possible. So, too, may the sick and the aged, though deprived of public ordinances, thus join in the general chorus of praise and thanksgiving. Especially should we attend to this duty and enjoy this privilege during the hours of the Lord's Day.

'And it came to pass at the time of the offering of the evening sacrifice, that Elijah the prophet came near.' But something else, something deeper, something more precious was denoted by Elijah's waiting until that particular time. That 'evening sacrifice' which was offered every day in the temple at Jerusalem, three hours before sunset, pointed forward to the antitypical burnt offering, which was to be slain when the fulness of time should come. Relying on that great sacrifice for the sins of God's people which the Messiah would offer at His appearing on earth, His servant now took his place by an altar which pointed forward to the Cross. Elijah, as well as Moses, had an intense interest in that great sacrifice, as was clear from the fact that they 'spake *of His decease* which He should accomplish at Jerusalem' when they appeared and talked with Christ on the mount of transfiguration, Luke 9. 30, 31. It was his faith depending upon, not the blood of a bullock, but the blood of Christ, that Elijah now presented his petitions unto God.

'And it came to pass at the time of the offering of the evening sacrifice, that Elijah the prophet *came near*': that is, unto the altar which he had built and on which he had laid the sacrifice. Yea, 'came near,' though expecting an answer by *fire!* yet not in the least afraid. Again we say, what holy confidence in God! Elijah was fully assured that the One whom he served, whom he was now honouring, would not hurt *him*. Ah, his long sojourn at the brook Cherith and the lengthy days spent in his upper room in the widow's house at Zarephath had not been wasted. He had improved the time by spending it in the secret place of the Most High, abiding under the shadow of the Almighty, and there he had learned precious lessons which none of the schools of men can impart. Fellow minister, suffer us to point out that power from God in *public* ordinances can only be acquired by drawing upon the power of God in *private*. Holy boldness before the people must be obtained by prostration of soul at the footstool of mercy in the secret place.

'And said, Lord God of Abraham, Isaac, and of Israel,' v. 36. This was far more than a reference to the ancestors of his people or the founders of his nation. It was something more than either a patriotic or sentimental utterance. It gave further evidence of the strength of his faith and made manifest the ground upon which it rested. It was the owning of Jehovah as the *covenant God* of His people, and who as such had promised never to forsake them. The Lord had entered into solemn covenant with Abraham, Gen. 17. 7, 8, which he had renewed with Isaac and Jacob. To that covenant the Lord made reference when He appeared unto Moses at the burning bush, Ex. 3. 6 and cf. 2. 24. When Israel was oppressed by the Syrians in the days of Jehoahaz we are told that, 'The Lord was gracious unto them, and had compassion upon them, and had respect unto them, because of His covenant with Abraham, Isaac, and Jacob,' 2 Kings 13. 23. Elijah's acting faith on the covenant in the hearing of the people reminded them of *the foundation* of their hope and blessing. O what a difference it makes when we are able to plead 'the blood of the everlasting covenant,' Heb. 13. 20.

'Lord God of Abraham, Isaac, and of Israel, let it be known this day that Thou are God in Israel,' v. 36. This was Elijah's first petition, and mark well the *nature* of it, for it makes clearly manifest his own character. The heart of the prophet was filled with a burning zeal for the glory of God. He could not bear to think of those wrecked altars and martyred prophets. He could not tolerate the land being defiled with the God-insulting and soul-destroying idolatry of the heathen. It was not himself that he cared about, but the horrible fact that the people of Israel were entertaining the idea that the God of Abraham, Isaac and Jacob had abdicated in favour of Baal. His spirit was stirred to its depths as he contemplated how blatantly and grievously Jehovah was dishonoured.

O that we were more deeply moved by the languishing state of Christ's cause upon earth today, by the inroads of the enemy and the awful desolation he has wrought in Zion! Alas that a spirit of indifference, or at least of fatalistic stoicism, is freezing so many of us.

The chief burden of Elijah's prayer was that God should vindicate Himself that day, that He would make known His mighty power, that He would turn the people's heart back unto Himself. It is only when we can look beyond personal interests and plead for the glory of God that we reach the place where He will not deny us. Alas, we are so anxious about the success of *our* work, the prosperity of *our* church or denomination, that we lose sight of the infinitely more wonderful matter of the vindication and honour of our Master. Is it any wonder that our circle enjoys so little of God's blessing? Our blessed Redeemer has set us a better example: 'I seek not Mine own glory,' John 8. 50, declared that One who was 'meek and lowly in heart.' 'Father, glorify *Thy* name,' John 12. 28, was the controlling desire of His heart. When longing for His disciples to bear fruit, it was that 'herein is My Father glorified,' John 15. 8. 'I have glorified Thee on the earth,' John 17. 4, said the Son at the completion of His mission. And now He declares, 'whatsoever ye shall ask in My name, that will I do, that *the Father* may be glorified in the Son,' John 14. 13.

'Let it be known this day that Thou art God in Israel, and that I am Thy *servant*.' How blessed to behold this man, by whose word the windows of heaven were closed, at whose prayers the dead was restored to life, before whom even the king quailed – how blessed, we say, to see him taking such a place before God. 'Let it be known . . . that I am thy servant.' It was the subordinate place, the *lowly* place, the place where he was under orders. A 'servant' is one whose will is entirely surrendered to another, whose personal interests are completely subservient to those of his master, whose desire and joy it is to please and honour the one who employs him. And this was the attitude and habitude of Elijah: he was completely yielded unto God, seeking His glory and not his own. 'Christian service' is not doing something for

Christ: it is doing *those* things which *He* has appointed and assigned us.

Fellow ministers, is this *our* character? Are our wills so surrendered to God that we can truly say, 'I am Thy *servant?*' But note another thing here. 'Let it *be known* that . . . I am Thy servant': own me as such by the manifestation of Thy power. It is not enough that the minister of the Gospel be God's servant, it must be *made manifest* that he is such. How? By his separation from the world, by his devotedness to his Master, by his love for and care of souls, by his untiring labours, his self-denial and self-sacrifice, by spending himself and being spent in ministering to others; and, by the Lord's *seal* on his ministry. 'By their fruits ye shall know them': by the holiness of their character and conduct, by the working of God's Spirit in and through them, by the walk of those who sit under their ministry. How we need to pray, 'Let it be known that I *am* Thy servant.'

CHAPTER EIGHTEEN

Effectual Prayer

———

At the close of our last chapter we were occupied with the prayer offered by Elijah on Mount Carmel. This supplication of the prophet requires to be examined attentively, for it was a prevalent one, securing a miraculous answer. There are two chief reasons why so many of the prayers of God's people are unavailing: first, because they fail to meet the requirements of acceptable prayer; second, because their supplications are unscriptural, not patterned after the prayers recorded in Holy Writ. It would take us too far afield to enter into full detail as to what requirements we must meet and what conditions have to be fulfilled by us in order to obtain the ear of God, so that He will show Himself strong on our behalf; yet we feel this is a suitable place to say something on this highly important and most practical subject, and at least mention some of the principal requirements for success at the throne of grace.

Prayer is one of the outstanding privileges of the Christian life. It is the appointed means for experimental access to God, for the soul to draw nigh unto its Maker, for the Christian to have spiritual communion with his Redeemer. It is the channel through which we are to seek all needed supplies of spiritual grace and temporal mercies. It is the avenue through which we are to make known our need unto the Most High and look for Him to minister to the same. It is the channel through which faith ascends to Heaven and in response thereto miracle descends to earth. But if that channel be choked, those supplies are withheld; if faith be dormant, miracles do not take place. Of old, God had to say of His people, 'Your iniquities have separated between you and your God, and your sins have hid His face from you, that He will not hear,' Isa. 59. 2. And is it any different today? Again He declared, 'Your sins have withholden good things from you,' Jer. 5. 25. And is not this the case with most of us now? Have we not occasion to acknowledge, 'We have transgressed and have rebelled : Thou hast not pardoned. Thou hast covered thyself with a cloud, that our prayer should not pass through,' Lam. 3. 42, 44. Sad, sad, indeed when such be the case.

If the professing Christian supposes that, no matter what the character of his walk may be, he has but to plead the name of Christ and his petitions are assured of an answer, he is sadly deluded. God is ineffably holy, and His Word expressly declares, 'If I regard iniquity in my heart, the Lord will not hear me,' Psa. 66. 18. It is not sufficient to believe in Christ, or plead His name, in order to ensure answers to prayer : there must be practical subjection to and daily fellowship with Him : 'If ye abide in Me and My words abide in you, ye shall ask what ye will, and it shall be done unto you,' John 15. 7. It is not sufficient to be a child of God and call upon our heavenly Father : there must be an ordering of our lives according to His revealed will : 'Whatsoever we ask we receive of Him, because we keep His commandments and do those things that are pleasing in His sight,' 1 John 3. 22. It is not sufficient to come boldly unto the throne of grace : we must 'draw near with a true heart in full assurance of faith, having our hearts sprinkled from an evil conscience, and our bodies washed with pure water,' Heb. 10. 22 – that which defiles being removed by the cleansing precepts of the Word, see Psa. 119. 9.

Apply the principles briefly alluded to above and mark how those requirements were met and those conditions fulfilled in the case of Elijah. He had walked in strict separation from the evil which abounded in Israel, refusing to compromise or have any fellowship with the unfruitful works of darkness. In a day of spiritual degeneracy and apostasy he had maintained personal communion with the Holy One, as his 'The Lord God of Israel . . . *before whom I stand*,' 1 Kings 17. 1, clearly attested. He walked in practical subjection to God, as his refusing to move until the 'word of the Lord came unto him,' 17. 8, bore definite witness. His life was ordered by the revealed will of his Master, as was manifested by his obedience to the Divine command to dwell with a widow woman in Zarephath. He shrank not from discharging the most unpleasant duties, as was plain from his prompt compliance with the Divine order, 'Go, show thyself to Ahab,' 18. 1. And *such a one* had the ear of God, had power with God.

Now if what has just been pointed out serves to explain the prevalency of Elijah's intercession, does it not (alas) also furnish the reason why so many of us have not the ear of God, have not power with Him in prayer? It is 'the effectual fervent prayer of a *righteous* man' which 'availeth much' with God, James 5. 16, and that signifies something more than a man to whom the righteousness of Christ has been imputed. Let it be duly noted that this statement occurs not in Romans (where the legal benefits of the atonement are chiefly in view), but in James, where the practical and experimental side of the Gospel is unfolded. The 'righteous man' in James 5. 16 (as also throughout the book of Proverbs, and likewise the 'just') is one who is right with God *practically* in his daily life, whose ways 'please the Lord.' If we walk not in separation from the world, if we deny not self, strive not against sin, mortify not our lusts, but gratify our carnal nature, is there any wonder that our prayer-life is cold and formal and our petitions unanswered?

In examining the prayer of Elijah on Mount Carmel we have seen that, first, at the time of the evening sacrifice 'the prophet came near': that is, unto the altar on which the slain bullock lay: 'came near,' though expecting an answer by fire! There we behold his holy confidence in God, and are shown the foundation on which his confidence rested, namely, an atoning sacrifice. Second, we have heard him addressing Jehovah as the covenant God of His people: 'Lord God of Abraham, Isaac, and of Israel.' Third, we have pondered his first petition: 'Let it be known this day that Thou art God in Israel,' that is, that He would vindicate His honour and glorify His own great name. The heart of the prophet was filled with a burning zeal for the living God and he could not endure the sight of the land being filled with idolatry. Fourth, 'and that I am Thy servant,' whose will is entirely surrendered to Thee, whose interests are wholly subordinated to Thine. Own me as such by a display of Thy mighty power.

These are the elements, dear reader, which enter into the prayer which is acceptable to God and which meets with a response from Him. There must be more than going through the motions of devotion: there must be an actual drawing near of the soul unto the living God, and for *that*, there must be a putting away and forsaking of all that is offensive to Him. It is *sin* which alienates the heart from Him, which keeps the conscience at a guilty distance from Him; and that sin must needs be repented of and confessed if access is to be ours again. What we are now inculcating is not legalistic; we are insisting upon the claims of Divine holiness. Christ has not died in order to purchase for His people an indulgence for them to live in sin: rather did He shed His precious blood to redeem them from all iniquity and 'purify unto Himself a peculiar people, zealous of good works,' Titus 2. 14, and just so far as they neglect those good works will they fail to enter experimentally into the benefits of His redemption.

But in order for an erring and sinful creature to draw near the thrice Holy One with any measure of humble confidence, he must know something of the relation which he sustains unto Him, not by nature but by grace. It is the blessed privilege of the believer – no matter how great a failure he feels himself to be (provided he is *sincere* in mourning his failures and *honest* in his endeavours to please his Lord) – to remind himself that he is approaching One in covenant relationship with him, yea, to plead that covenant before Him. David – despite all his falls – acknowledged 'He hath made with me an everlasting covenant, ordered in all things, and sure,' 2 Sam. 23. 5, and so may the reader if he grieves over sins as David did, confesses them as contritely, and has the same pantings of heart after holiness. It makes a world of difference in our praying when we can '*take hold of* God's covenant,' assured of our personal interest in it. When we plead the fulfilment of covenant promises, Jer. 32. 40, 41; Heb. 10. 16, 17, for example, we present a reason God will not reject, for He cannot deny Himself.

Still another thing is essential if our prayers are to meet with the Divine approval: the motive prompting them and the petition itself must alike be right. It is at this point so many fail: as it is written, 'Ye ask, and receive not, because ye ask amiss, that ye may consume it upon your lusts,' James 4. 3. Not so was it with Elijah: it was not his own advancement or aggrandizement he sought, but the magnifying of his Master, and vindication of His holiness, which had been so dishonoured by His people's turning aside to Baal worship. We all need to test ourselves here: if the motive behind our praying proceeds from nothing higher than *self*, we must expect to be denied. Only when we truly ask for that which will promote God's glory, do we ask aright. 'This is the confidence that we have in Him, that, if we ask anything according to His will, He heareth us,' 1 John 5. 14, and we ask 'according to His will' when we make request for what will bring honour and praise to the Giver. Alas, how carnal much of our 'praying' is!

Finally, if our prayers are to be acceptable to God they must issue from those who can truthfully declare, 'I am Thy *servant*' – one submissive to the authority of another, one who takes the place of subordination, one who is under the orders of his master, one who has no will of his own, one whose constant aim is to please his master and promote his interests. And surely the Christian will make no demur against this. Is not this the very place into which his illustrious Redeemer entered? Did not the Lord of glory take upon Him 'the form of a servant,' Phil. 2. 7, and conduct Himself as such all the days of His flesh? If we maintain our *servant character* when we approach the throne of grace we shall be preserved from the blatant irreverence which characterizes not a little so-called 'praying' of today. In place of making demands or speaking to God as though we were His equals, we shall humbly present our 'requests.' And *what are* the main things a 'servant' desires? A knowledge of what his master requires, and needed supplies so that his orders may be carried out.

'And that I have done all these things at Thy word,' 1 Kings 18. 36. 'And it came to pass at the time of the offering of the evening sacrifice, that Elijah the prophet came near, and said, Lord God of Abraham, Isaac, and of Israel, let it be known this day that Thou art God in Israel, and that I have done all these things at Thy word.' This was advanced by the prophet as an additional plea: that God would send down fire from heaven in answer to his supplications, as an attestation of his fidelity to his Master's will. It was in response to Divine orders that the prophet had restrained rain from the earth, had now convened Israel and the false prophets together, and had suggested an open trial or contest, that by a visible sign from heaven it might be known who was the true God. All this he had done not of himself, but by direction from above. It adds great force to our petitions when we are able to plead before God our faithfulness to His commands. Said David to the Lord, 'Remove from me reproach and contempt; for I have kept Thy testimonies,' and again, 'I have stuck unto Thy testimonies: O Lord, put me not to shame,' Psa. 119. 22, 31. For a servant to act without orders from his master is self-will and presumption.

God's commands 'are not grievous' (to those whose wills are surrendered to Him), and 'in keeping of them there is great reward'! Psa. 19. 11 – in this life as well as in the next, as every obedient soul discovers for himself. The Lord has declared, 'them that honour Me, I will honour,' 1 Sam. 2. 30, and He is faithful in making good His promises. The way to honour Him is to walk in His precepts. This is what Elijah had done, and now he counted upon Jehovah honouring him by granting this petition. When the servant of God has the testimony of a good conscience and the witness of the Spirit that he is acting according to the Divine will, he may rightly feel himself to be invincible – that men, circumstances, and Satanic opposition, are of no more account than the chaff of the summer threshing-floor. God's Word shall not return unto Him void: His purpose shall be accomplished though heaven and earth pass away. This, too, was what filled Elijah with calm assurance in that crucial hour. God would not mock one who had been true to Him.

'Hear me, O Lord, hear me, that this people may know that Thou art the Lord God,' v. 37. How those words breathed forth the intensity and vehemency of the prophet's zeal for the Lord of hosts. No mere formal lip service was this, but real supplication, fervent supplication. This repetition intimates how truly and how deeply Elijah's heart was burdened. He could not endure the dishonour done to his Master on every side: he yearned to see Him vindicate Himself. 'Hear me, O Lord, hear me,' was the earnest cry of a pent-up soul. How his zeal and intensity puts to shame the coldness of our prayers! It is only the genuine cry of a burdened heart that reaches the ear of God. It is 'the effectual *fervent* prayer of a righteous man' that 'availeth much.' Oh, what need we have to seek the aid of the Holy Spirit, for He alone can inspire real prayer within us!

'That this people may know that Thou art the Lord God.' Here was the supreme longing of Elijah's soul: that it might be openly and incontrovertibly demonstrated that Jehovah, and not Baal or any idol, was the true God. That which dominated the prophet's heart was a yearning that God would be glorified. And is it not thus with all His genuine servants? They are willing to endure any hardships, glad to spend themselves and be spent, if so be that their Lord is magnified. 'For I am ready not to be bound only, but also to die at Jerusalem for the name of the Lord Jesus,' Acts 21. 13: how many since the apostle have actually died in His service and for the praise of His holy name! Such, too, is the deepest and most constant desire of each Christian who is not in a backslidden condition: all his petitions issued from and centre in this – that God may be glorified. They have, in their measure, drunk of the spirit of their Redeemer: 'Father, glorify Thy Son, that Thy Son also may glorify Thee,' John 17. 1: when such is the motive behind our petition it is certain of an answer.

'And that Thou hast turned their heart back again,' v. 37 – back from wandering after forbidden objects unto Thyself, back from Baal to the service and worship of the true and living God. Next to the glory of his Master, the deliverance of Israel from the deceits of Satan was the deepest longing of Elijah's heart. He was no selfish and self-centred individual who was indifferent to the fate of his fellows: rather was he anxious that they should have for their portion and supreme good that which so fully satisfied his own soul. And again we say, is not the same thing true of all genuine servants and saints of God? Next to the glory of their Lord, that which lies nearest their hearts and forms the constant subject of their prayers is the salvation of sinners, that they may be turned from their evil and foolish ways unto God. Note well the two words we place in italics: 'that *Thou* hast turned their *hearts* back again' – nothing short of the heart being turned unto God will avail anything for eternity, and nothing short of God's putting forth His mighty power can effect this change.

Having considered in detail and at some length each petition in Elijah's prevailing prayer, let us call attention to one other feature which marked it, and that is its noticeable *brevity*. It occupies but two verses in our Bibles and contains only sixty-three words in the English translation: still fewer in the original Hebrew. What a contrast is this from the long-drawn-out and wearisome prayers in many pulpits today! 'Be not rash with thy mouth, and let not thine heart be hasty to utter anything before God: for God is in heaven, and thou upon earth: therefore let thy words be few,' Eccl. 5. 2. Such a verse as this appears to have no weight with the majority of ministers. One of the marks of the scribes and Pharisees was, that they 'for a pretence (to impress the people with their piety) make *long* prayers,' Mark 12. 40. We would not overlook the fact that when the Spirit's unction is enjoyed, the servant of Christ may be granted much liberty to pour out his heart at length, yet this is the exception rather than the rule, as God's Word clearly proves.

One of the many evils engendered by lengthy prayers in the pulpit is the discouraging of simple souls in the pew: they are apt to conclude that if their private devotions are not sustained at length, then the Lord must be witholding from them the spirit of prayer. If any of our readers be distressed because of this, we would ask them to make a study of the prayers recorded in Holy Writ – in Old and New Testaments alike – and they will find that almost all of them are exceedingly *short ones*. The prayers which brought such remarkable responses from Heaven were like this one of Elijah's: brief and to the point, fervent but definite. No soul is heard because of the multitude of his words, but only when his petitions come from the heart, are prompted by a longing for God's glory, and are presented in childlike faith. The Lord mercifully preserve us from hypocrisy and formality, and make us feel our deep need of crying to Him, 'Teach us (not *how* to, but) *to pray*.'

CHAPTER NINETEEN

The Answer by Fire

———

In our last chapter we sought to make practical application unto ourselves of the prayer that was offered unto God by Elijah upon Mount Carmel. It has been recorded for our learning, Rom. 15. 4, and encouragement, and many valuable lessons are contained therein, if only we have hearts to receive them. With rare exceptions the modern pulpit furnishes little or no help on this important matter, rather is it a stumbling block to those desirous of knowing the way of the Lord more perfectly. If young Christians are anxious to discover the secrets of acceptable and effectual prayer, they must not be guided by what they now hear and see going on in the religious world: instead, they must turn to that Divine revelation which God has graciously designed as a lamp unto their feet and a light unto their path. If they humbly seek instruction from God's Word and trustfully count upon His Holy Spirit's aid, they will be delivered from that anomaly which is now called prayer.

On the one hand, we need to be delivered from a cold, mechanical and formal type of praying which is merely a lip service, in which there is no actual approach unto the Lord, no delighting of ourselves in Him, no pouring out of the heart before Him. On the other hand, we need to be preserved from that unseemly, wild and fanatical frenzy which in some quarters is mistaken for spiritual warmth and earnestness. There are some who too much resemble the worshippers of Baal when they pray, addressing God as though He were deaf. They seem to regard excitement of their animal spirits and violent contortions of body as the essence of supplication, and despise those who speak unto God in a calm

[163]

and composed, meet and orderly manner. Such irreverent frenzy is even worse than formality. Noise is not to be mistaken for fervour, nor raving for devotion. 'Be ye therefore *sober*, and watch unto prayer,' 1 Pet. 4. 7, is the Divine corrective for this evil.

Now we turn to and consider the remarkable sequel to the beautiful but simple prayer of Elijah. And again we would say to the reader, let us attempt to visualize the scene, and as far as we can, take our place on Carmel. Cast your eye over the vast concourse of people there assembled. View the large company of the now exhausted and defeated priests of Baal. Then seek to catch the closing words of the Tishbite's prayer : 'Hear me, O Lord, hear me, that this people may know that Thou art the Lord God, and that Thou hast turned their heart back again,' 1 Kings 18. 37. What an awful moment follows! What intense eagerness on the part of the assembled multitude to behold the issue! What breathless silence must there have been! What shall be the outcome? Will the servant of Jehovah be baffled as had been the prophets of Baal? If no answer follow, if no fire come down from Heaven, then the Lord is no more entitled to be regarded as God than Baal. Then all that Elijah had done, all his testimony to his Master being the only true and living God, would be looked upon as a delusion. Solemn, intensely solemn moment!

But the short prayer of Elijah had scarcely ended when we are told, 'Then the fire of the Lord fell, and consumed the burnt sacrifice, and the wood, and the stones, and the dust, and licked up the water that was in the trench,' v. 38. By that fire the Lord avouched Himself to be the only true God, and by it He bore witness to the fact that Elijah was His prophet and Israel His people. Oh, the amazing condescension of the Most High in repeatedly making demonstration of the most evident truths concerning His being, perfections, the Divine authority of His Word, and the nature of His worship. Nothing is more wonderful than this, unless it be the perverseness of men who reject such repeated demonstrations. How gracious of God to furnish such proofs and make all doubting utterly unreasonable and excuseless! Those who receive the teachings of Holy Writ without a question are not credulous fools, for so far from following cunningly devised fables, they accept the unimpeachable testimony of those who were the eye-witnesses of the most stupendous miracles. The Christian's faith rests upon a foundation that need not fear the closest investigation.

'Then the fire of the Lord fell.' That this was no ordinary but rather supernatural fire was plainly evident from the effects of it. It descended from above. Then it consumed the pieces of the sacrifice, and then the wood on which they had been laid – this order making it clear that it was not by means of the wood the flesh of the bullock was burnt. Even the twelve stones of the altar were consumed, to make it further manifest this was no common fire. As though that were not sufficient attestation of the extra-ordinary nature of this fire, it consumed 'the dust and licked up the water that was in the trench,' thus making it quite obvious that this was a fire whose agency nothing could resist. In each instance the action of this fire was *downwards*, which is contrary to the nature of all earthly fire. No trickery was at work here, but a supernatural power that removed every ground of suspicion in the spectators, leaving them face to face with the might and majesty of Him they had so grievously slighted.

'Then the fire of the Lord fell, and consumed the burnt sacri-fice.' Exceedingly blessed, yet unspeakably solemn was this. First, this remarkable incident should encourage weak Christians to put their trust in God, to go forth in *His* strength to meet the gravest dangers, to face the fiercest enemies, and to undertake the most arduous and hazardous tasks to which He may call them. If our confidence be fully placed in the Lord Himself, He will not fail us. He will stand by us, though no others do; He will deliver us out of the hands of those who seek our hurt; He will put to confusion those who set themselves against us; and He will honour us in the sight of those who have slandered or reproached us. Look not on the frowning faces of worldlings, O trembling believer, but fix the eye of faith upon Him who has all power in heaven and in earth. Be not discouraged because you meet with so few who are like-minded, but console yourself with the grand fact that if *God* be for us it matters not who is against us.

How this incident should cheer and strengthen the tried servants of God! Satan may be telling you that *compromise* is the only wise and safe policy in such a degenerate day as this. He may be moving you to ask yourself the question, What is to become of me and my family if I persevere in preaching what is so unpopular? Then recall the case of the apostle, and how he was supported by the Lord in the most trying circumstances. Referring to his being called upon by that monster Nero to vindicate his conduct as a servant of Christ, he says, 'At my first answer no man stood with me, but all men forsook me: I pray God that it may not be laid to their charge. Notwithstanding, the Lord stood with me, and strengthened me: that by me the preaching might be fully known, and that all the Gentiles might hear: and I was delivered out of the mouth of the lion. And the Lord shall deliver me from every evil work, and will preserve me unto His heavenly kingdom: to whom be glory for ever and ever. Amen,' 2 Tim. 4. 16-18. And the Lord has not changed! Put yourself unreservedly in His hands, seek only His glory, and He will not fail you. Trust Him fully as to the outcome, and He will not put you to confusion, as this writer has fully proved.

How blessedly this incident exemplifies *the power of faith* and the efficacy of prayer. We have already said quite a little upon the prayer offered by Elijah on this momentous occasion, but let us call attention to one other essential feature that marked it, and which must mark our prayers if they are to call down responses from Heaven. 'According to your faith be it unto you,' Matt. 9. 29, is one of the principles which regulates God's dealings with us. 'If thou canst believe, all things are possible to him that believeth,' Mark 9. 23. Why? Because faith has to do directly with God: it brings *Him* into the scene, it puts Him upon His faithfulness, laying hold of His promises and saying, 'Do as Thou hast said,' 2 Sam. 7. 25. If you want to see some of the marvels and miracles which faith can bring to pass, read slowly through Hebrews 11.

And prayer is the principal channel through which faith is to operate. To pray without faith is to insult and mock God. It is written, 'The prayer *of faith* shall save the sick,' James 5. 15. But what is it to pray in faith? It is for the mind to be regulated and the heart to be affected by what God has said to us: it is a laying hold of His Word and then counting upon Him to fulfil His promises. This is what Elijah had done, as is plain from his 'I have done all these things *at Thy word*,' v. 36. Some of those things appeared utterly contrary to carnal reason – such as his venturing into the presence of the man who sought his life and ordering him to convene a vast assembly on Carmel, his pitting himself against the hundreds of false prophets, his pouring water on the sacrifice and the wood; nevertheless, he acted on God's Word and trusted Him as to the outcome. Nor did God put him to confusion: He honoured his faith and answered his prayer.

Once again we would remind the reader: this incident is recorded for our learning and for our encouragement. The Lord God is the same today as He was then – ready to show Himself strong on the behalf of those who walk as Elijah and trust Him as he did. Are you faced with some difficult situation, some pressing emergency, some sore trial? Then place it not between yourself and God, but rather put God between it and you. Meditate afresh on His wondrous perfections and infinite sufficiency; ponder His precious promises which exactly suit your case; beg the Holy Spirit to strengthen your faith and call it into action. So too with God's servants: if they are to accomplish great things in the name of their Master, if they are to put to confusion His enemies and gain the victory over those who oppose, if they are to be instrumental in turning the hearts of men back to God, then they must look to Him to work in and by them, they must rely on His almighty power both to protect and carry them fully through the discharge of arduous duties. They must have a single eye to God's glory in what they undertake, and give themselves to believing and fervent prayer.

'Then the fire of the Lord fell, and consumed the burnt sacrifice.' As we have said above, this was not only exceedingly blessed, but also unspeakably solemn. This will be the more evident if we call to mind those awful words: 'our God is *a consuming fire*,' Heb. 12. 29. How rarely is this text quoted, and more rarely still preached upon! The pulpit often declares that 'God is love,' but maintains a guilty silence upon the equally true fact that He is 'a consuming fire.' God is ineffably holy, and therefore does His pure nature burn against sin. God is inexorably righteous, and therefore He will visit upon every transgression and disobedience 'a just recompense of reward,' Heb. 2. 2. 'Fools make a mock at sin,' Prov. 14. 9, but they shall yet discover that they cannot mock God with impunity. They may defy His authority and trample upon His laws in this life, but in the next they shall curse themselves for their madness. In this world God deals mercifully and patiently with His enemies, but in the world to come they shall find out to their eternal undoing that He is 'a consuming fire.'

There upon Mount Carmel God made public demonstration of the solemn fact that He *is* 'a consuming fire.' For years past He had been grievously dishonoured, His worship being supplanted by that of Baal; but here before the assembled multitude He vindicated His holiness. That fire which descended from heaven in response to the earnest supplication of Elijah was a Divine *judgment*: it was the execution of the sentence of God's outraged Law. God has sworn that 'the soul that sinneth it shall die,' and He will not belie Himself. Sin's wages must be paid, either to the sinner himself or to an innocent substitute, which takes his place and endures his penalty. Side by side with the moral law there was the ceremonial law given unto Israel, in which provision was made whereby mercy could be shown the transgressor and yet at the same time the claims of Divine justice be satisfied. An animal, without spot or blemish, was slain in the sinner's stead. Thus it was here on Carmel: 'The fire of the Lord fell and consumed *the burnt sacrifice*,' and so the idolatrous Israelites were spared.

O what a wondrous and marvellous scene is presented to us here on Mount Carmel! A holy God must deal with all sin by the fire of His judgment. And here was a guilty nation steeped in evil which God must judge. Must then the fire of the Lord fall immediately upon and consume that disobedient and guilty people? Was no escape possible? Yea, blessed be God, it was. An innocent victim was provided, a sacrifice to represent that sin-laden nation.

On it the fire fell, consuming it, and the people were spared. What a marvellous foreshadowing was that of what took place almost a thousand years later upon another mount, even Calvary. There the Lamb of God substituted Himself in the place of His guilty people, bearing their sins in His own body on the tree, 1 Pet. 2. 24. There the Lord Jesus Christ suffered, the Just for the unjust, that He might bring them to God. There He was made a curse, Gal. 3. 13, that eternal blessing might be their portion. There 'the fire of the Lord' fell upon His sacred head, and so intense was its heat, He cried 'I thirst.'

'And when all the people saw it, they fell on their faces: and they said, The Lord, He is the God; the Lord, He is the God,' v. 39. 'They could no longer doubt the existence and the omnipotence of Jehovah. There could be no deception as to the reality of the miracle: they saw with their own eyes the fire come down from heaven and consume the sacrifice. And whether they had respect to the greatness of the miracle itself, or to the fact of its having been foretold by Elijah and wrought for a special purpose; or whether they contemplated the occasion as being one worthy of the extraordinary interposition of the supreme Being, viz, to recover His people who had been seduced into apostasy by the influence of those who were in authority, and to prove Himself to be the God of their fathers; all these things combined to demonstrate its Divine Author and to establish the commission of Elijah' (John Simpson).

'And when all the people saw it, they fell on their faces: and they said, The Lord, He is the God.' The Lord is known by His ways and works: He is described as 'glorious in holiness, fearful in praises, doing wonders.' Thus the controversy was settled between Jehovah and Baal. But the children of Israel soon forgot what they had seen and – like their fathers who had witnessed the plagues upon Egypt and the overthrow of Pharaoh and his hosts in the Red Sea – they soon relapsed into idolatry. Awful displays of the Divine justice may terrify and convince the sinner, may extort confessions and resolutions, and even dispose to many acts of obedience, *while* the impression lasts: but something more is

[169]

needed to change his heart and convert his soul. The miracles wrought by Christ left the Jewish nation still opposed to the truth: there must be a supernatural work within him for man to be born again.

'And Elijah said unto them, Take the prophets of Baal; let not one of them escape. And they took them: and Elijah brought them down to the brook Kishon, and slew them there,' v. 40. Very solemn is this: Elijah had not prayed for the false prophets (but for 'this people'), and the sacrificed bullock availed not for them. So too with the atonement: Christ died for His people, 'the Israel of God,' and shed not His blood for reprobates and apostates. God has caused this blessed truth – now almost universally denied – to be illustrated in the types as well as expressed definitely in the doctrinal portions of His Word. The paschal lamb was appointed for and gave shelter to the Hebrews, but none was provided for the Egyptians! And, my reader, unless your name is written in the Lamb's book of life there is not the slightest ray of hope for you.

There are those actuated by false notions of liberality, who condemn Elijah for his slaying of Baal's prophets, but they err greatly, being ignorant of the character of God and the teachings of His Word. False prophets and false priests are the greatest enemies a nation can have, for they bring both temporal and spiritual evils upon it, destroying not only the bodies but the souls of men. To have permitted those prophets of Baal an escape would have licensed them as the agents of apostasy, and exposed Israel to further corruption. It must be remembered that the nation of Israel was under the direct government of Jehovah, and to tolerate in their midst those who seduced His people into idolatry, was to harbour men who were guilty of high treason against the Majesty of heaven. Only by their destruction could the insult to Jehovah be avenged and His holiness vindicated.

Degenerate times call for witnesses who have in view the glory of God and are not swayed by sentimentality, who are uncompromising in dealing with evil. Those who consider Elijah carried his sternness to an extreme length, and imagine he acted in ruthless cruelty by slaying the false prophets, know not Elijah's God. The Lord is glorious in holiness, and He never acts more gloriously than when He is 'a consuming fire' to the workers of iniquity. But Elijah was only a man! True, yet he was the Lord's servant, under bonds to carry out His orders, and in slaying these false prophets he did what God's Word required: see Deuteronomy 13. 1-5; 18. 20-22. Under the Christian dispensation we must not slay those who have deceived others into idolatry, for 'the weapons of our warfare are not carnal,' 2 Cor. 10. 4. The application to us today is this: we must unsparingly judge whatever is evil in our lives and shelter in our hearts no rivals to the Lord our God – 'let not one of them escape!'

CHAPTER TWENTY

The Sound of Abundance of Rain

Not a little is said in the Scriptures about *rain*, yet is such teaching quite unknown today even to the vast majority of people in Christendom. In this atheistic and materialistic age God is not only not accorded His proper place in the hearts and lives of the people, but He is banished from their thoughts and virtually excluded from the world which He has made. His ordering of the seasons, His control of the elements, His regulating of the weather, is now believed by none save an insignificant remnant who are regarded as fools and fanatics. There is need then for the servants of Jehovah to set forth the relation which the living God sustains to His creation and His superintendence of and government over all the affairs of earth, to point out first that the Most High foreordained in eternity past all which comes to pass here below, and then to declare that He is now executing His predetermination and working 'all things after the counsel of His own will."

That God's foreordination reaches to material things as well as spiritual, that it embraces the elements of earth as well as the souls of men, is clearly revealed in Holy Writ. 'He made a decree (the same Hebrew word as in Psa. 2. 7) for the rain,' Job 28. 26 – predestinating when, where and how little or how much it should rain: just as 'He gave to the sea His decree, that the waters should not pass His commandment,' Prov. 8. 29, and He hath 'placed the sand for the bound of the sea by a perpetual decree, that it cannot pass it: and though the waves thereof toss themselves, yet can they not prevail,' Jer. 5. 22. The precise number, duration and quantity of the showers have been eternally and unalterably fixed by the Divine will, and the exact bounds of each ocean and river expressly determined by the fiat of the Ruler of heaven and earth.

In accordance with His foreordination we read that God 'prepareth rain for the earth,' Psa. 147. 8. 'I will cause it to rain,' Gen. 7. 4, says the King of the firmament, nor can any of His creatures say Him nay. 'I will give you rain in due season,' Lev. 26. 4, is His gracious promise, yet how little is its fulfilment recognized or appreciated. On the other hand, He declares 'I have *withholden* the rain from you . . . I caused it to rain upon one city, and caused it not to rain upon another city: one piece was rained upon, and the piece whereupon it rained not withered,' Amos 4. 7 and cf. Deut. 11. 17; and again, 'I will also command the clouds that they rain no rain,' Isa. 5. 6, and all the scientists in the world are powerless to reverse it. And therefore does He require of us, '*Ask ye* of the Lord rain,' Zech. 10. 1, that our dependence upon Him may be acknowledged.

What has been pointed out above receives striking and convincing demonstration in the part of Israel's history which we have been considering. For the space of three and a half years there had been no rain or dew upon the land of Samaria, and that was the result neither of chance nor blind fate, but a Divine judgment upon a people who had forsaken Jehovah for false gods. In surveying the drought-stricken country from the heights of Carmel it would have been difficult to recognize that garden of the Lord which had been depicted as 'a land of brooks of water, of fountains and depths that spring out of valleys and hills; a land of wheat, and barley, and vines, and fig trees; a land wherein thou shalt eat bread without scarceness, thou shalt not lack anything in it,' Deut. 8. 7-9. But it had also been announced, 'And thy heaven that is over thy head shall be brass, and the earth that is under thee shall be iron. The Lord shall make the rain of thy land *powder and dust*,' Deut. 28. 23, 24. That terrible curse had been literally inflicted, and therein we may behold the horrible consequences of sin. God endures with much longsuffering the waywardness of a nation as He does of an individual, but when both leaders and people apostatize and set up idols in the place which belongs to Himself alone, sooner or later He makes it unmistakably evident that He will not be mocked with impunity, and 'indignation and wrath, tribulation and anguish' become their portion.

Alas that those nations which are favoured with the light of God's Word are so slow to learn this salutary lesson: it seems that the hard school of experience is the only teacher. The Lord had fulfilled His awful threat by Moses and had made good His word through Elijah, 1 Kings 17. 1. Nor could that fearful judgment be removed till the people at least avowedly owned Jehovah as the true God. As we pointed out at the close of a previous chapter, till the people were brought back into their allegiance to God, no favour could be expected from Him; and in another chapter, neither Ahab nor his subjects were yet in any fit state of soul to be made the recipients of His blessings and mercies. God had been dealing with them in judgment for their awful sins, and thus far His rod had not been acknowledged, nor had the occasion of His displeasure been removed.

But the wonderful miracle wrought on Carmel had entirely changed the face of things. When the fire fell from heaven in answer to Elijah's prayer, all the people 'fell on their faces, and they said, The Lord, He is the God; the Lord, He is the God.' And when Elijah ordered them to arrest the false prophets of Baal and to let not one of them escape, they promptly complied with his orders, nor did they or the king offer any resistance when the Tishbite brought them down to the brook Kishon and slew them there, 1 Kings 18. 39, 40. Thus was the evil put away from them and the way opened for God's outward blessing. He graciously accepted this as their reformation and accordingly removed His scourge from them. This is ever the order: judgment prepares the way for blessing; the awful fire is followed by the welcome rain. Once a people take their place on their faces and render to God the homage which is His due, it will not be long ere refreshing showers are sent down from heaven.

As Elijah acted the part of executioner to the prophets of Baal who had been the principal agents in the national revolt against God, Ahab must have stood by, a most unwilling spectator of that fearful deed of vengeance, not daring to resist the popular outburst of indignation or attempting to protect the men whom he had introduced and supported. And now their bodies lay in ghastly death before his eyes on the banks of the Kishon. When the last of Baal's prophets had bitten the dust, the intrepid Tishbite turned to the king and said, 'Get thee up, eat and drink; for there is a sound of abundance of rain,' 1 Kings 18. 41. What a load would his words lift from the heart of the guilty king! He must have been greatly alarmed as he stood helplessly by, watching the slaughter of his prophets, tremblingly expecting some terrible sentence to be pronounced upon him by the One whom he had so openly despised and blatantly insulted. Instead, he is allowed to depart unharmed from the place of execution; nay, bidden to go and refresh himself!

How well Elijah knew the man he was dealing with! He did not bid him humble himself beneath the mighty hand of God and publicly confess his wickedness, still less did he invite the king to join him in returning thanks for the wondrous and gracious miracle which he had witnessed. Eating and drinking was all this Satan-blinded sot cared about. As another has pointed out, it was as though the servant of the Lord had said, 'Get thee up to where thy tents are pitched on yon broad upland sweep. The feast is spread in thy gilded pavilion, thy lackeys await thee; go, feast on thy dainties. But "be quick" for now that the land is rid of those traitor priests and God is once more enthroned in His rightful place, the showers of rain cannot be longer delayed. Be quick then! Or the rain may interrupt thy carouse.' The appointed hour for sealing the king's doom had not yet arrived: meanwhile he is suffered, as a beast, to fatten himself for the slaughter. It is useless to expostulate with apostates; compare John 13. 27.

'For there is a sound of abundance of rain.' It should scarcely need pointing out that Elijah was not here referring to a natural phenomenon. At the time when he spoke, a cloudless sky appeared as far as the eye could reach, for when the prophet's servant looked out towards the sea for any portent of approaching rain, he declared 'there is nothing,' v. 43, and later when he looked a seventh time all that could be seen was 'a little cloud.' When we are told that Moses 'endured as seeing Him who is invisible,' Heb. 11. 27, it was not because he beheld God with the natural eye, and when Elijah announced 'there is a sound of abundance of rain,' that sound was not audible to the outward ear. It was by 'the hearing of faith,' Gal. 3. 2, that the Tishbite knew the welcome rain was nigh at hand. 'The Lord God will do nothing, but He revealeth His secret unto His servants the prophets,' Amos 3. 7, and the Divine revelation now made known to him was received by faith.

While Elijah yet abode with the widow at Zarephath the Lord had said to him, 'Go show thyself to Ahab; and I will send rain upon the earth,' 18. 1, and the prophet believed that God would do as He had said, and in the verse we are considering he speaks accordingly as if it were now being done, so certain was he that his Master would not fail to make good His word. It is thus that a spiritual and supernatural faith ever works: 'Now faith is the substance of things hoped for, the evidence of things not seen,' Heb. 11. 1. It is the nature of this God-given grace to bring distant things close to us: faith looks upon things promised as though they were actually fulfilled. Faith gives a present subsistence to things that are yet future: that is, it realizes them to the mind, giving a reality and substantiality to them. Of the patriarchs it is written, 'These all died in faith, not having received the promises, but having seen them afar off,' Heb. 11. 13: though the Divine promises were not fulfilled in their lifetime, yet the eagle eyes of faith saw them, and it is added they 'were persuaded of them and embraced them' – one cannot 'embrace' distant objects, true, but faith being so sure of their verity makes them nigh.

'There is a sound of abundance of rain.' Does not the reader now perceive the spiritual purport of this language? That 'sound' was certainly not heard by Ahab, nor even by any other person in the vast concourse on Mount Carmel. The clouds were not then gathered, yet Elijah hears that which shall be. Ah, if *we* were more separated from the din of this world, if we were in closer communion with God, our ears would be attuned to His softest whispers: if the Divine Word dwelt in us more richly, and faith was exercised more upon it, we should hear that which is inaudible to the dull comprehension of the carnal mind. Elijah was as sure that promised rain would come as if he now heard its first drops splashing on the rocks or as if he saw it descending in torrents. O that writer and reader may be fully assured of God's promises and embrace them: living on them, walking by faith in them, rejoicing over them, for He is faithful who has promised. Heaven and earth shall pass away before one word of His shall fail.

'So Ahab went up to eat and to drink,' v. 42. The views expressed by the commentators on this statement strike us as being either carnal or forced. Some regard the king's action as being both logical and prudent: having had neither food nor drink since early morning, and the day being now far advanced, he naturally and wisely made for home, that he might break his long fast. But there is a *time* for everything, and immediately following a most remarkable manifestation of God's power was surely not the season for indulging the flesh. Elijah, too, had had nothing to eat that day, yet *he* was far from looking after his bodily needs at this moment. Others see in this notice the evidence of a subdued spirit in Ahab: that he was now meekly obeying the prophet's orders. Strange indeed is such a concept: the last thing which characterized the apostate king was submission to God or His servant. The reason why he acquiesced so readily on this occasion was because compliance suited his fleshly appetites and enabled him to gratify his lusts.

"So Ahab went up to eat and to drink.' Has not the Holy Spirit rather recorded this detail so as to show us the hardness and insensibility of the king's heart? For three and a half years drought had blighted his dominions and a fearful famine had ensued. Now that he knew rain was about to fall, surely he would turn unto God and return thanks for His mercy. Alas! he had seen the utter vanity of his idols, he had witnessed the exposure of Baal, he had beheld the awful judgment upon his prophets, but no impression was made upon him: he remained obdurate in his sin. God was not in his thoughts: his one idea was, the rain is coming, so I can enjoy myself without hindrance; therefore, he goes to make merry.

While his subjects were suffering the extremities of the Divine scourge he cared only to find grass enough to save his stud, 18. 5, and now that his devoted priests have been slain by the hundreds, he thought only of the banquet which awaited him in his pavilion. Gross and sensual to the last degree, though clad with the royal robes of Israel!

Let it not be supposed that Ahab was exceptional in his sottishness, but rather regard his conduct on this occasion as an illustration and exemplification of the spiritual deadness that is common to all the unregenerate – devoid of any serious thoughts of God, unaffected by the most solemn of His providences or the most wondrous of His works, caring only for the things of time and sense. We have read of Belshazzar and his nobles feasting at the very hour that the deadly Persians were entering the gates of Babylon. We have heard of Nero fiddling while Rome was burning, and even of the royal apartment of Whitehall being filled with a giddy crowd that gave itself up to frivolity while William of Orange was landing at Tor Bay. And we have lived to behold the pleasure-intoxicated masses dancing and carousing while enemy planes were raining death and destruction upon them. Such is fallen human nature in every age: if only they can eat and drink, people act regardless of the judgments of God and are indifferent to their eternal destiny. Is it otherwise with you, my reader? Though preserved outwardly, is there any difference *within*?

'And Elijah went up to the top of Carmel; and he cast himself down upon the earth, and put his face between his knees.' v. 42. Does not this unmistakably confirm what has been said above? How striking the contrast here presented: so far from the prophet desiring the convivial company of the world, he longed to get alone with God; so far from thinking of the needs of his body, he gave himself up to spiritual exercises. The contrast between Elijah and Ahab was not merely one of personal temperament and taste, but was the difference there is between life and death, light and darkness. But that radical antithesis is not always apparent to the eye of man: the regenerate may walk carnally, and the unregenerate can be very respectable and religious. It is the *crises of life* which reveal the secrets of our hearts and make it manifest whether we are really new creatures in Christ or merely white-washed worldlings. It is our reaction to the interpositions and judgments of God which brings out what is within us. The children of this world will spend their days in feasting and their nights in revelry though the world be hastening to destruction; but the children of God will betake themselves to the secret place of the Most High and abide under the shadow of the Almighty.

'And Elijah went up to the top of Carmel; and he cast himself down upon the earth, and put his face between his knees.' There are some important lessons here for ministers of the Gospel to take to heart. Elijah did not hang around that he might receive the congratulations of the people upon the successful outcome of his contest with the false prophets, but retired from man to get alone with God. Ahab hastens to his carnal feast, but the Tishbite, like his Lord, has 'meat to eat' which others knew not of, John 4. 32. Again, Elijah did not conclude that he might relax and take his ease following upon his public ministrations, but desired to thank his Master for His sovereign grace in the miracle He had wrought. The preacher must not think his work is done when the congregation is dismissed: he needs to seek further communion with God, to ask His blessing upon his labours, to praise Him for what He has wrought, and to supplicate Him for further manifestations of His love and mercy.

CHAPTER TWENTY-ONE

Persevering in Prayer

'And Elijah went up to the top of Carmel; and he cast himself down upon the earth, and put his face between his knees,' 1 Kings 18. 42. We closed our last chapter by pointing out that this verse sets forth some important lessons which ministers of the Gospel do well to take to heart, the principal of which is the importance and need of their retiring from the scene of their ministry that they may commune with their Lord. When public work is over they need to betake themselves to private work with God. Ministers must not only preach, but pray; not only before and while preparing their sermons, but afterwards. They must not only attend to the souls of their flock, but look after their own souls also, particularly that they may be purged from pride or resting on their own endeavours. Sin enters into and defiles the best of our performances. The faithful servant, no matter how honoured of God with success in his work, is conscious of his defects and sees reason for abasing himself before his Master. Moreover, he knows that God alone can give the increase to the seed he has sown, and for that he needs to supplicate the throne of grace.

In the passage which is now to be before us there is most blessed and important instruction not only for ministers of the Gospel but also for the people of God in general. Once again it has pleased the Spirit here to let us into the secrets of prevailing prayer, for it was in that holy exercise the prophet was now engaged. It may be objected that it is not expressly stated in 1 Kings 18. 42-46 that Elijah did any praying on this occasion. True, and here is where we discover afresh the vital importance of comparing Scripture with Scripture. In James 5 we are told 'Elijah was a man subject to like passions as we are, and he prayed earnestly that it might not rain: and it rained not on the earth by the space of three years and six months. And he *prayed again*, and the heaven gave rain,' vv.17, 18. The latter verse clearly has reference to the incident we are now considering: as truly as the heavens were closed in response to Elijah's prayer, so were they now opened in answer to his supplication. Thus we have before us again the conditions which must be met if our intercessions are to be effectual.

Once more we emphasize the fact that what is recorded in these Old Testament passages is written both for our instruction and consolation, Rom. 15. 4, affording as they do invaluable illustrations, typifications and exemplifications of what is stated in the New Testament in the form of doctrine or precept. It might be thought that after so recently devoting almost the whole of two chapters in this book on the life of Elijah to showing the secrets of prevailing intercession there was less need for us to take up the same subject again. But it is a *different aspect* of it which is now in view: in 1 Kings 18. 36, 37 we learn how Elijah prayed in *public*, here we behold how he prevailed in *private* prayer, and if we are really to profit from what is said in verses 42-46 we must not skim them hurriedly, but study them closely. Are you anxious to conduct your secret devotions in a manner that will be acceptable to God and which will produce answers of peace? Then attend diligently to the details which follow.

First, this man of God *withdrew* from the crowds and 'went up to the top of Carmel.' If we would hold audience with the Majesty on high, if we would avail ourselves of that 'new and living way' which the Redeemer has consecrated for His people, and 'enter into the holiest,' Heb. 10. 19, 20, then we must needs retire from the mad and distracting world around us and get alone with God. This was the great lesson laid down in our Lord's first word on the subject before us: 'But thou, when thou prayest, enter into thy closet, and when thou hast shut thy door, pray to thy Father which is in secret; and thy Father which seeth in secret shall reward thee openly,' Matt. 6. 6. Separation from the godless, and the shutting out of all sights and sounds which take the mind off God is absolutely indispensable. But the entering of the closet and the shutting of its door denotes more than physical isolation: it also signifies the calming of our spirit, the quieting of our feverish flesh, the gathering in of all wandering thoughts, that we may be in a fit frame to draw nigh unto and address the Holy One. '*Be still*, and know that I am God' is His unchanging requirement. How often the *failure* of this 'shut door' renders our praying ineffectual! The atmosphere of the world is fatal to the spirit of devotion and we must get alone if communion with God is to be enjoyed.

Second, observe well *the posture* in which we now behold this man of God: 'And he cast himself down upon the earth, and put his face between his knees,' v. 42. Very, very striking is this! As one has put it: 'We scarcely recognize him, he seems so to have lost his identity. A few hours before, he stood erect as an oak of Bashan: now he is bowed as a bulrush.' As he confronted the assembled multitude, Ahab, and the hundreds of false prophets, he carried himself with majestic mien and becoming dignity; but now he would draw nigh unto the King of kings, the utmost humility and reverence marks his demeanour. There as God's ambassador he had pleaded with Israel, here as Israel's intercessor he is to plead with the Almighty. Facing the forces of Baal he was as bold as a lion; alone with God most high, he hides his face and by his actions owns his nothingness. It has ever been thus with those most favoured of Heaven: Abraham declared 'Behold now, I have taken upon me to speak unto the Lord, which am but dust and ashes,' Gen. 18. 27. When Daniel beheld an anticipation of God incarnate, he declared, 'my comeliness was turned in me into corruption,' Dan. 10. 8. The seraphim veil their faces in His presence, Isa. 6. 2.

That to which we are now directing attention is greatly needed by this most irreverent and blatant generation. Though so highly favoured of God and granted such power in prayer, this did not cause Elijah to take liberties with Him or approach Him with indecent familiarity. No, he bowed his knees before the Most High and placed his head between his knees, betokening his most profound veneration for that infinitely glorious Being whose messenger he was. And if *our* hearts be right, the more we are favoured of God the more shall we be humbled by a sense of our unworthiness and insignificance, and we shall deem no posture too lowly to express our respect for the Divine Majesty. We must not forget that though God be our Father He is also our Sovereign, and that while we be His children we are likewise His subjects. If it be an act of infinite condescension on His part for the Almighty even to '*behold* the things which are in heaven and in earth,' Psa. 113. 6, then we cannot sufficiently abase ourselves before Him.

How grievously have those words been perverted: 'Let us therefore come *boldly* unto the Throne of grace,' Heb. 4. 16! To suppose they give licence for us to address the Lord God as though we were His equals is to put darkness for light and evil for good. If we are to obtain the ear of God then we must take our proper place before Him, and that is, in the dust. 'Humble yourselves therefore under the mighty hand of God, that He may exalt you in due time' *comes before* 'Casting all your care upon Him, for He careth for you,' 1 Pet. 5. 6, 7. We must abase ourselves under a sense of our meanness. If Moses was required to remove his shoes ere he approached the burning bush in which the Shekinah glory appeared, we too must conduct ourselves in prayer as befits the majesty and might of the great God. It is true that the Christian is a redeemed man and accepted in the Beloved, yet in himself he is still *a sinner*. As another has pointed out, 'The most tender love which casts out the fear that hath torment, begets a fear that is as delicate and sensitive as that of John's, who, though he had laid his head on the bosom of Christ, scrupled too hastily to intrude upon the grave where He had slept.'

Third, note particularly that this prayer of Elijah's was *based upon a Divine promise*. When commanding his servant to appear again before Ahab, the Lord had expressly declared, "And I will send rain upon the earth,' 18. 1. Why then, should he now be found earnestly begging Him for rain? To natural reason a Divine assurance of anything seems to render asking for it unnecessary: would not God make good His word and send the rain irrespective of further prayer? Not so did Elijah reason: nor should we. So far from God's promises being designed to exempt us from making application to the throne of grace for the blessings guaranteed, they are designed to instruct us what things to ask for, and to encourage us to ask for them believingly, that we may have their fulfilment *to ourselves*. God's thoughts and ways are ever the opposite of ours – and infinitely superior thereto. In Ezekiel 36. 24-36 will be found a whole string of promises, yet in immediate connection therewith we read, 'I will yet for this *be inquired of* by the house of Israel, *to do it* for them,' v. 37.

By asking for those things which God has promised, we own Him as the Giver, and are taught our dependence upon Him: faith is called into exercise and we appreciate His mercies all the more when they are received. God will do what He undertakes, but He requires us to sue for all which we would have Him do for us. Even to His own beloved Son God says, '*Ask of Me, and I shall give Thee the heathen for Thine inheritance,*' Psa. 2. 8: His reward must be claimed. Even though Elijah heard (by faith) 'a sound of abundance of rain,' nevertheless he must pray for it, Zech. 10. 1. God has appointed that if we would receive, we must ask; that if we would find, we must seek; that if we would have the door of blessing opened, we must knock; and if we fail so to do, we shall prove the truth of those words, 'ye have not, because ye ask not,' James 4. 2. God's promises then are given us to incite to prayer, to become the mould in which our petitions should be cast, to intimate the extent to which we may expect an answer.

Fourth, his prayer was *definite* or to the point. Scripture says, 'Ask ye of the Lord rain,' Zech. 10. 1, and for that very thing the prophet asked: he did not generalize but particularized. It is just here that so many fail. Their petitions are so vague they would scarcely recognize an answer if it were given: their requests are so lacking in precision that the next day the petitioner himself finds it difficult to remember what he asked for. No wonder such praying is profitless to the soul, and brings little to pass. Letters which require no answer contain little or nothing in them of any value or importance. Let the reader turn to the four Gospels with this thought before him and observe how very definite in his requests and detailed in describing his case was each one who came to Christ and obtained healing, and remember they are recorded for our learning. When His disciples asked the Lord to teach them to pray He said, 'Which of you shall have a friend and shall go to him at midnight and say unto him; Friend, lend me three loaves,' Luke 11. 5 – not simply 'food,' but specifically '*three* loaves!'

Fifth, his prayer was *fervent*: 'he prayed earnestly,' James 5. 17. It is not necessary for a man to shout and scream in order to prove he is in earnest, yet on the other hand cold and formal askings must not expect to meet with any response. God grants our requests only for Christ's sake, nevertheless unless we supplicate Him with warmth and reality, with intensity of spirit and vehemency of entreaty, we shall not obtain the blessing desired. This importunity is constantly inculcated in Scripture, where prayer is likened unto seeking, knocking, crying, striving. Remember how Jacob wrestled with the Lord, and how David panted and poured out his soul. How unlike them is the listless and languid petitioning of most of our moderns! Of our blessed Redeemer it is written that He 'offered up prayers and supplications with strong crying and tears,' Heb. 5. 7. It is not the half-hearted and mechanical asking which secures an answer, but 'the effectual fervent prayer of a righteous man (that) availeth much,' James 5. 16.

Sixth, note well Elijah's *watchfulness* in prayer: 'And said to his servant, Go up now, look toward the sea,' v. 43. While we are instant in prayer and waiting for an answer, we must be on the look-out to see if there be any token for good. Said the Psalmist, 'I wait for the Lord, my soul doth wait, and in His Word do I hope. My soul waiteth for the Lord more than they that watch for the morning: I say, more than they that watch for the morning,'

Psa. 130. 5, 6. The allusion is to those who were stationed on the watch-tower gazing eastward for the first signs of the break of day, that the tidings might be signalled (trumpeted) to the temple, so that the morning sacrifice might be offered right on time. In like manner the suppliant soul is to be on the alert for any sign of the approach of the blessing for which he is praying. 'Continue in prayer, *and* watch in the same with thanksgiving,' Col. 4. 2. Alas, how often we fail at this very point, because hope does not hold up the head of our holy desires. We pray, yet do not look out expectantly for the favours we seek. How different was it with Elijah!

Seventh, Elijah's *perseverance* in his supplication. This is the most noticeable feature about the whole transaction and it is one which we need particularly to heed, for it is at this very point most of us fail the worst. 'And he said to his servant, Go up now, look toward the sea. And he went up, and looked, and said, There is nothing.' 'Nothing': nothing in the sky, nothing arising out of the sea to intimate the approach of rain. Does not both writer and reader know the meaning of this from personal experience? We have sought the Lord, and then hopefully looked for His intervention, but instead of any token from Him that He has heard us, there is 'nothing'! And what has been our response? Have we petulantly and unbelievingly said, 'Just as I thought,' and ceased praying about it? If so, that was a wrong attitude to take. First make sure your petition is grounded upon a Divine promise, and then believingly wait God's time to fulfil it. If you have no definite promise, commit your case into God's hands and seek to be reconciled to His will as to the outcome.

'And he went up, and looked, and said, There is nothing.' Even Elijah was not always answered *immediately,* and who are we to demand a prompt answer to our first asking? The prophet did not consider that because he had prayed once and there was no response, therefore he need not continue to pray; rather did he persevere in pressing his suit until he received. Such was the persistency of the patriarch Jacob, 'I will not let Thee go except Thou bless me,' Gen. 32. 26. Such was the Psalmist's mode of praying: 'I waited patiently for the Lord; and He inclined unto me, and heard my cry,' 40. 1. 'And he said, Go again seven times,' v. 43, was the prophet's command to his servant. He was convinced that sooner or later God would grant his request, yet he was persuaded he should 'give Him no rest,' Isa. 62. 7. Six times the servant returned with his report that there was no portent of rain, yet the prophet relaxed not his supplication. And let *us* not be faint-hearted when no immediate success attends our praying, but be importunate, exercising faith and patience until the blessing comes.

To ask once, twice, thrice, nay six times, and then be denied, was no slight test of Elijah's endurance, but grace was granted him to bear the trial. 'Therefore will the Lord wait, that He may be gracious unto you,' Isa. 30. 18. Why? To teach us that we are not heard for our fervour or urgency, or because of the justness of our cause : we can claim nothing from God – all is *of grace,* and we must wait *His* time. The Lord waits, not because He is tyrannical, but 'that He may be gracious.' It is for our good that He waits : that our graces may be developed, that submission to His holy will may be wrought in us; then He lovingly turns to us and says, 'Great is thy faith, be it unto thee as thou wilt,' Matt. 15. 28. 'This is the confidence that we have in Him, that, if we ask anything according to His will, He heareth us : and if we know that He hear us, whatsoever we ask, we know that we have the petitions that we desired of Him,' John 5. 14, 15. God cannot break His own Word, but we must abide His time and, refusing to be discouraged, continue supplicating Him until He appears on our behalf.

'And it came to pass at the seventh time, that he said, Behold, there ariseth a little cloud out of the sea, like a man's hand,' v. 44. The prophet's perseverance in prayer had not been in vain, for here was a token from God that he was heard. God does not often give a full answer to prayer all at once, but a little at first and then gradually more and more as He sees that to be good for us. What the believer has now is nothing to what he shall yet have if he continues instant in prayer, believing and earnest prayer. Though God was pleased to keep the prophet waiting for a time, He did not disappoint his expectation, nor will He fail us if we continue in prayer and watch in the same with thanksgiving. Then let us be ready to receive with cheerfulness and gratitude the least indication of an answer to our petitions, accepting it as a token for good and an encouragement to persevere in our requests till there be full accomplishment of those desires which are grounded upon the Word. Small beginnings often produce wonderful effects, as the parable of the grain of mustard seed clearly teaches, Matt. 13. 31, 32. The feeble efforts of the apostles met with remarkable success as God owned and blessed them. We regard the words, 'like a man's hand,' as possessing a symbolic meaning: a man's hand had been raised in supplication and had, as it were, left its shadow on the heavens!

'And he said, Go up, say unto Ahab, Prepare thy chariot and get thee down, that the rain stop thee not,' v. 44. Elijah did not disdain the significant omen, little though it was, but promptly took encouragement from the same. So convinced was he that the windows of heaven were about to be opened and plentiful showers given that he sent his servant with an urgent message to Ahab, that he should get away at once ere the storm burst and the brook Kishon be so swollen that the king would be prevented from making his journey homeward. What holy confidence in a prayer-hearing God did that display! Faith recognized the Almighty behind that 'little cloud.' A 'handful of meal' had been sufficient under God to sustain a household for many months, and a cloud 'like a man's hand' could be counted upon to multiply and furnish an abundant downpour. 'And it came to pass in the meanwhile, that the heaven was black with clouds and wind, and there was a great rain,' v. 45. Should not this speak loudly to us? O sorely-tried believer, take heart from what is here recorded: the answer to your prayers may be much nearer than you think.

'And Ahab rode, and went to Jezreel,' v. 45. The king had responded promptly to the prophet's message. How much sooner are the ministers of the Lord attended to when giving temporal advice than they are when offering *spiritual* counsel. Ahab had no doubt now that the rain was about to fall. He was satisfied that

He who answered Elijah with fire was on the point of answering him with water; nevertheless, his heart remained as steeled against God as ever. O how solemn is the picture here presented: Ahab was convinced but not converted. How many like him there are in the churches today, who have religion in the head but not in the heart: convinced that the Gospel is true, yet rejecting it; assured that Christ is mighty to save, yet not surrendering to Him.

CHAPTER TWENTY-TWO

In Flight

———

In passing from 1 Kings 18 to 1 Kings 19 we meet with a sudden and strange transition. It is as though the sun was shining brilliantly out of a clear sky and the next moment, without any warning, black clouds drape the heavens and crashes of thunder shake the earth. The contrasts presented by these chapters are sharp and startling. At the close of the one 'the hand of the Lord was on Elijah' as he ran before Ahab's chariot: at the beginning of the other he is occupied with self and 'went for his life.' In the former we behold the prophet at his best: in the latter we see him at his worst. There he was strong in faith and the helper of his people: here he is filled with fear and is the deserter of his nation. In the one he confronts the four hundred prophets of Baal undaunted: in the other he flees panic-stricken from the threats of one woman. From the mountain top he betakes himself into the wilderness, and from supplicating Jehovah that He would vindicate and glorify His great name to begging Him to take away his life. Who would have imagined such a tragic sequel?

In the startling contrasts here presented we have a striking proof of the Divine inspiration of the Scriptures. In the Bible human nature is painted in its true colours: the characters of its heroes are faithfully depicted, the sins of its noteworthy persons are frankly recorded. True, it is human to err, but equally true it is human to conceal the blemishes of those we most admire. Had the Bible been a human production, written by uninspired historians, they had magnified the virtues of the most illustrious men of their nation, and ignored their vices, or if mentioned at all, glossed over them and made attempts to extenuate the same. Had some human admirer chronicled the history of Elijah, his sad failure would have been omitted. The fact that it *is* recorded, that no effort is made to excuse it, is evidence that the characters of the Bible are painted in the colours of truth and reality, that they were not sketched by human hands, but that the writers were controlled by the Holy Spirit.

'And the hand of the Lord was on Elijah; and he girded up his loins, and ran before Ahab to the entrance of Jezreel,' 1 Kings 18. 46. This is most blessed. The 'hand of the Lord' is often used in Scripture to denote His power and blessing. Thus Ezra said, 'the hand of our God was upon us, and he delivered us from the hand of the enemy,' 8. 31; 'The hand of the Lord was with them: and a great number believed, and turned unto the Lord, Acts 11. 21. This word coming in here points an instructive sequel to what was before us in verse 42: there we beheld the prophet cast down on the earth in self-abasement before God, here we see God honouring and miraculously sustaining His servant – if we would have the power and blessing of God rest upon us, we must take a lowly place before Him. In this instance the 'hand of the Lord' communicated supernatural strength and fleetness of foot to the prophet, so that he covered the eighteen miles so swiftly as to overtake and pass the chariot: thus did God further honour the one who had honoured Him and at the same time supply Ahab with yet another evidence of Elijah's Divine commission. This was illustrative of the Lord's way: where there is a man who takes his place in the dust before the Most High, it will soon be made apparent before others that a power beyond his own energizes him.

'And he girded up his loins, and ran before Ahab to the entrance of Jezreel.' Each detail contains an important lesson for us. The power of God resting upon Elijah did not render him careless and negligent of his own duty: he gathered up his garment so that his movements might be unimpeded. And if *we* are to run with patience the race that is set before us we need to 'lay aside every weight,' Heb. 12. 1. If we are to 'stand against the wiles of the Devil' we must have our 'loins girt about with truth,' Eph. 6. 14. By running 'before Ahab' Elijah took the lowly place of a common footman, which should have shown the monarch that his zeal against idolatry was prompted by no disrespect for himself, but actuated only by jealousy for God. The Lord's people are required to 'honour the king' in all civil matters, and here too it is the duty of ministers to set their people an example. Elijah's conduct on this occasion served as another test of Ahab's character: if he had had any respect for the Lord's servant he would have invited him into his chariot, as the eminent Ethiopian did Philip, Acts 8. 31, but it was far otherwise with this son of Belial.

Onward sped the wicked king toward Jezreel where his vile consort awaited him. The day must have been a long and trying one for Jezebel, for many hours had passed since her husband had gone forth to meet Elijah at Carmel. The peremptory command he had received from Jehovah's servant to gather all Israel together unto that mount, and the prophets of Baal as well, intimated that the crisis had been reached. She would therefore be most anxious to know how things had gone. Doubtless she cherished the hope that her priests had triumphed, and as the rain clouds blotted out the sky would attribute the welcome change to some grand intervention of Baal in response to their supplications. If so, all was well: her heart's desire would be realized, her scheming crowned with success, the undecided Israelites would be won over to her idolatrous régime and the last vestiges of the worship of Jehovah would be stamped out. For the troublesome famine Elijah was solely to blame; for the ending thereof she and her gods should have the credit. Probably such thoughts as these occupied her mind in the interval of waiting.

And now the suspense is over: the king has arrived and hastens to make report to her. 'And Ahab told Jezebel all that Elijah had done, and withal how he had slain all the prophets with the sword,' 19. 1. The first thing which strikes us about these words is their noticeable omission: the Lord Himself was left out entirely. Nothing is said of the wonders *He* had wrought that day, how that He had not only caused fire to come down from heaven, and consume the sacrifice, but even the very stones of the altar, and how it had licked up great quantities of water in the trench around it; and how in response to the prayer of His servant, rain was sent in abundance. No, God has no place in the thoughts of the wicked, rather do they put forth their utmost efforts to banish Him from their minds. And even those who, from some form of self-interest, take up with religion, and make a profession and attend the public services, yet to talk of God and His wondrous works with their wives in their *homes*, is one of the last things we should find them doing. With the vast majority of professors, religion is like their Sunday clothes – worn that day and laid by for the rest of the week.

'And Ahab told Jezebel all that *Elijah* had done.' As God is not in the thoughts of the wicked so it is the way of unbelief to fix upon secondary causes or attribute unto the human instrument what the Lord is the doer of. It matters not whether He act in judgment or in blessing, God himself is lost sight of and only the means He employs or the instruments He uses are seen. If a man of insatiable ambition be the Divine instrument for chastising nations laden with iniquity, that instrument becomes the object of universal hatred, but there is no humbling of the nations before the One who wields that rod. If a Whitefield or a Spurgeon be raised up to preach the Word with exceptional power and blessing, he is worshipped by the religious masses and men talk of *his* abilities and *his* converts. Thus it was with Ahab: first he ascribed the drought and famine to the prophet – 'art thou he that troubleth Israel!' 18. 17, instead of perceiving that it was *the Lord* who had a controversy with the guilty nation and that he was the one mainly responsible for its condition; and now he is still occupied with what 'Elijah had done.'

'And Ahab told Jezebel all that Elijah had done.' He would relate how Elijah had mocked her priests, lashed them with his biting irony, and held them up to the scorn of the people. He would describe how he had put them to confusion by his challenge, and how he, as if by some spell or charm, had brought down fire from heaven. He would enlarge upon the victory gained by the Tishbite, of the ecstasy of the people thereon, how they had fallen on their faces, saying, 'Jehovah, He is the God; Jehovah, He is the God.' That he recounted these things unto Jezebel, not to convince her of her error, but rather to incense her against God's servant, is clear from his designed climax: 'and withal how he had slain all the prophets with the sword.' How this revealed once more what an awful character Ahab was! As the protracted drought with the resultant famine had not turned him unto the Lord, so this Divine mercy of sending the rain to refresh his dominions led him not to repentance. Neither Divine judgments nor Divine blessings will of themselves reclaim the unregenerate: nothing but a miracle of sovereign grace can turn souls from the power of sin and Satan unto the living God.

It is not difficult to imagine the effect which would be produced upon the haughty, domineering and ferocious Jezebel when she heard Ahab's report: it would so hurt her pride and fire her furious temper that nothing but the speedy dispatch of the object of her resentment could pacify it. 'Then Jezebel sent a messenger unto Elijah, saying, So let the gods do to me, and more also, if I make not thy life as the life of one of them by tomorrow about this time,' v. 2. If Ahab's heart was unaffected by what had transpired on Carmel, remaining steeled against God, still less was his heathen consort softened thereby. He was sensual and materialistic, caring little about religious matters: so long as he had plenty to eat and drink, and his horses and mules were cared for, he was content. But Jezebel was of a different type, as resolute as he was weak. Crafty, unscrupulous, merciless, Ahab was but a tool in her hands, fulfilling her pleasure, and therein, as Rev. 2. 20 intimates, she was a fore-shadowing of the woman riding the scarlet-coloured beast, Rev. 17. 3. The crisis was one of gravest moment, and policy as well as indignation prompted her to act at once. If this national reformation were permitted to develop it would overthrow what she had worked for years to establish.

'So let the gods do to me, and more also, if I make not thy life as the life of one of them (her slain prophets) by tomorrow.'

Behold the implacable and horrible enmity against God of a soul that has been abandoned by Him. Utterly incorrigible, her heart was quite insensible of the Divine presence and power. Behold how that awful hatred expressed itself: unable to hurt Jehovah directly, her malice vents itself on His servant. It has ever been thus with those whom God has given up to a reprobate mind. Plague after plague was sent upon Egypt, yet so far from Pharaoh throwing down his weapons of rebellion, after the Lord brought His people out with a high hand, that wretch declared. 'I will pursue, I will overtake, I will divide the spoil; my lust shall be satisfied upon them; I will draw my sword, my hand shall destroy them,' Ex. 15. 9. When the Jewish council beheld Stephen and 'saw his face as it had been the face of an angel,' irradiated with heavenly glory, instead of receiving his message when they heard his words "they were cut to the heart and they gnashed on him with their teeth,' and like so many raging maniacs 'cried out with a loud voice, and stopped their ears, and ran upon him with one accord, and cast him out of the city, and stoned him,' Acts 7. 54-58.

Beware of resisting God and rejecting His Word, lest you be abandoned by Him and He suffers your madness to hasten your destruction. The more it was manifest that God was with Elijah, the more was Jezebel exasperated against him. Now that she learned he had slain her priests, she was like a lioness robbed of her cubs. Her rage knew no bounds; Elijah must be slain at once. Boastful of the morrow, swearing by her gods, she pronounced a fearful imprecation upon herself if Elijah does not meet the same end. The resolution of Jezebel shows the extreme hardness of her heart. It solemnly illustrates how wickedness grows on people. Sinners do not reach such fearful heights of defiance in a moment, but as conscience resists convictions, as light is again and again rejected, the very things which should soften and humble come to harden and make more insolent, and the more plainly God's will be set before us, the more will it work resentment in the mind and hostility in the heart; then it is but a short time until that soul is consigned to the everlasting burnings.

But see here *the overruling hand of God*. Instead of ordering her officers to slay the prophet forthwith, Jezebel sent a servant to announce her sentence upon him. How often mad passions defeat their own ends, fury blinding the judgment so that prudence and caution are not exercised. Possibly she felt so sure of her prey that she feared not to announce her purpose. But future events lie not at the disposal of the sons of men, no matter what positions of worldly power be occupied by them. Probably she thought that Elijah was so courageous, there was no likelihood of his attempting an escape: but in this she erred. How often God takes 'the wise in their own craftiness,' Job 5. 13, and defeats the counsels of the wicked Ahithophels, 2 Sam. 15. 31! Herod had murderous designs on the infant Saviour, but 'being warned of God in a dream,' His parents carried Him down to Egypt, Matt. 2. 12. The Jews 'took counsel' to kill the apostle Paul, but 'their laying wait was known to him' and the disciples delivered him out of their hands, Acts 9. 23. So here: Elijah is given warning before Jezebel wreaks her vengeance on him.

This brings us to the saddest part of the narrative. The Tishbite is notified of the queen's determination to slay him: what was his response thereto? He was the Lord's servant, does he then look unto his Master for instructions? Again and again we have seen in the past how 'the Word of the Lord came' to him, 17. 2, 8; 18. 1, telling him what to do: will he now wait upon the Lord for the necessary guidance? Alas, instead of spreading his case before God, he takes matters into his own hands; instead of waiting patiently for Him, he acts on hasty impulse, deserts the post of duty, and flees from the one who sought his destruction. 'And when he saw that, he arose and went for his life, and came to Beersheba which belongeth to Judah, and left his servant there,' v. 3. Notice carefully the 'when he saw, he arose and went for his life.' His eyes were fixed on the wicked and furious queen: his mind was occupied with her power and fury, and therefore his heart was filled with terror. Faith in God is the only deliverer from carnal fear: 'Behold, God is my salvation: I will trust, and not be afraid'; 'Thou wilt keep him in perfect peace, whose mind is stayed on Thee: because he trusteth in Thee,' Isa. 12. 2; 26. 3. Elijah's mind was no longer stayed upon Jehovah, and therefore fear took possession of him.

Hitherto Elijah had been sustained by faith's vision of the living God, but now he lost sight of the Lord and saw only a furious woman. How many solemn warnings are recorded in Scripture of the disastrous consequences of walking by sight. 'Lot lifted up his eyes and beheld all the plain of Jordan, that it was well watered everywhere,' Gen. 13. 10, and made choice thereof: but very shortly after it is recorded of him that he 'pitched his tent toward Sodom!' The majority-report of the twelve men sent by Moses to spy out the land of Canaan was, 'we *saw* the giants, the sons of Anak, which come of the giants; and we were in our own *sight* as grasshoppers, and so we were in their sight, Num. 13. 33. In consequence of which 'all the congregation lifted up their voice, and cried; and the people wept that night.' Walking by sight magnifies difficulties and paralyses spiritual activity. It was when Peter '*saw* the wind boisterous' that 'he was afraid and began to sink, Matt. 14. 30. How striking the contrast between Elijah here and Moses, who '*By faith* forsook Egypt, not fearing the wrath of the king: for he endured, as seeing Him who is invisible,' Heb. 11. 27, and nothing but the eye of faith fixed steadily upon God will enable anyone to 'endure.'

'And when he saw that, he arose, and went for *his life*' – not for God, nor for the good of His people; but because he thought only of self. The man who had faced the four hundred and fifty false prophets, now fled from one woman; the man who hitherto had been so faithful in the Lord's service now deserted his post of duty, and that at a time when his presence was most needed by the people, if their convictions were to be strengthened and the work of reformation carried forward and firmly established. Alas, what is man! As Peter's courage failed him in the presence of the maid, so Elijah's strength wilted before the threatenings of Jezebel. Shall we exclaim, 'How are the mighty fallen!'? No, indeed, for that would be a carnal and erroneous conception. The truth is that 'It is only as God vouchsafes His grace and Holy Spirit that any man can walk uprightly. Elijah's conduct on this occasion shows that the spirit and courage he had previously manifested were of the Lord, and not of himself : and that those who have the greatest zeal and courage for God and His truth, if left to themselves, become weak and timorous' (John Gill).

CHAPTER TWENTY-THREE

In the Wilderness

━━━

The lot of God's people is a varied one and their case is marked
by frequent change. We cannot expect that it should be otherwise
while they are left in this scene, for there is nothing stable here:
mutability and fluctuation characterizes everything under the
sun. Man is born unto trouble as the sparks fly upward, and the
common experience of saints is no exception to this general rule.
'In the world ye shall have tribulation' John 16. 33, Christ plainly
warned His disciples: yet He added, 'but be of good cheer; I have
overcome the world,' and therefore ye shall share in My victory.
Yet though victory be sure, they suffer many defeats along the
way. They do not enjoy unbroken summer in their souls; nor is it
always winter with them. Their voyage across the sea of life is
similar to that encountered by mariners on the ocean: 'They mount
up to the heaven, they go down again to the depths: their soul
is melted because of trouble . . . Then they cry unto the Lord in
their trouble, and He bringeth them out of their distresses,' Psa.
107. 26, 28.

Nor is it any otherwise with God's public servants. True, they
enjoy many privileges which are not shared by the rank and file
of the Lord's people, and for these they must yet render an
account. Ministers of the Gospel do not have to spend most of
their time and strength amid the ungodly, toiling for their daily
bread; instead they are shielded from constant contact with the
wicked, and much of their time may be and should be spent in
quiet study, meditation and prayer. Moreover, God has bestowed
special spiritual gifts on them: a larger measure of His Spirit, a
deeper insight into His Word, and therefore they should be far

better fitted to cope with the trials of life. Nevertheless, 'tribulation' is also *their* portion while left in this wilderness of sin. Indwelling corruptions give them no rest day or night and the Devil makes them the special objects of his malice, ever busy seeking to disturb their peace and impair their usefulness, venting upon them the full fury of his hatred.

More may rightly be expected from the minister of the Gospel than from others. He is required to be 'an example of the believers in word, in conversation (behaviour), in charity (love), in spirit, in faith, in purity,' 1 Tim. 4. 12; 'in all things showing thyself a pattern of good works; in doctrine showing uncorruptness, gravity, sincerity,' Titus 2. 7. But though a 'man of God,' he *is* a 'man' and not an angel, compassed with infirmity and prone to evil. God has placed His treasure in 'earthen vessels' – not steel or gold – easily cracked and marred, worthless in themselves: 'that' adds the apostle, 'the excellency of the power may be of God, and not of us,' 2 Cor. 4. 7: that is, the glorious Gospel proclaimed by ministers is no invention of *their* brains, and the blessed effects which it produces are in no wise due to *their* skill. They are but instruments, weak and valueless in themselves; their message is God-given and its fruits are entirely of the Holy Spirit, so that they have no ground whatever for self-glorification, nor have those who are benefited by their labours any reason to make heroes out of them or look up to them as a superior order of beings, who are to be regarded as little gods.

The Lord is very jealous of His honour and will not share His glory with another. His people profess to believe that as a cardinal truth, yet they are apt to forget it. They, too, are human, and prone to hero-worship, prone to idolatry, prone to render unto the creatures that to which the Lord alone is entitled. Hence it is they so frequently meet with disappointment, and discover their beloved idol is, like themselves, made of clay. For his own people, God has chosen 'the foolish things of this world,' the 'weak things,' the 'base things' and 'things which are not' (mere 'nobody's'), 'that no flesh should glory in His presence,' 1 Cor. 1. 27-29. And he has called sinful though regenerated men, and not holy angels, to be the preachers of His Gospel, that it might fully appear that 'the excellency of the power' in calling sinners out of darkness into His marvellous light lies not in them nor proceeds from them, but that He alone gives the increase to the seed sown by them: 'So then neither is he that planteth (the evangelist) anything, neither he that watereth (the teacher), but *God*,' 1 Cor. 3. 7.

It is for this reason that God suffers it to appear that the best of men are but men at the best. No matter how richly gifted they may be, how eminent in God's service, how greatly honoured and used of Him, let His sustaining power be withdrawn from them for a moment and it will quickly be seen that they *are* 'earthen vessels.' No man stands any longer than he is supported by Divine grace. The most experienced saint, if left to himself, is immediately seen to be as weak as water and as timid as a mouse. 'Man at his best estate is altogether vanity,' Psa. 39. 5. Then why should it be thought a thing incredible when we read of the failings and falls of the most favoured of God's saints and servants? Noah's drunkenness, Lot's carnality, Abraham's prevarications, Moses' anger, Aaron's jealousy, Joshua's haste, David's adultery, Jonah's disobedience, Peter's denial, Paul's contention with Barnabas, are so many illustrations of the solemn truth that 'there is not a just man upon earth that doeth good, and sinneth not,' Eccl. 7. 20. Perfection is found in Heaven, but nowhere on earth except in the Perfect Man.

Yet let it be pointed out that the failures of these men are not recorded in Scripture for us to hide behind, as though we may use them to excuse our own infidelities. Far from it: they are set before us as so many danger signals for us to take note of, as solemn warnings for us to heed. The reading thereof should humble us, making us more distrustful of ourselves. They should impress upon our hearts the fact that our strength is found alone in the Lord, and that without Him we can do nothing. They should be translated into earnest prayer that the workings of pride and self-sufficiency may be subdued within us. They should cause us to cry constantly, 'Hold *Thou* me up, and I shall be safe,' Psa. 119. 117. Not only so, they should wean us from undue confidence in the creatures and deliver us from expecting too much of others, even of the fathers in Israel. They should make us diligent in prayer for our brethren in Christ, especially for our pastors, that it may please God to preserve them from everything which would dishonour His name and cause His enemies to rejoice.

The man at whose prayers the windows of heaven had been fast closed for three and a half years, and at whose supplication they had again been opened, was no exception: he too was made of flesh and blood, and this was permitted to be painfully manifest. Jezebel sent a message to inform him that on the morrow he should suffer the same fate as had overtaken her prophets. 'And when he saw that, he arose and went for his life.' In the midst of his glorious triumph over the enemies of the Lord, at the very time the people needed him to lead them in the total overthrow of idolatry and the establishment of true worship, he is terrified by the queen's threat, and flees. It was 'the hand of the Lord' which had brought him to Jezreel, 1 Kings 18. 46, and he received no Divine intimation to move from there. Surely it was both his privilege and duty to look unto his Master to protect him from Jezebel's rage as He had before done from Ahab's. Had he committed himself into the hands of God *He* had not failed him and great good had probably been accomplished if he now remained at the post where the Lord had put him.

But his eyes were no longer fixed upon God, instead they saw only a furious woman. The One who had miraculously fed him at the brook Cherith, who had so wondrously sustained him at the widow's home in Zarephath, and who so signally strengthened him on Carmel, is forgotten. Thinking only of himself he flees from the place of testimony. But how is this strange lapse to be accounted for? Obviously his fears were excited by the queen's threat coming to him *so unexpectedly*. Was there not good reason for him now to be anticipating with great joy and exultation the co-operation of all Israel in the work of reformation? Would not the whole nation, who had cried, 'Jehovah, He is the God,' be deeply thankful for his prayers having procured the much-needed rain? And in a moment his hope seemed to be rudely shattered by this message from the incensed queen. Had he then lost all faith in God to protect him? Far be it from us so to charge him: rather does it seem that he was momentarily overwhelmed, panic-stricken. He gave himself no time to think: but taken completely by surprise, he acted on the spur of the moment. How that gives point to 'he that believeth shall not make haste,' Isa. 28. 16.

While what has been pointed out above accounts for Elijah's hurried action, yet it does not explain his strange lapse. It was the absence of faith which caused him to be filled with fear. But let it be stated that the exercise of faith lies not at the disposal of the believer, so that he may call it into action whenever he pleases. Not so: faith is a Divine gift and the exercise of it is solely by Divine power, and both in its bestowment and its operations God acts sovereignly. Yet though God ever acts sovereignly, He never acts capriciously. He afflicts not willingly, but because we give Him occasion to use the rod; He withholds grace because of our pride, withdraws comfort because of our sins. God permits His people to experience falls along the road for various reasons, yet in every instance the outward fall is preceded by some failure or other on their part, and if we are to reap the full benefit from the recorded sins of such as Abraham, David, Elijah and Peter, we need to study attentively what led up to and was the occasion of them. This is generally done with Peter's case, yet rarely so with the others.

In most instances the preceding contexts give plain intimation of the first signs of declension, as a spirit of self-confidence signally marked the approaching fall of Peter. But in the case before us the previous verses supply no clue to the eclipse of Elijah's faith, yet the verses which follow indicate the cause of his relapse. When the Lord appeared unto him and asked, 'What doest thou here, Elijah?' 19. 9, the prophet answered, 'I have been very jealous for the Lord God of hosts: for the children of Israel have forsaken Thy covenant, thrown down Thine altars, and slain Thy prophets with the sword; and I, even I only, am left, and they seek my life to take it away.' Does not that tell us, first, that he had been entertaining too great a regard of his own importance; second, that he was unduly occupied with his service: 'I, even I only am left' – to maintain Thy cause; and third, that he was chagrined at the absence of those results he had expected? The workings of pride – his threefold 'I' – choke the exercises of faith. Observe how Elijah repeated those statements, v. 14, and how God's response seems by His very corrective to specify the disease – Elisha was appointed in his stead!

God then withdrew His strength for the moment that Elijah might be seen in his native weakness. He did so righteously, for grace is promised only to the humble, James 4. 6. Yet in this God acts sovereignly, for it is only by His grace that any man is kept humble. He gives more faith to one than to another, and maintains it more evenly in certain individuals. How great the contrast from Elijah's flight was Elisha's faith: when the king of Syria sent a great host to arrest the latter and his servant said, 'Alas, my master! how shall we do?' the prophet answered, 'Fear not: for they that be with us are more than they that be with them,' 2 Kings 6. 15, 16. When the Empress Eudoxia sent a threatening message to Chrysostom, he bade her officer, 'Go tell her I fear nothing but sin.' When the friends of Luther earnestly begged him not to proceed to the Diet of Worms to which he had been summoned by the Emperor, he replied, 'Though every tile on the houses of that city were a devil I will not be deterred,' and he went, and God delivered him out of his enemies' hands. Yet the infirmities of Chrysostom and Luther were manifested on other occasions.

It was his being occupied with circumstances which brought about Elijah's sad fall. It is a dictum of the world's philosophy that 'man is the creature of his circumstances.' No doubt this is largely the case with the natural man, but it should not be true of the Christian, nor is it so while his graces remain in a healthy condition. Faith views the One who orders our circumstances, hope looks beyond the present scene, patience gives strength to endure trials, and love delights in Him whom no circumstances affect. While Elijah set the Lord before him he feared not though a host encamped against him. But when he looked upon the creature and contemplated his peril he thought more of his own safety than of

God's cause. To be occupied with circumstances is to walk by sight, and that is fatal both to our peace and spiritual prosperity. However unpleasant or desperate be our circumstances, God is able to preserve us in them, as He did Daniel in the lion's den and his companions in the fiery furnace; yea, He is able to make the heart triumph over them, as witness the singing of the apostles in the Philippian dungeon.

Oh, what need have we to cry, 'Lord, increase our faith,' for we are only strong and safe while exercising faith in God. If He be forgotten and His presence with us be not realized at the time when great dangers menace us, then we are certain to act in a manner unworthy of our Christian profession. It is by faith we stand, 2 Cor. 1. 24, as it is through faith we are kept by the power of God unto salvation, 1 Pet. 1. 5. If we truly set the Lord before us and contemplate Him as being at our right hand, nothing will move us, none can make us afraid; we may bid defiance to the most powerful and malignant. Yet as another has said, 'But where is the faith that never staggers through unbelief? the hand that never hangs down, the knee that never trembles, the heart that never faints?' Nevertheless, the fault is *ours*, the blame is ours. Though it lies not in our power to strengthen faith or call it into exercise, we may weaken it and can hinder its operations. After saying, 'Thou standest by faith,' the apostle at once added, 'Be not high-minded, but fear,' Rom. 11. 20 – be distrustful of self, for it is pride and self-sufficiency which stifle the breathings of faith.

Many have thought it strange when they read of the most note-worthy of Biblical saints failing in the very graces which were their strongest. Abraham is outstanding for his faith, being called 'the father of all them that believe'; yet his faith broke down in Egypt when he lied to Pharaoh about his wife. We are told that 'Moses was very meek, above all the men who were upon the face of the earth,' Num. 12. 3, yet he was debarred from entering Canaan because he lost his temper and spoke unadvisedly with his lips. John was the apostle of love, yet in a fit of intolerance he and his brother James wanted to call down fire from heaven so that the Samaritans be destroyed, for which the Saviour rebuked them,

Luke 9. 54, 55. Elijah was renowned for his boldness, yet it was his courage which now failed him. What proofs are these that none can exercise those graces which most distinguish their characters without the immediate and constant assistance of God, and that, when in danger of being exalted above measure, they are often left to struggle with temptation without their accustomed support. Only by conscious and acknowledged weakness are we made strong.

A few words only must suffice in making application of this sad incident. Its outstanding lesson is obviously a solemn warning unto those occupying public positions in the Lord's vineyard. When He is pleased to work through and by them there is sure to be bitter and powerful opposition stirred up against them. Said the apostle, 'A great and effectual door is opened unto me, and there are many adversaries,' 1 Cor. 16. 9 – the two ever go together; yet if the Lord be our confidence and strength, there is nothing to fear. A heavy and wellnigh fatal blow had been given to Satan's kingdom that day on Carmel, and had Elijah stood his ground, would not the seven thousand secret worshippers of Jehovah have been emboldened to come forth on his side, the language of Micah 4. 6, 7, been accomplished, and the captivity and dispersion of his people spared? Alas, one false step and such a bright prospect was dashed to the ground, and never returned. Seek grace, O servant of God, to 'withstand in the evil day, and having done all, to stand,' Eph. 6. 13.

But does not this sad incident also point a salutary lesson which *all* believers need take to heart? This solemn fall of the prophet comes also immediately after the marvels which had been accomplished in response to his supplications. How strange! Rather, how searching! In the preceding chapters we emphasized that the glorious transactions wrought upon Mount Carmel supply the Lord's people with a most blessed illustration and demonstration of the efficacy of prayer, and surely this pathetic sequel shows what need they have to be on their guard when they have received some notable mercy from the Throne of Grace. If it was needful that the apostle should be given a thorn in the flesh, the messenger of Satan to buffet him, lest he should be 'exalted above measure through the abundance of the revelations' vouchsafed him, 2 Cor. 12. 7, then what need have we to 'rejoice *with trembling*,' Psa. 2. 11, when we are elated over receiving answers to our petitions.

CHAPTER TWENTY-FOUR

Dejected

We are now to behold the effects which Elijah's giving way to fear had upon him. The message which had come from Jezebel, that on the morrow she would take revenge upon him for his slaying of her prophets, rendered the Tishbite panic-stricken. For the moment God saw fit to leave him to himself, that we might learn the strongest are weak as water when He withholds His support, as the powerful Samson was as impotent as any other man as soon as the Spirit of the Lord departed from him. It matters not what growth has been made in grace, how well experienced we may be in the spiritual life, or how eminent the position we have occupied in the Lord's service, when *He* withdraws His sustaining hand the madness which is in our hearts by nature at once asserts itself, gains the upper hand, and leads us into a course of folly. Thus it was now with Elijah. Instead of taking the angry queen's threat unto the Lord and begging Him to undertake, he took matters into his own hands and 'went for his life,' 1 Kings 19. 3.

In the preceding chapter we intimated why it was that the Lord suffered His servant to experience a lapse at this time: in addition to what was there said we believe the prophet's flight was *a punishment on Israel*, for the insincerity and inconstancy of their reformation. 'One would have expected after such a public and sensible manifestation of the glory of God, and such a clear decision of the contest pending between him and Baal, to the honour of Elijah, the confusion of Baal's prophets, and the universal satisfaction of the people, after they had seen both fire and water come from heaven at the prayer of Elijah, and both in mercy to them: the one as a sign of the acceptance of their offering, the other as it refreshed their inheritance, that they should now all as one man have returned to the worship of the God of Israel and taken Elijah for their guide and oracle, that he should henceforth have been their prime minister of state and his directions laws both to king and kingdom. But it is quite otherwise: he is neglected whom God honoured; no respect is paid to him nor any use made of him; on the contrary, the land of Israel to which he had been and might yet have been a great blessing, is soon made too hot for him' (Matthew Henry). His departure from Israel was a judgment upon them.

In the Scriptures God's children are exhorted again and again *not to fear*: 'Neither fear ye their fear, nor be afraid,' Isa. 8. 12. But how are weak and trembling souls to render obedience to this precept? The very next verse tells us: 'Sanctify the Lord of hosts Himself, and let *Him* be your fear, and let Him be your dread.' It is the fear of the Lord in our hearts which delivers from the fear of man: the filial awe of displeasing and dishonouring Him who is our refuge and strength, a very present help in trouble. 'Be not afraid of their faces,' said God to another of His servants, adding, 'for I am with thee to deliver thee, saith the Lord,' Jer. 1. 8. Ah, it is the consciousness of His presence which faith must realize if fear is to be stilled. Christ admonished His disciples for their fear: 'Why are ye fearful, O ye of little faith?' Matt. 8. 26. 'Be not afraid of their terror, neither be troubled,' 1 Pet. 3. 14, is the word which we are required to take to heart.

In connection with Elijah's flight from Jezebel we are told first that he 'came to Beersheba, which belongeth to Judah,' 1 Kings 19. 3. There it might be thought a safe asylum would be secured, for he was now outside the territory governed by Ahab, but it was only a case (as the old saying goes) of 'jumping out of the frying-pan into the fire.' For at that time the kingdom of Judah was ruled over by Jehoshaphat, and his son had married 'the daughter of Ahab,' 2 Kings 8. 18, and so closely were the two houses of Jehoshaphat and Ahab united that when the former was asked to join the latter in an expedition against Ramoth-gilead, Jehoshaphat declared, 'I am as thou art, my people as thy people, my horses as thy horses,' 1 Kings 22. 4. Thus Jehoshaphat would have had no compunction in delivering up the one who had fled to his land as soon as he received command from Ahab and Jezebel to that effect. So tarry in Beersheba Elijah dare not, but flees yet farther.

Beersheba lay towards the extreme south of Judea, being situated in the inheritance of Simeon, and it is estimated that Elijah and his companion covered no less than ninety miles in their journey thither from Jezreel. Next we are told that he 'left his servant there.' Here we behold the prophet's thoughtfulness and compassion for his lone retainer: anxious to spare him the hardships of the dreary wilderness of Arabia, which he now proposed to enter. In this considerate act the prophet sets an example for masters to follow, who should not require their dependents to encounter unreasonable perils nor perform services above their strength. Moreover, Elijah now wished to be alone with his trouble and not give vent to his feelings of despair in the presence of another. This, too, is worthy of emulation: when fear and unbelief fill his heart and he is on the point of giving expression to his dejection, the Christian should retire from the presence of others lest he infect them with his morbidity and petulance – let him unburden his heart to *the Lord*, and spare the feelings of his brethren.

'But he himself went a day's journey into the wilderness,' v. 4. Here we are given to see another effect of fear and unbelief: it produces perturbation and agitation, so that a spirit of *restlessness* seizes the soul. And how can it be otherwise? Rest of soul is to be found nowhere but in the Lord, by communing with and confiding in Him. 'The wicked are like the troubled sea, when it cannot rest,' Isa. 57. 20: necessarily so, for they are utter strangers to the Rest-Giver – 'the way of peace have they not known,' Rom. 3. 17. When the Christian is out of fellowship with God, when he takes matters into his own hands, when faith and hope are no longer in exercise, his case is no better than that of the unregenerate, for he has cut himself off from his comforts and is thoroughly miserable. Contentment and delighting in the Lord's will is no longer his portion: instead, his mind is in a turmoil, he is thoroughly demoralized, and now vainly seeks to find relief in a ceaseless round of diversions and the feverish activities of the flesh. He must be on the move, for he is completely discomposed: he wearies himself in vain exercises, till his natural strength gives out.

Follow the prophet with your mind's eye. Hour after hour he plods along beneath the burning sun, his feet blistered by the scorching sands, alone in the dreary desert. At last fatigue and anguish overcame his sinewy strength and he 'came and sat under a juniper tree and requested for himself that he might die,' v. 4. The first thing we would note in this connection is that, disheartened and despondent as he was, Elijah made no attempt to lay violent hands on himself. Though now for a season God had withdrawn His comforting presence, and in a measure withheld His restraining grace, yet He did not and never does wholly deliver one of His own into the power of the Devil.

'And he requested for himself that he might die.' The second thing we would note is the *inconsistency* of his conduct. The reason why Elijah left Jezreel so hurriedly on hearing of Jezebel's threat was that he 'went for his life,' and now he longs that his life might be taken from him. Herein we may perceive still another effect when unbelief and fear possess the heart. Not only do we then act foolishly and wrongly, not only does a spirit of unrest and discontent take possession of us, but we are thrown completely off our balance, the soul loses its poise, and consistency of conduct is at an end. The explanation of this is simple: truth is uniform and harmonious, whereas error is multiform and incongruous; but for the truth to control us effectually *faith* must be in constant exercise – when faith ceases to act we at once become erratic and undependable and, as men speak, we are soon a 'bundle of contradictions.' Consistency of character and conduct is dependent upon a steady walking with God.

Probably there are few of God's servants but who at some time or other are eager to cast off their harness and cease from the toils of conflict, particularly when their labours seem to be in vain and they are disposed to look upon themselves as cumberers of the ground. When Moses exclaimed, 'I am not able to bear all this people alone, because it is too heavy for me,' he at once added, 'And if Thou deal thus with me, kill me, I pray Thee, out of hand,' Num. 11. 14, 15. So, too, Jonah prayed, 'Therefore now, O Lord, take, I beseech Thee, my life from me; for it is better for me to die than to live,' 4. 3. Nor is a longing to be removed from this world of trouble peculiar to the ministers of Christ. Many of the rank and file of His people also are at times moved to say with David, 'Oh that I had wings like a dove! for then would I fly away, and be at rest,' Psa. 55. 6. Short as is our sojourn down here, it seems long, too long for some of us, and though we cannot vindicate Elijah's peevishness and petulance, yet this writer can certainly sympathize with him under the juniper tree, for he has often been there himself.

It should, however, be pointed out that there is a radical difference between desiring to be delivered from a world of disappointment and sorrow and a longing to be delivered from this body of death in order that we may be present with the Lord. The latter was the case with the apostle when he said, 'Having a desire to depart, and to be with Christ; which is far better,' Phil. 1. 23. A desire to be freed from abject poverty or a bed of languishing is only natural, but a yearning to be delivered from a world of iniquity and a body of death so that we may enjoy unclouded communion with the Beloved is truly spiritual. One of the greatest surprises of our own Christian life has been to find how few people give evidence of the latter. The majority of professors appear to be so wedded to this scene, so in love with this life, or so fearful of the physical aspect of death, that they cling to life as tenaciously as do non-professors. Surely Heaven cannot be very real to them. True, we ought submissively to wait God's time, yet that should not preclude or override a desire to 'depart, and be with Christ.'

But let us not lose sight of the fact that in his dejection Elijah *turned to God* and said, 'It is enough; now, O Lord, take away my life; for I am not better than my fathers,' v. 4. No matter how cast down we be, how acute our grief, it is ever the privilege of the believer to unburden his heart unto that One who 'sticketh closer than a brother,' and pour out our complaint into His sympathetic ear. True, He will not wink at what is wrong, nevertheless He is touched with the feeling of our infirmities. True, He will not always grant us our request, for oftentimes we 'ask amiss,' James 4. 3, yet if He withholds what we desire it is because He has something better for us. Thus it was in the case of Elijah. The Lord did not take away his life from him at that time: He did not do so later, for Elijah was taken to Heaven without seeing death. Elijah is one of the only two who have entered Heaven without passing through the portals of the grave. Nevertheless, for God's chariot Elijah had to wait God's appointed time.

'It is enough; now, O Lord, take away my life; for I am not better than my fathers.' He was tired of the ceaseless opposition which he encountered, weary of the strife. He was disheartened in his labours, which he felt were of no avail. I have striven hard, but it has been in vain; I have toiled all night and caught nothing. It was the language of disappointment and fretfulness: 'It is enough' – I am unwilling to fight any longer, I have done and suffered sufficient: let me go hence. We are not sure what he signified by his 'I am not better than my fathers.' Possibly he was pleading his weakness and incapacity: I am not stronger than they, and no better able to cope with the difficulties they encountered. Perhaps he alluded to the lack of fruit in his ministry: nothing comes of my labours, I am no more successful than they were. Or maybe he was intimating his disappointment because God had not fulfilled his expectations. He was thoroughly despondent and anxious to quit the arena.

See here once more the consequences which follow upon giving way to fear and unbelief. Poor Elijah was now in the slough of despond, an experience which most of the Lord's people have at some time or other. He had forsaken the place into which the Lord had brought him, and now was tasting the bitter effects of a course of self-will. All pleasure had gone out of life: the joy of the Lord was no longer his strength. O what a rod do we make for our backs when we deliberately depart from the path of duty. By leaving the paths of righteousness we cut ourselves off from the springs of spiritual refreshment, and therefore the 'wilderness' is now our dwelling-place. And there we sit down in utter dejection alone in our wretchedness, for there is none to comfort us while we are in such a state. Death is now desired that an end may be put to our misery. If we try to pray it is but the murmurings of our hearts which find expression: my will, and not Thine, be done being the substance thereof.

And what was the Lord's response? Did He turn with disgust from such a sight and leave His erring servant to reap what he had sown and suffer the full and final deserts of his unbelief? Ah, shall the good Shepherd refuse to take care of one of His strayed sheep, lying helpless by the wayside? Shall the great Physician refuse assistance to one of His patients just when he needs Him most? Blessed be His name, the Lord is 'long-suffering to us-ward, not willing that any should perish.' 'Like as a father pitieth his children, so the Lord pitieth them that fear Him,' Psa. 103. 13. Thus it was here: the Lord evidenced His pity for His overwrought and disconsolate servant in a most gracious manner, for the next thing that we read of is that he '*slept* under a juniper tree,' v. 5. But the force of that is apt to be lost upon us, in this God-dishonouring day, when there are few left who realize that '*He* giveth His beloved sleep,' Psa. 127. 2. It was something better than 'nature taking its course': it was the Lord refreshing the weary prophet.

How often is it now lost sight of that the Lord cares for the bodies of His saints as well as for their souls. This is more or less recognized and owned by believers in the matter of food and clothing, health and strength, but it is widely ignored by many concerning the point we are here treating of. Sleep is as imperative for our physical well-being as is food and drink, and the one is as much the *gift* of our heavenly Father as is the other. We cannot put ourselves to sleep by any effort of will, as those who suffer with insomnia quickly discover. Nor does exercise and manual labour of itself ensure sleep: have you ever lain down almost exhausted and then found you were 'too tired to sleep'? Sleep is a Divine gift, but the nightly recurrence of it blinds us to the fact.

When it so pleases Him, God withholds sleep, and then we have to say with the Psalmist, 'Thou holdest mine eyes waking,' 77. 4.

But that is the exception rather than the rule, and deeply thankful should we be that it is so. Day by day the Lord feeds us, and night by night He 'giveth His beloved sleep.' Thus in this little detail – of Elijah's sleeping under the juniper tree – which we are likely to pass over lightly, we should perceive the gracious hand of God ministering in tenderness to the needs of one who is dear unto Him. Yes, 'the Lord pitieth them that fear Him,' and why? '*for* He knoweth our frame; He remembereth that we are dust,' Psa. 103. 14. He is mindful of our frailty, and tempers His winds accordingly; He is aware when our energies are spent, and graciously renews our strength. It was not God's design that His servant should die of exhaustion in the wilderness after his long, long flight from Jezreel, so He mercifully refreshes his body with sleep. And thus compassionately does He deal with us.

Alas, how little are we affected by the Lord's goodness and grace unto us. The unfailing recurrence of His mercies both temporally and spiritually inclines us to take them as a matter of course. So dull of understanding are we, so cold our hearts Godward, it is to be feared that most of the time we fail to realize *whose* loving hand it is which is ministering to us. Is not this the very reason why we do not begin really to value our health until it is taken from us, and not until we spend night after night tossing upon a bed of pain do we perceive the worth of regular sleep with which we were formerly favoured? And such vile creatures are we that, when illness and insomnia come upon us, instead of improving the same by repenting of our former ingratitude, and humbly confessing the same to God, we murmur and complain at the hardness of our present lot and wonder what we have done to deserve such treatment. O let those of us who are still blessed with good health and regular sleep fail not daily to return thanks for such privileges and earnestly seek grace to use the strength from them to the glory of God.

CHAPTER TWENTY-FIVE

Refreshed

━━━━

'There hath no temptation (trial: whether in the form of seductions or afflictions, solicitations to sin, or hardships) taken you but such as is common to man,' 1 Cor. 10. 13. There hath no trial come upon you but such as human nature is liable unto and has often been subject to: you have not been called upon to experience any super-human or unprecedented temptation. But how generally is this fact lost sight of when the dark clouds of adversity come our way! Then we are inclined to think, none was ever so severely tried as I am. It is well at such a moment to remind ourselves of this truth and ponder the records of those who have gone before us. Is it excruciating suffering of body which causes you to suppose your anguish is beyond that of any other? Then recall the case of Job 'with sore boils from the sole of his foot unto his crown'! Is it bereavement, the unexpected snatching away of loved ones? Then remember also that Job lost all his sons and daughters in a single day. Is it a succession of hardships and persecutions encountered in the Lord's service? Then read 2 Corinthians 11. 24-27 and note the multiplied and painful experiences through which the chief of the apostles was called upon to pass.

But perhaps that which most overwhelms some reader is *the shame* he feels over his breakdown under trials. He knows that others have been tried as severely as he has, yea, much more severely, yet they bore them with courage and composure, whereas he has been crushed by them: instead of drawing comfort from the Divine promises, he has given way to a spirit of despair; instead of bearing the rod meekly and patiently, he has rebelled and murmured; instead of plodding along the path of duty, he has deserted it. Was there ever such a sorry failure as I am? is now his lament. Rightly should we be humbled and mourn over such failures to quit ourselves 'like men,' 1 Cor. 16. 13; contritely should we confess such sins unto God. Yet we must not imagine that all is now lost. Even this experience is not unparalleled in the lives of others. Though Job cursed not God, yet he did the day of his birth. So, too, did Jeremiah, 20. 14. Elijah deserted his post of duty, lay down under the juniper tree and prayed for death. What a mirror is Scripture in which we may see ourselves!

'But God is faithful, who will not suffer you to be tempted above that ye are able; but will with the temptation also make a way to escape, that ye may be able to bear it,' 1 Cor. 10. 13. Yes, God is faithful even if we are faithless: He is true to His covenant engagements, and though He visits our iniquities with stripes, yet His loving kindness will He never utterly take from one of His own, Psa. 89. 32, 33. It is in the hour of trial, just when the clouds are blackest and a spirit of dejection has seized us, that God's faithfulness appears most conspicuously. He knows our frame and will not suffer us to be unduly tried, but will 'with the temptation also make a way to escape.' That is to say, He will either lighten the burden or give increased strength to bear it, so that we shall not be utterly overwhelmed by it. 'God is faithful': not that He is engaged to secure us if we deliberately plunge into temptations. No, but rather, if we seek to resist temptation, if we call upon Him in the day of trouble, if we plead His promises and count upon Him to undertake for us, He most certainly will not fail us. Thus, though on the one hand we must not presume and be reckless, on the other hand we should not despair and give up the fight. Weeping may endure for a night, but joy cometh in the morning.

How strikingly and how blessedly was 1 Corinthians 10. 13, illustrated and exemplified in the case of Elijah! It was a sore temptation or trial, when after all his fidelity in the Lord's service his life should be threatened by the wicked Jezebel, and when all his efforts to bring back Israel to the worship of the true God seemed to be entirely in vain. It was more than he could bear: he was weary of such a one-sided and losing fight, and he prayed to be removed from the arena. But God was faithful and with the sore temptation 'also made a way to escape' that he might be able to bear it. In Elijah's experience, as is so often the case with us, God did not remove the burden, but He gave fresh supplies of grace so that the prophet could bear it. He neither took away Jezebel nor wrought a mighty work of grace in the hearts of Israel, but He renewed the strength of His overwrought servant. Though Elijah had fled from his post of duty, the Lord did not now desert the prophet in his hour of need. 'If we believe not, yet He abideth faithful: He cannot deny Himself,' 2 Tim. 2. 13. O what a God is ours! No mere fair-weather friend is the One who shed his blood to redeem us, but a Brother 'born for adversity,' Prov. 17. 17. He has solemnly sworn 'I will never leave thee nor forsake thee,' and therefore may we triumphantly declare, 'The Lord is my Helper, and I will not fear what man shall do unto me,' Heb. 13. 5, 6.

As we pointed out in our last chapter, the first thing which the Lord did in renewing the strength of Elijah was to give His beloved sleep, thereby refreshing his weary and travel-worn body. How inadequately do we value this Divine blessing, not only for the rest it brings to our physical frames but for the relief it affords to a worried mind! What a mercy it is for many harassed souls that they are not awake the full twenty-four hours! Those who are healthy and ambitious may begrudge the hours spent in slumber as so much 'necessary waste of time,' but others who are wracked with pain or who are distressed must regard a few hours of un-consciousness each night as a great boon. None of us are as grateful as we should be for this constantly recurring privilege, nor as hearty in returning thanks unto its Bestower. That this *is* one of the Creator's gifts unto us is seen from the very first occurrence of the word in Scripture: 'The Lord caused a deep sleep to fall upon Adam,' Gen. 2. 21.

'And as he lay and slept under a juniper tree, *behold*, then, an angel touched him,' 1 Kings 19. 5. Here was the second proof of the Lord's tender care for His servant and an inexpressibly blessed one was it. Each separate word calls for devout attention. 'Behold:' a note of wonderment to stimulate our interest and stir us to reverent amazement. 'Behold' *what?* Some token of the Lord's displeasure, as we might well expect: a drenching rain for example, to add to the prophet's discomfort? No, far otherwise. Behold a grand demonstration of that truth, 'For my thoughts are not your thoughts, neither are your ways My ways, saith the Lord. For as the heavens are higher than the earth so are My ways higher than your ways, and My thoughts than your thoughts,' Isa. 55. 8, 9. These verses are often quoted, yet few of the Lord's people are familiar with the words which immediately precede them and of which they are an amplification: 'Let us return to the Lord and He will have mercy upon us, and to our God for He will *abundantly pardon.*' Thus it is not the loftiness of his wisdom but the infinitude of his mercy which is there in view.

'Behold *then.*' This time-mark gives additional emphasis to the amazing phenomenon which is here spread before our eyes. It was not on the summit of Carmel, but here in the wilderness that Elijah received this touching proof of his Master's care. It was not immediately after his conflict with the prophets of Baal, but following upon his flight from Jezreel that he received this distinguishing favour. It was not while he was engaged in importunate prayer, begging God to supply his need, but when he had petulantly asked that his life should be taken from him, that provision was now made to preserve it. How often God is better to us than our fears. We look for judgment, and behold mercy! Has there not been just such a 'then' in our lives? Certainly there has been – more than once in the writer's experience; and we doubt not in each of our Christian reader's. Well, then, may we unite together in acknowledging, 'He hath not dealt with us after our sins, nor rewarded us according to our iniquities,' Psa. 103. 10. Rather has He dealt with us after His covenant faithfulness and according to His knowledge-passing love.

'Behold, then an *angel* touched him.' It was not a fellow-traveller whose steps God now directed toward the juniper tree and whose heart He moved to have compassion unto the exhausted one who lay beneath it. That had been a signal mercy, but here we gaze upon something far more amazing. God dispatched one of those celestial creatures who surround His throne on high to comfort the dejected prophet and supply his wants. Verily this was not 'after the manner of men,' but blessed be His name it *was* after the manner of Him who is 'the God of all grace,' 1 Pet. 5. 10. And grace, my reader, takes no account of our worthiness or unworthiness, of our undeservedness, or ill-deservedness. No, grace is free and sovereign and looks not outside itself for the motive of its exercise. Man often deals harshly with his fellows, ignoring their frailty and forgetting that he is liable to fall by the wayside as they are, and therefore he frequently acts hurriedly, inconsistently, and unkindly towards them. But not so did God: He ever deals patiently with His erring children, and shows the deepest pity and tenderness.

'Behold, then an angel touched him,' gently rousing him from his sleep, that he might see and partake of the refreshment which had been provided for him. How this reminds us of that word, 'are they not all (the holy angels) ministering spirits, sent forth to minister for them who shall be heirs of salvation?' Heb. 1. 14. This is something about which we hear little in this materialistic and sceptical age, but concerning which the Scriptures reveal much for our comfort. It was an angel who came and delivered Lot from Sodom ere that city was destroyed by fire and brimstone, Gen. 19. 15, 16. It was an angel which 'shut the lions' mouths' when Daniel was cast into their den, 6. 22. It was angels who conveyed the soul of the beggar into 'Abraham's bosom,' Luke 16. 22. It was an angel which visited Peter in the prison, smote the chains from his hands, caused the iron gate of the city to 'open of his own accord,' Act 12. 7, 10, and thus delivered him from his enemies. It was an angel who assured Paul that none on the ship should perish, Acts. 27. 23. Nor do we believe for a moment that the ministry of angels is a thing of the past, though they no longer manifest themselves in visible form as in Old Testament times – Hebrews 1. 14, precludes such an idea.

"Then an angel touched him, and said unto him, Arise and eat. And he looked, and behold, there was a cake baken on the coals, and a cruse of water at his head,' vv. 5, 6. Here was the third provision which the Lord so graciously made for the refreshment of

His exhausted servant. Once more we note the thought-provoking 'behold.' And well may we ponder this sight and be moved to wonderment at it – wonderment at the amazing grace of Elijah's God, and our God. Twice before, the Lord provided sustenance for the prophet in a miraculous manner; by the ravens at the brook Cherith, by the widow woman at Zarephath; but here none less than an angel ministered to him! Behold *the constancy* of God's love, which all Christians profess to believe in but few seem to realize in moments of depression and darkness. As another has said, 'It is not difficult to believe that God loves us when we go with the multitude to the house of God with joy and praise and stand in the sunlit circle: but it is hard for us to believe that He feels as much love for us when, exiled by our sin to the land of Jordan and of the Hermonites our soul is cast down within us, and deep calls to deep and His waves and billows surge around.

'It is not difficult to believe that God loves us when, like Elijah at Cherith and Carmel, we do his commandments hearkening unto the voice of His Word; but it is not so easy when, like Elijah in the desert, we lie stranded, or as dismantled and rudderless vessels roll in the trough of the waves. It is not difficult to believe in God's love when, like Peter, we stand on the mount of glory and in the rapture of joy propose to share a tabernacle with Christ for evermore; but it is well-nigh impossible when, with the same apostle, we deny our Master with oaths, and are abashed by a look in which grief masters rebuke.' Most necessary is it for our peace and comfort to know and believe that the love of God abides unchanging as Himself. What proof did Elijah here receive of the same! Not only was he not forsaken by the Lord, but there was no upbraiding of him nor word of reproach upon his conduct. Ah, who can fathom, yea even understand, the amazing grace of our God: the more sin abounds the more does His grace superabound!

Not only did Elijah receive unmistakable proof of the constancy of God's love at this time, but it was manifested in a specially tender manner. He had drunk of the brook Cherith, but never of water drawn by angelic hands from the river of God. He had eaten of bread foraged for him by ravens and of meal multiplied by a miracle, but never of cakes manufactured by celestial fingers. And why these *special* proofs of tenderness? Certainly not because God condoned His servant, but because a special manifestation of love was needed to assure the prophet that he was still the object of Divine love, to soften his spirit and lead him to repentance. How this reminds us of that scene portrayed in John 21, where we behold a breakfast prepared by the risen Saviour and a fire of coals to warm the wet seamen; and He did this for the very men who, on the night of His betrayal, all forsook Him and fled, and who refused to believe in His triumph when the women told them of the empty tomb and of His appearing unto them in tangible form!

'And he looked, and behold, there was a cake baken on the coals and a cruse of water at his head.' Not only does this 'behold' emphasize the riches of God's grace in ministering to His wayward servant, but it also calls attention to a marvel of His power. In their petulance and unbelief, Israel of old had asked, 'Can God furnish a table in the wilderness?' Psa. 78. 19; yea, they affirmed, 'It had been better for us to serve the Egyptians, than that we should die in the wilderness,' Ex. 14. 12. And here was Elijah, not merely on the fringe of this desolate and barren wilderness but 'a day's journey' into its interior. Nothing grew there save a few shrubs, and no stream moistened its parched sands. But adverse circumstances and unpropitious conditions present no obstacles to the Almighty. Though means be wanting to us, the lack of them presents no difficulty to the Creator; He can produce water from the flinty rock and turn stones into bread. Therefore no good thing shall they lack whom the Lord God has engaged to provide for: His mercy and His power are equally pledged on their behalf. Remember then, O doubting one, the God of Elijah still lives and whether thy lot be cast in a time of war or famine, thy bread and thy water are sure.

'And he looked, and behold, there was a cake baken on the coals, and a cruse of water at his head.' There is yet another direction to which this 'behold' points us, which seems to have escaped the notice of the commentators, namely, the kind of service which the angel here performed. What an amazing thing that so dignified a creature should be engaged in such a lowly task: that the fingers of a celestial being should be employed in preparing and baking a cake! It would appear a degrading task for one of those exalted beings which surround the throne of the Most High to minister unto one who belonged to an inferior and fallen race, who was undutiful and out of temper: to leave a spiritual occupation to prepare food for Elijah's body – how abasing! Well may we marvel at such a sight, and admire the angel's obedience in complying with his Master's order. But more, it should encourage us to heed that precept and 'condescend to men of low estate,' Rom. 12. 16, to regard no employment beneath us by which we may benefit a fellow creature who is dejected in mind and whose spirit is overwhelmed within him. Despise not the most menial duty when an angel disdained not to cook food for a sinful man.

'And he did eat and drink, and laid him down again,' v. 6. Once again it is evident that these narratives of Holy Writ are drawn by an impartial hand and are painted in the colours of truth and reality. The Holy Spirit has depicted the conduct of men, even of the most eminent, not as it should have been but as it actually was. That is why we find our own path and experiences therein so accurately depicted. Had some religious idealist invented the story, *how had he portrayed* Elijah's response to this amazing display of the Lord's grace, of the constancy of His love, and of the special tenderness now shown him? Why obviously he would have pictured the prophet as overwhelmed by such Divine favour, thoroughly melted by such loving kindness, and prostrated before Him in adoring worship. How different the Spirit's description of fact! There is no intimation that the petulant prophet was moved at heart, no mention of his bowing in worship, not so much as a word that he returned thanks: merely that he ate and drank and laid himself down again.

Alas, what is man? What is the best of men looked at apart from Christ? How does the maturest saint act the moment the Holy Spirit suspends His operations and ceases to work in and through him? Not differently from the unregenerate, for the flesh is no better in him than in the former. When he is out of communion with God, when his will has been crossed, he is as peevish as a spoiled child. He is no longer capable of appreciating Divine mercies, because he considers himself hardly dealt with, and instead of expressing gratitude for temporal favours he accepts them as a matter of course. If the reader feels we are putting an unwarranted construction on this silence of the narrative, that we should not assume Elijah failed to return thanks, we would ask him to read the sequel and ascertain whether or not it shows that the prophet *continued* in a fretful mood. The omission of Elijah's worship and giving thanks for the refreshment is only too sadly true to life. How this should rebuke us for similar omissions! How this absence of praise should remind us of *our* ingratitude at Divine favours when our wills are crossed, and humble us at the recollection thereof.

CHAPTER TWENTY-SIX

The Cave in Mount Horeb

───

Two things are made prominent in the opening verses of 1 Kings 19, the one serving to enhance the other: the bitter fruits of the prophet's panic and the superabounding grace of the Lord unto his erring servant. The threatening message sent by the furious Jezebel had filled Elijah with consternation, and in his subsequent actions we are given to behold *the effects* which follow when the heart is filled with unbelief and fear. Instead of spreading the queen's message before his Master, Elijah took matters into his own hands; instead of waiting patiently for Him, he acted on hasty impulse. First, he deserted his post of duty and fled from Jezreel, whither 'the hand of the Lord' had brought him. Second, occupied solely with self, he 'went for his life,' being no longer actuated by the glory of God nor the good of His people. Third, folly now possessed him, for in rushing to Beersheba he entered the territory of Jehoshaphat, whose son had married 'the daughter of Ahab' – not even does 'common sense' regulate those who are out of fellowship with God.

Elijah dare not remain at Beersheba, so he goes ' a day's journey into the wilderness,' illustrative of the fact that when unbelief and fear take possession, a spirit of restlessness fills the soul so that it is no longer capable of being still before God. Finally, when his feverish energy had spent itself, the prophet flung himself beneath a juniper tree and prayed for death. He was now in the slough of despond, feeling that life was no longer worth living. And it is on *that* dark background we behold the glories of Divine grace which now shone forth so blessedly. In the hour of his despair and need, the Lord did not forsake His poor servant. No, first He gave His

[225]

beloved sleep, to rest his jaded nerves. Second, He sent an angel to minister unto him. Third, He provided refreshments for his body. This was grace indeed; not only undeserved but entirely unsought by the Tishbite. Wondrous indeed are the ways of Him with whom we have to do, who is 'longsuffering to us-ward.'

And what was Elijah's response to these amazing overtures of God's mercy? Was he overwhelmed by the Divine favour? melted by such lovingkindness? Cannot the reader, yea the Christian reader, supply the answer from his own sad experience? When you have wandered from the Lord and forsaken the paths of righteousness, and He has borne with your waywardness, and instead of visiting your transgressions with the rod has continued to shower His temporal blessings upon you, has a sense of His goodness led you to repentance, or while still in a backslidden state have you not rather accepted God's benefits as a matter of course, unmoved by the most tender mercies? Such is fallen human nature the world over, in every age: 'As in water face answereth to face, so the heart of man to man, Prov. 27. 19. And Elijah was no exception, for we are told 'he did eat and drink, and *laid him down again*,' v. 6, – no sign of repentance for the past, no hint of gratitude for present mercies, no exercise of soul about future duty.

Ah, in this line of the picture we are shown yet another effect which follows upon the heart's giving way to unbelief and fear, and that is *insensibility of soul*. When the heart is estranged from God, when self becomes the centre and circumference of our interests, a hardness and deadness steals over us so that we are impervious unto the Lord's goodness. Our vision is dimmed, so that we no longer appreciate the benefits bestowed upon us. We become indifferent, callous, unresponsive. We descend to the level of the beasts, consuming what is given us with no thought of the Creator's faithfulness. Does not this short sentence sum up the life of the unregenerate: 'They eat and drink and lie down again' – without any regard for God, care for their souls, or concern for eternity? And my reader, that is the case with a backsliding believer: he comes down to the level of the ungodly, for God no longer has the chief place in his heart and thoughts.

And what was the Lord's response to such gross ingratitude on the part of His servant? Did He now turn from him in disgust, as deserving no further consideration from Him? Well He might, for despising grace is no ordinary sin. Yet while grace does not make light of sin – as the sequel here will make evident – yet if sin were able to thwart grace it would cease to be *grace*. As grace can never be attracted by 'well-desert' so it is never repelled by 'ill-desert.' And God was dealing in grace, sovereign grace, with the prophet. Wherefore we read, 'And the angel of the Lord came again the *second* time, and touched him, and said, Arise and eat; because the journey is too great for thee,' 1 Kings 19. 7. Truly we must exclaim with the Psalmist, 'He hath not despised nor abhorred the affliction of the afflicted, neither hath He hid his face from him,' 22. 24. And why? Because God is love, and love 'suffereth long and is kind . . . is not easily provoked . . . beareth all things,' 1 Cor. 13. 4-7.

'And the angel of the Lord came again the second time.' How wondrous is the Lord's patience! 'God hath spoken once' and that should be sufficient for us, yet it rarely is so, and therefore is it added '*twice* have I heard this; that power belongeth unto God,' Psa. 62. 11. The first time the cock crew Peter paid no heed to it, but 'the *second* time it crew' he 'called to mind the word which Jesus said unto him . . . and when he thought thereon, he wept,' Mark 14. 72. Alas, how slow we are to respond to the Divine advances: 'And the voice spake unto him again the *second* time, What God hath cleansed, that call not thou common,' Acts 10. 15. 'Rejoice in the Lord alway:' surely the Christian needs not to have such a word repeated! The apostle knew better: '*Again* I say, Rejoice!' is added, Phil. 4. 4. What dull scholars we are: 'When for the time ye ought to be teachers, ye have need that one teach you *again*,' Heb. 5. 12, and thus it has to be 'line upon line, precept upon precept.'

'And the angel of the Lord came again the second time.' It seems most probable that it was evening when the angel came to Elijah the first time and bade him arise and eat, for we are told he had gone 'a day's journey into the wilderness' before he sat down under the juniper bush. After he had partaken of the refreshment provided by such august hands, Elijah had lain him down again and night had spread her temporary veil over the scorched sands. When the angel came and touched him the second time, day had dawned: through the intervening hours of darkness the celestial messenger had kept watch and ward while the weary prophet slept. Ah, the love of God knows no change – it fainteth not, neither is weary. Darkness makes no difference and serves not to conceal its object from it. Unfailing love watches over the believer during the hours when he is insensible to its presence. 'Having loved His own which were in the world He loved them unto the end' – unto the end of all their wanderings and unworthiness.

'And said, Arise and eat; because the journey is too great for thee.' May we not perceive here a gentle rebuke for the prophet? 'The journey is too great for thee.' What journey? He had not been directed to take any! It was a journey undertaken of his own accord, a devising of his own self-will. It was a journey away from the post of duty, which he ought, at that hour, to have been occupying. It was as though this heavenly messenger said to the prophet: See what comes of your self-will; it has reduced you to weakness and starvation. Nevertheless God has taken pity on you and furnished refreshment: He will not break the bruised reed nor quench the smoking flax. The Lord is full of kindness: He foresees the further demands which are going to be made upon your frame, so 'Arise and eat.' Elijah had fixed his mind on the distant Horeb, and so God anticipates his needs, even though they were the needs of a truant servant and rebellious child. O what a God is ours!

But there is a practical lesson here for each of us, even for those whom grace hath preserved from backsliding. 'The journey is too great for thee.' Not only life's journey as a whole, but each daily segment of it will make demands above and beyond our own unaided powers. The faith required, the courage demanded, the patience needed, the trials to be borne, the enemies to be overcome, are 'too great' for mere flesh and blood. What then? Why, begin the day as Elijah began this one: 'Arise and eat.' You do not propose to go forth to a day's work without first supplying your body with food and drink, and is the *soul* more able to do without nourishment? God does not ask *you* to provide the spiritual food, but has graciously placed it by your side. All He asks is, 'Arise and eat:' feed on the heavenly manna that your strength may be renewed; begin the day by partaking of the Bread of Life, that you may be thoroughly furnished for the many demands that will be made upon your graces.

'And he arose, and did eat and drink,' v. 8. Ah, though his case was such a sad one, yet 'the root of the matter' was in him. He did not scorn the provision supplied him nor despise the use of means. Though there is yet no sign of gratitude, no returning of thanks to the gracious Giver, yet when bidden to eat, Elijah obediently complied. Though he had taken matters into his own hands, he did not now defy the angel to his face. As he had refused to lay violent hands upon himself, asking the Lord to take his life from him, so now he did not deliberately starve himself but ate the food set before him. The righteous may fall, yet he will not be 'utterly cast down.' The flax may not burn brightly, yet smoke will evidence that it has not quite gone out. Life in the believer may wane to a low ebb, yet sooner or later it will give proof that it is still there.

'And went in the strength of that meat forty days and forty nights unto Horeb the mount of God,' v. 8. In His grace the Lord passes over the infirmities of those whose hearts are upright with Him and who sincerely love Him, though there still be that in them which ever seeks to oppose His love. Very blessed is the particular detail now before us: God not only reviewed the flagging energy of His servant but He caused the food which he had eaten to supply him with strength for a long time to come. Should the sceptic ask, How could that single meal nourish the prophet for almost six weeks? it would be sufficient answer to bid him explain *how* our food supplies us with energy for a single day! The greatest philosopher cannot explain the mystery, but the simplest believer knows that it is by the power and blessing of God upon it. No matter how much food we eat, or how choice it be, unless the Divine blessing attend it, it nourishes us not a single whit. The same God who can make a meal energize us for forty minutes can make it do so for forty days when He so pleases.

'Horeb the mount of God' was certainly a remarkable place for Elijah to make for, for there is no spot on earth where the presence of God was so signally manifested as *there*, at least in Old Testament times. It was there that Jehovah had appeared unto Moses at the burning bush, Ex. 3. 1-4. It was there the Law had been given to Israel, Deut. 4. 15, under such awe-inspiring phenomena. It was there that Moses had communed with Him for forty days and nights. Yet, though Israel's prophets and poets were wont to draw their sublimest imagery from the splendours and terrors of that scene, strange to say there is no record in Scripture of any Israelite visiting that holy mount from the time the Law was given until Elijah fled there from Jezebel. Whether it was his actual intention to proceed thither when he left Jezreel we know not. Why he went there we cannot be sure. Perhaps, as Matthew Henry suggested, it was to indulge his melancholy, saying with Jeremiah, 'O that I had in the wilderness a lodging place of wayfaring men; that I might leave my people, and go from them!' 9. 2.

Strangely enough there are some who think that the prophet wended his way across the wilderness to Horeb because he had received instructions from the angel to do so. But surely this view is negatived by the sequel: the Lord had not twice uttered that searching and rebuking, 'What doest thou here, Elijah?', had he come thither in obedience to the celestial messenger. That his steps were Divinely guided thither we doubt not, for there was a striking propriety that he who was peculiarly the legal reformer should meet with Jehovah in the place where the Law had been promulgated – compare Moses *and* Elijah appearing with Christ on the mount of transfiguration. Though Elijah came not to Horeb by the *command* of God, he was directed there by the secret *providence* of God: 'A man's heart deviseth his way, but the Lord directeth his steps,' Prov. 16. 9. And *how*? By a secret impulse from within which destroys not his freedom of action. 'The king's heart is in the hand of the Lord as the rivers of water: He turneth it whithersoever He will,' Prov. 21. 1, – the waters of a river flow freely, yet is their course determined by Heaven!

'And he came thither into a cave, and lodged there,' v. 9. At last the prophet was contented with the distance he had put between himself and the one who had sworn to avenge the death of her prophets: there in that remote mountain, concealed in some dark cave amid its precipices, he felt secure. How he now employed himself we are not told. If he tried to engage in prayer we may be sure he had no liberty and still less delight therein. More probably he sat and mused upon his troubles. If his conscience accused him that he had acted too hastily in fleeing from Jezreel, that he ought not to have yielded to his fears, but rather put his trust in God and proceeded to instruct the nation, yet the sequel indicates he would have stifled such humiliating convictions instead of confessing to God his failure. 'The backslider in heart shall be filled with his own ways,' Prov. 14. 15: in the light of such a scripture who can doubt that Elijah was now engaged in pitying and vindicating himself, reflecting on the ingratitude of his fellow-countrymen and aggrieved at the harsh treatment of Jezebel?

'And, behold, the word of the Lord came to him,' v. 9. God had spoken to him personally on previous occasions. The word of the Lord had ordered him to hide by the brook Cherith, 17. 2, 3. It had come to him again, bidding him betake himself to Zarephath, 17. 8, 9. And yet again it had commanded him to show himself unto Ahab, 18. 1. But it seems to the writer that here we have something different from the other instances. As the fugitive lurked in the cave, we are told 'and, *behold,* the Word of the Lord came to him.' That expressive term does not occur in any of the previous passages and its employment here is the Spirit's intimation that something extraordinary is before us. On this occasion it was something more than a Divine *message* which was communicated to the prophet's ear, being nothing less than a visit from a Divine *person* which the prophet now received. It was none other than the second Person of the Trinity, the Eternal 'Word,' John 1. 1, who now interrogated the erring Tishbite. This is unmistakably clear from the next clause: 'and *He* said unto him.' Very remarkable, very solemn is this.

'And He said unto him, What doest thou here, Elijah?', v. 9. Elijah had turned aside from the path of duty, and his Master knew it. The living God knows where His servants are, what they are doing and not doing. None can escape His omniscient gaze, for His eyes are in every place, Prov. 15. 3. The Lord's question was a rebuke, a searching word addressed to his conscience. As we do not know which particular word the Lord accentuated, we will emphasize each one separately. '*What* doest thou?': is it good or evil, for totally inactive, in either mind or body, man cannot be. 'What *doest* thou?': art thou employing thy time for the glory of God and the good of His people, or is it being wasted in peevish repinings? 'What doest *thou?*': thou who art the servant of the Most High who hast been so highly honoured, who hast received such clear tokens of His aid and depended upon the Almighty for protection! 'What doest thou *here?*': away from the land of Israel, away from the work of reformation.

'And he said, I have been very jealous for the Lord God of hosts: for the children of Israel have forsaken Thy covenant, thrown down Thine altars, and slain Thy prophets with the sword; and I, even I only, am left; and they seek my life, to take it away,' v. 10. As we ponder these words we find ourselves out of accord with the commentators, most of whom severely criticize the prophet for seeking to excuse himself and throw the blame on others. That which impresses the writer first is the ingenuousness of Elijah: there were no evasions and equivocations, but a frank and candid explanation of his conduct. True, what he here advanced furnished no sufficient reason for his flight, yet it was the truthful declaration of an honest heart. Well for both writer and reader if *he* can always give as good an account of himself when challenged by the Holy One. If we were as open and frank with the Lord as Elijah was, we could expect to be dealt with as graciously as he was; for note it well, the prophet received no rebuke from God in answer to his outspokenness.

'I have been very jealous for the Lord God of hosts' was a statement of fact: he had not shrunk from the most difficult and dangerous service for his Master and his people. It was not because his zeal had cooled that he had fled from Jezreel. 'For the children of Israel have forsaken Thy covenant, thrown down Thine altars, and slain Thy prophets with the sword.' Elijah had been deeply distressed to behold how grievously the Lord was dishonoured by the nation which was called by His name. God's glory lay very near his heart, and it affected him deeply to see His laws broken, His authority flouted, His worship despised, the homage of the people given to senseless idols and their tacit consent to the murder of His servants. 'And I, even I only, am left.' He had, at imminent peril of his life, laboured hard to put a stop to Israel's idolatry and to reclaim the nation; but to no purpose. So far as he could perceive, he had laboured in vain and spent his strength for nought. 'And they seek my life, to take it away:' what then is the use of my wasting any more time on such a stiffnecked and unresponsive people!

CHAPTER TWENTY-SEVEN

A Still Small Voice

‘And He said, Go forth, and stand upon the mount before the Lord. And, behold, the Lord passed by, and a great and strong wind rent the mountains, and brake in pieces the rocks before the Lord; but the Lord was not in the wind: and after the wind an earthquake; but the Lord was not in the earthquake: and after the earthquake a fire; but the Lord was not in the fire: and after the fire a still small voice,’ 1 Kings 19. 11, 12. Elijah was now called upon to witness a most remarkable and awe-inspiring display of God’s power. The description which is here given of the scene, though brief, is so graphic that any words of ours would only serve to blunt its forcefulness. What we desire to do is rather to ascertain the *meaning and message* of this sublime manifestation of God: its message to Elijah, to Israel, and to ourselves. Oh, that our eyes may be anointed to discern, our heart so affected as to appreciate, our thoughts controlled by the Holy Spirit, and our pen directed unto the glory of the Most High and the blessing of His dear people.

In seeking to discover the spiritual significance of what the prophet here witnessed upon the mount, we must ponder the scene in connection with what has preceded it both in the history of Israel and in the experience of Elijah himself. Then we must consider it in relation to what immediately follows, for there is undoubtedly a close connection between the startling scenes depicted in verses 11 and 12 and the solemn message contained in verses 15 to 18, the latter serving to interpret the former. Finally, we need to examine this striking incident in the light of the analogy of faith, the Scriptures as a whole, for one part of them serves to explain another. It is as we become better acquainted with the 'ways' of God, as revealed in His Word, that we are able to enter more intelligently into the meaning of His 'acts,' Psa. 103. 7.

How then are we to consider this manifestation of God upon the mount with regard to Elijah himself? First, as the Lord's dealing with him *in grace*. This should be evident from the context. There we have seen the touching response which God made to His servant's failure. So far from forsaking him in his hour of weakness and need, the Lord had ministered most tenderly to him, exemplifying that precious promise, 'Like as a father pitieth his children, so the Lord pitieth them that fear Him,' Psa. 103. 13. And Elijah *did* fear the Lord, and though his faith was for the moment eclipsed, the Lord did not turn His back upon him on that account. Sleep was given to him; an angel supplied him with food and drink; supernatural strength was communicated to his frame, so that he was enabled to do without any further nourishment for forty days and nights. And when he reached the cave, Christ Himself, the eternal 'Word' had stood before him in theophanic manifestation. What *high favours* were those! What proofs that we have to do with One who is 'the God of all grace'!

Of what has just been pointed out it may be said, True, but then Elijah *slighted* that grace: instead of being suitably affected thereby he remained petulant and peevish; instead of confessing his failure he attempted to justify the forsaking of his post of duty. Even so, then what? Why, does not the Lord here teach the refractory prophet a needed lesson? Does He not appear before him in a terrifying manner for the purpose of rebuking him? Not so do we read this incident. Those who take such a view must have little experimental acquaintance with the wondrous grace of God. He is not fickle and variable as we are: He does not at one time deal with us according to His own compassionate benignity and at another treat with us according to our ill deserts. When God *begins* to deal in grace with one of His elect, He *continues* dealing with him in grace, and nothing in the creature can impede the outflow of His lovingkindness.

One cannot examine the wonders which occurred here on Horeb without seeing in them an intended reference to the awful solemnities of Sinai with its 'thunders and lightnings,' when the Lord 'descended upon it in fire' and the whole mount 'quaked greatly,' Ex. 19. 16, 18. Yet we miss the force of the allusion unless we heed carefully the words, 'the Lord was *not in* the wind,' 'the Lord was *not in* the earthquake,' 'the Lord was *not in* the fire.' God was not dealing with Elijah on the ground of the legal covenant. That threefold negative is the Spirit saying to us, Elijah had 'not come unto the mount that might be touched, and that burned with fire, nor unto blackness, and darkness, and tempest,' Heb. 12. 18. Rather was the prophet addressed by the 'still small voice,' which was plain intimation that he had 'come unto mount Zion,' Heb. 12. 22 – the Mount of grace. That Jehovah should reveal Himself thus to Elijah was a mark of Divine favour, conferring upon him the same sign of distinction which He had vouchsafed unto Moses in that very place, when He showed him His glory and made all His goodness pass before him.

Second, the method which the Lord chose to take with His servant on this occasion was designed for his *instruction*. Elijah was dejected at the failure of his mission. He had been jealous for the Lord God of hosts, but what had come of all his zeal? He had prayed as probably none before him had ever prayed, yet though miracles had been wrought in answer thereto, that which lay nearest to his heart had not been attained. Ahab had been quite unaffected by what he had witnessed. The nation was not reclaimed unto God. Jezebel was as defiant as ever. Elijah appeared to be entirely alone, and his utmost efforts were unavailing. The enemy still triumphed in spite of all. The Lord therefore sets before His servant an object lesson. By solemn exhibitions of His mighty power He impressively reminds Elijah that He is not confined to any one agent in the carrying out of His designs. The elements are at His disposal when He is pleased to employ them: a gentler method and milder agent if such be His will.

It was quite natural that Elijah should have formed the conclusion that the whole work was to be done by himself, coming as he did with all the vehemence of a mighty wind; that under God all obstacles would be swept away – idolatry abolished and the nation brought back to the worship of Jehovah. The Lord now graciously makes known unto the prophet that He has other arrows in His quiver which He will discharge in due time. The 'wind,' the 'earthquake,' 'the fire,' should each play their appointed part, and thereby make way more distinctly and effectively for the milder ministry of the 'still small voice.' Elijah was but one agent among several. 'One soweth, and another reapeth,' John 4. 37, Elijah had performed his part and soon would he be grandly rewarded for his faithfulness. Nor had he laboured in vain, yet another man and not himself should enter into his labours. How gracious of the Lord thus to take His servants into His confidence!

'Surely the Lord God will do nothing, but He revealeth His secret unto His servants the prophets,' Amos 3. 7. This is exactly what occurred there on Horeb. By means of what we may term a panoramic parable God revealed the future unto Elijah. Herein we may discover the bearing of this remarkable incident *upon Israel*. In the immediate sequel we find the Lord bidding Elijah anoint Hazael over Syria, Jehu over Israel, and Elisha prophet in his own room, assuring him that 'it shall come to pass, that him that escapeth the sword of Hazael shall Jehu slay, and him that escapeth from the sword of Jehu shall Elisha slay,' v. 17. In the work of those men we may perceive the prophetic meaning of the solemn phenomena Elijah beheld – they were symbols of the dire calamities with which God would punish the apostate nation. Thus the strong 'wind' was a figure of the work of judgment which Hazael performed on Israel, when he 'set their strongholds on fire and slew their young men with the sword,' 2 Kings 8. 12; the 'earthquake,' of the revolution under Jehu, when he utterly destroyed the house of Ahab, 2 Kings 9. 7-10; and the 'fire,' the work of judgment completed by Elisha.

Third, the incident as a whole was designed for the *consolation* of Elijah. Terrible indeed were the judgments which would fall upon guilty Israel, yet in wrath Jehovah would remember mercy. The chosen nation would not be utterly exterminated, and therefore did the Lord graciously assure His despondent servant, 'Yet will I leave Me seven thousand in Israel, all the knees which have not bowed unto Baal and every mouth which hath not kissed him,' v. 18. As the 'strong wind,' the 'earthquake,' and the 'fire' were emblematic portents of the judgments which God was shortly to send upon His idolatrous people, so the 'still small voice' which followed them looked forward to the *mercy* He had in store after His 'strange work' had been accomplished. For we read that, after Hazael had oppressed Israel all the days of Jehoahaz, 'the Lord was gracious unto them, and had respect unto them because of His covenant with Abraham, Isaac and Jacob, and would not destroy them, neither cast He them from His presence as yet,' 2 Kings 13. 23. Once again we say, how gracious of the Lord to make known unto Elijah 'things to come,' and thus acquaint him with what should be the sequel to his labours.

If we consider the remarkable occurrences of Horeb in the light of the Scriptures as a whole, we shall find they were indicative and illustrative of one of the general principles in the Divine government of this world. The *order* of the Divine manifestations before Elijah was analogous to the general tenor of the Divine proceedings. Whether it be with regard to a people or an individual, it is usual for the bestowment of Divine mercies to be preceded by awe-inspiring displays of God's power and displeasure against sin. First the plagues upon Egypt and the destruction of Pharaoh and his hosts at the Red Sea, and then the deliverance of the Hebrews. The majesty and might of Jehovah exhibited on Sinai and then the blessed proclamation, 'The Lord, the Lord God, merciful and gracious, long-suffering, and abundant in goodness and truth, keeping mercy for thousands, forgiving iniquity and transgression and sin,' Ex. 34. 6, 7.

Fourth, the method followed by the Lord on this occasion was meant to *furnish Elijah for further service*. The 'still small voice,' 'speaking quietly and gently, was designed to calm and sooth his ruffled spirit. It evidenced afresh the kindness and tenderness of the Lord, who would assuage Elijah's disappointment and cheer his heart. Where the soul is reassured of His Master's love the servant is nerved to face fresh dangers and oppositions for His sake and to tackle any task He may assign him. It was thus also He dealt with Isaiah: first abasing him with a vision of His glory, which made the prophet conscious of his utter sinfulness and insufficiency, and then assuring him of the remission of his sins: and in consequence Isaiah went forward on a most thankless mission, Isa. 6. 1-12. The sequel here shows the Lord's measures were equally effective with Elijah; he received a fresh commission and obediently he discharged it.

'And it was so, when Elijah heard it, that he wrapped his face in his mantle, and went out, and stood in the entering in of the cave,' v. 13. This is remarkable. So far as we can gather from the inspired record, Elijah stood unmoved at the varied displays of Jehovah's power, fearful as they were to behold – surely a clear intimation that his conscience was not burdened by guilt! But when the still small voice sounded, he was at once affected. The Lord addressed His servant, not in an angry and austere manner, but with gentleness and tenderness, to show him what a compassionate and gracious God he had to do with, and his heart was touched. The Hebrew word for 'still' is the one employed in Psalm 107. 29, 'He maketh the storm a *calm*.' The wrapping of his face in his mantle betokened two things: his reverence for the Divine majesty and a sense of his own unworthiness – as the seraphim are represented as covering their faces in the Lord's presence, Isa. 6. 2, 3. When Abraham found himself in the presence of God, he said, 'I am dust and ashes,' Gen. 18. When Moses beheld Him in the burning bush, he 'hid his face,' Ex. 3.

Many and profitable are the lessons *for us* in this remarkable incident. First, from it we may perceive *it is God's way to do the unexpected*. Were we to put it to a vote as to which they thought the more likely, for the Lord to have spoken to Elijah through the mighty wind and earthquake or the still small voice, we suppose the great majority would say the former. And is it not much the same in our own spiritual experience? We earnestly beg Him to grant us a more definite and settled assurance of our acceptance in Christ, and then look for His answer in a sort of electric shock imparted to our souls or in an extraordinary vision; when instead, it is by the still small voice of the Spirit bearing witness with our spirit that we are the children of God. Again, we beseech the Lord that we may grow in grace, and then expect His answer in the form of more conscious enjoyment of His presence; whereas He quietly gives us to see more of the hidden depravity of our hearts. Yes, God often does the unexpected in His dealings with us.

Second, *the pre-eminence of the Word*. Reduced to a single word we may say that the varied phenomena witnessed by Elijah upon the mount were a matter of the Lord *speaking* to him. When it is said, 'The Lord was not in' the wind, the earthquake, and the fire, we are to understand it was not through *them* He addressed Himself to the prophet's heart; rather was it by the 'still small voice.' In regarding this last agent as the emblem of the Word, we find confirmation in the striking fact that the Hebrew word for 'small' is the self-same one used in 'a small round thing' in Exodus 16. 14, and we need hardly add, the manna whereby the Lord fed Israel in the wilderness was a type of the food He has provided for our souls. Though the wondrous wisdom and potent power of God are displayed in creation, yet it is not through nature that God may be understood and known, but through the Word applied by His Spirit.

Third, in the phenomena of the mount we may perceive *a striking illustration of the vivid contrast* between the Law and the Gospel. The rock-rending wind, the earthquake and the fire figured the terror-producing Law (as may be seen from their presence at Sinai), but the 'still small voice' was a fit emblem of 'the Gospel of peace' which soothes the troubled breast. As the plough and the harrow are necessary in order to break up the hard earth and prepare it for the seed, so a sense of the majesty, holiness and wrath of God is the harbinger which prepares us to appreciate truly His grace and love. The careless must be awakened, the soul made sensible of its danger, the conscience convicted of the sinfulness of sin, ere there is any turning unto God and fleeing from the wrath to come. Yet those experiences are not saving ones: they do but prepare the way, as the ministry of John the Baptist fitted men to behold the Lamb of God.

Fourth, thus we may see in this incident a figure of *God's ordinary manner of dealing with souls*, for it is customary for Him to use the Law before the Gospel. In spite of much which is now said to the contrary, this writer still believes that it is usual for the Spirit to wound before He heals, to shake the soul over hell before He communicates a hope of heaven, to bring the heart to despair before it is brought to Christ. Self-complacency has to be rudely shattered and the rags of self-righteousness torn off if a sense of deep need is to fill the heart. The Hebrews had to come under the whip of their masters and to be made to groan in the brick kilns before they longed to be delivered from Egypt. A man must know himself to be utterly lost before he will crave salvation. The wind and fire must do their work before we can appreciate the 'joyful sound,' Psa. 89. 15. Sentence of death has to be written upon us ere we turn to Christ for life.

Fifth, this is often *God's method of answering prayer*. Christians are very apt to look for God to respond unto their petitions with striking signs and spectacular wonders, and because these are not given in a marked and permanent form they conclude He heeds them not. But the presence and power of God are not to be gauged by abnormal manifestations and extraordinary visitations. The wonders of God are rarely wrought with noise and vehemence. Whose ear can detect the falling of the dew? Vegetation grows silently but none the less surely. In grace as in nature God usually works gently, softly, unperceived, except through the effects produced. The greatest fidelity and devotion to God are not to be found where excitement and sensationalism hold forth. The blessing of the Lord attends the unobtrusive and persevering use of His appointed means which attracts not the attention of the vulgar and carnal.

Sixth, this scene on Horeb, contains *a timely message for preachers*. How many ministers of the Gospel have become thoroughly discouraged, though with far less provocation than Elijah. They have been untiring in their labours, zealous for the

Lord, faithful in preaching His Word, yet nothing comes of it, there is no response, all appears to be in vain. Even so, granted that such be the case, then what? Seek to lay hold afresh on the grand truth that the purpose of the Lord shall not fail, and that purpose includes *tomorrow* as well as today! The Most High is not confined to any one agent. Elijah thought the whole work was to be accomplished through *his* instrumentality, but was taught that he was only one factor among several. Do your duty where God has stationed you: plough up the fallow ground and sow the seed, and though there be no fruit in your day, who knows but an Elisha may follow you and do the reaping.

Seventh, there is *a solemn warning here to the unsaved*. God will not be mocked with impunity. Though He be longsuffering, there is a limit to His patience. Those who improved not the day of their visitation and opportunity under the ministry of Elijah were made to feel what a terrible thing it is to flout the Divine warnings. Mercy was followed by judgment, drastic and devastating. The strongholds of Israel were overthrown and their young men slain by the sword. Is this to be the awful fate of the present generation? Is it devoted by God to destruction? It looks more and more like it. The masses are given up to a spirit of madness. The most solemn portents of the approaching storm are blatantly disregarded. The words of God's servants fall upon deaf ears. O my unsaved readers, flee to Christ without further delay ere the flood of God's wrath engulfs you.

CHAPTER TWENTY-EIGHT

Elijah's Recovery

The failure of Elijah had been of a different character from that of Jonah. It does not appear that he had done any moral wrong in quitting Jezreel; rather was his conduct in line with Christ's direction to His disciples: 'But when they persecute you in this city, flee ye into another,' Matt. 10. 23. They were not to expose themselves rashly to danger, but if they could do so honourably, avoid it and thus preserve themselves for future service – as numbers of our Reformers and members of their flocks took refuge on the Continent in the days of wicked Queen Mary. God had given Elijah no express order to remain at Jezreel and continue the work of reformation, and 'where no law is, there is no transgression,' Rom. 4. 15. It was more a case of the Lord's testing His servant with 'circumstances,' leaving him to himself, to show us what was in his heart, allowing him to exercise his own judgment and follow his own inclinations. Had there been something more involved than this, had the prophet been guilty of deliberate disobedience, the Lord's dealings with him at Horeb would have been quite different from what they were.

What has been said above is not for the purpose of excusing Elijah, but to view his fault in a fair perspective. Some have unfairly magnified his failure, charging him with that which cannot justly be laid to his account. We certainly believe he made a lamentable mistake in deserting the post of duty to which 'the hand of the Lord' had brought him, 1 Kings 18. 46, for he received no word from his Master to leave there. Nor can we justify his petulancy under the juniper tree and his request for the Lord to take away his life – *that* is for Him to decide, and not for us at any time. Moreover, the question put to him twice at Horeb, 'What doest thou here, Elijah?' evidently implied a gentle rebuke: yet it was more an error of judgment which he had committed than a sin of the heart. He had felt at liberty to exercise his own discretion and to act according to the dictates of his own feelings. God permitted this that we might know the strongest characters are as weak as water the moment He withdraws His upholding hand.

We have already seen how tenderly Jehovah dealt with His erring servant in the wilderness, let us now admire the grace He exercised toward him at Horeb. That which is to be before us reminds us much of the Psalmist's experience: the Lord who was his Shepherd had not only made him to lie down in green pastures, but 'He restoreth my soul,' 23. 2, 3, he acknowledged. The One who had refreshed and fed His servant under the juniper tree now recovers him from his useless repinings, reclaims him from his wanderings, and raises him to a position of honour in His service. Elijah was incapable of restoring himself, and there was no human being who could have delivered him from the slough of despond, so when there was none other eye to pity him the Lord had compassion upon him. And is it not thus, at some time or other, in the experience of all God's servants and people? He who first delivered us from a horrible pit continues to care for us, and when we wander from Him He restores our souls and leads us back into the paths of righteousness.

'And the Lord said unto him, Go, return on thy way to the wilderness of Damascus,' 1 Kings 19. 15. 'The prophet was bemoaning the failure of all his efforts to glorify God, and the obstinate determination of his people to continue in their apostasy. It was thus he spent his time in the cave at Horeb, brooding over his disappointment, and lashing himself, by reflecting upon the conduct of the people. A solitary place, with nothing to do, might be congenial with such a disposition; it might foster it, but would never heal it: and thus Elijah might have succumbed to a settled melancholy or raving madness. The only hope for persons in such circumstances is to come out from their lonely haunts, and to be actively employed in some useful and benevolent occupation. This is the best cure for melancholy: to set about doing something which will require muscular exertion, and which will benefit others. Hence God directed Elijah to quit this present lonely abode, which only increased the sadness and irritation of his spirit; and so He gave him a commission to execute a long way off' (John Simpson).

'And the Lord said unto him, Go, *return* on thy way to the wilderness of Damascus,' v. 15. This is the course God takes when He restores the soul of one of His erring people, causing him to retrace his steps and return to the place of duty. When Abraham left Egypt – whither he had gone 'down' in the time of famine: Genesis 12. 10 – we read that 'he went on his journeys from the south even to Bethel, unto the place where his tent had been at the beginning,' Gen. 13. 3. When the church at Ephesus 'left her first love,' Christ's message to her was 'Remember from whence thou art fallen, and repent, and do the first works,' Rev. 2. 4. So now Elijah is required to go back the way he had come, through the wilderness of Arabia, which was part of the course he would traverse on his way to Damascus. This is still God's word to His strayed sheep: '*Return*, thou backsliding Israel, saith the Lord; I will not cause Mine anger to fall upon you: for I am merciful,' Jer. 3. 12.

When Peter repented for his great sin, the Lord not only forgave him, but recommissioned His servant: 'Feed My sheep,' John 21. 16. So here, the Lord not only restored the prophet's soul, but appointed him to fresh work in His service. 'And when thou comest, anoint Hazael to be king over Syria,' v. 15. This was a high honour for Jehovah to confer upon Elijah, such as He had bestowed upon Samuel, 1 Sam. 16. 13. How gracious is our God! how patiently He bears with our infirmities! Observe how these passages teach that it is not by the people but by God that kings reign, Prov. 8. 15. 'There is no power but of God: the powers that be are ordained of God,' and therefore does He require of us, 'let every soul be subject unto the higher powers,' Rom. 13. 1. In this 'democratic' age it is necessary that ministers of the Gospel should press this truth: 'Submit yourselves to every ordinance of man *for the Lord's sake*: whether it be to the king, as supreme; or unto governors, as unto them that are sent by him for the punishment of evildoers,' 1 Pet. 2. 13, 14. Said the apostle to Titus, 'Put them in mind to be subject to principalities and powers, to obey magistrates,' 3. 1.

'And Jehu the son of Nimshi shalt thou anoint to be king over Israel,' v. 16. None can reign except those whom God makes kings, and they only so long as He pleases. This 'anointing' or unction proclaimed their Divine designation to this office and the qualification with which they should be endowed for their work. The Lord Jesus, who was 'anointed with the Holy Spirit,' Acts 10. 38, united in Himself the offices of prophet, priest and king: the only persons ordered to be anointed in the Scriptures. Infidels have raised an objection against our present verse by pointing out that Jehu was anointed, not by Elijah, but by a young prophet under the direction of Elisha, 2 Kings 9. 1-6. This objection may be disposed of in two ways. First, Jehu may have been anointed *twice*, as David was, 1 Sam. 16. 13; 2 Sam. 2. 4; or, as 'Jesus made and baptized more disciples than John, though Jesus Himself baptized not, but His disciples,' John 4. 1, 2, so Jehu is said to be anointed by Elijah because what took place in 2 Kings 9 was according to *his orders*.

'And Elisha the son of Shaphat of Abel-meholah shalt thou anoint to be prophet in thy room,' v. 16. Here was an additional favour bestowed upon Elijah, that he should have the almost unique honour of ordaining his successor. That which had so quenched the Tishbite's spirit was the failure which attended his efforts: no impression seemed to be made on the idolatrous nation, he alone appeared to be concerned about the glory of the Lord God, and now his own life was imperilled. How his heart must have been comforted by the Divine assurance that another was appointed to carry on the mission he had prosecuted so zealously! Hitherto there had been none to help him, but in the hour of his despondency God provides him with a suitable companion and successor. It has ever been a great consolation to godly ministers and their flocks to think that God will never lack instruments to conduct

His work, that when *they* are removed *others* will be brought forward to carry on. One of the saddest and most solemn features of this degenerate age is that the ranks of the righteous are so depleted and scarcely any are being raised up to fill their places. It is this which makes the outlook doubly dark.

'And it shall come to pass, that him that escapeth the sword of Hazael shall Jehu slay, and him that escapeth from the sword of Jehu shall Elisha slay,' v. 17. Elijah had wrought faithfully, but Israel had to be dealt with by other agents too: the three men whom he was bidden to anoint would in their turn bring down judgment upon the land. God was infinitely more jealous of His own honour than His servant could be, and He would by no means desert His cause or suffer His enemies to triumph as the prophet feared. But mark the *variety* of the instruments which God was pleased to employ: Hazael, king of Syria; Jehu, the rude captain of Israel; and Elisha, a young farmer – great differences here! And yet each one was needed for some special work in connection with that idolatrous people at that time. Ah, 'the eye cannot say to the hand, I have no need of thee; nor again the head to the feet, I have no need of you,' 1 Cor. 12. 21. Yea, as some of the smaller and frailer members of the body perform the most useful and essential offices, so it is often by the most unlettered and apparently unqualified men that God accomplishes the chief exploits in His kingdom.

We may also perceive here how God exercises His high sovereignty in the instruments He employs. Neither Hazael nor Jehu was a pious man: the former came to the throne by foully murdering his predecessor, 2 Kings 8. 15, while of the latter we read, 'But Jehu took no heed to walk in the law of the Lord God of Israel with all his heart: for he departed not from the sins of Jeroboam,' 2 Kings 10. 31. It is often His way to make use of wicked men to thrash those who have enjoyed but spurned particular favours at His hands. It is indeed remarkable how the Most High accomplishes His purpose through men whose only thought is to gratify their own evil lusts. True, their sin is neither diminished nor condoned because they are executing the decrees of Heaven;

[247]

indeed, they are held fully accountable for the evil, yet they do only that which *God's* hand and counsel determined before to be done, serving as His agent to inflict judgment upon His apostate people.

'And it shall come to pass, that him that escapeth the sword of Hazael shall Jehu slay, and him that escapeth from the sword of Jehu shall Elisha slay.' Unspeakably solemn is this. Though God bears 'with much longsuffering' the vessels of wrath fitted to destruction, yet there is a limit to His patience; 'He that being often reproved hardeneth his neck, shall suddenly be destroyed, and that without remedy,' Prov. 29. 1. Long had God endured that horrible insult to His majesty, but the worshippers of Baal should shortly discover that His wrath was as great as His power. They had been faithfully warned: for three and a half years there had been a fearful drought and famine upon their land. A notable miracle had been wrought on Carmel, but only a fleeting impression had been made on the people. And now God announces that the 'sword' shall do its fearful work, not mildly but thoroughly, until the land was completely purged of this great evil. And this is placed on record for all succeeding generations to ponder! The Lord has not changed: even as we write, His judgments are upon most of the world. O that the nations may heed His voice ere it be too late!

'Yet I will leave Me seven thousand in Israel, all the knees which have not bowed unto Baal, and every mouth which hath not kissed him,' v. 18. On this verse we take decided exception to the interpretation given by the great majority of the commentators, who see in it a Divine *rebuke* unto the prophet's dark pessimism, supposing it was God's reply to his despondent 'I only am left,' when in reality there was a multitude in Israel who refused to join in the general idolatry. For several reasons we cannot accept any such view. Is it thinkable that there could actually be thousands in Israel who remained loyal to Jehovah and yet the prophet be totally unaware of their existence? It is not surprising to find one writer of note saying, 'It has often been a subject of wonder to me how those seven thousand secret disciples could

[248]

keep so close as to be unknown by their great leader: attar of roses will always betray its presence, hide it as we may' – but he creates his own difficulty. Moreover, such a view is quite out of harmony with the context: why, after bestowing honour upon the prophet, should the Lord suddenly reprove him?

The careful reader will observe that the marginal reading opposite 'Yet I have left Me seven thousand' is, 'Yet *I will* leave Me seven thousand.' The Hebrew allows of either, but we much prefer the latter, for it not only removes the difficulty of Elijah's ignorance (which the former necessarily involves), but it accords much better with the context. The Lord was graciously *comforting* His despondent servant. First, the Lord informed the prophet that another should take his place and carry on his mission. Next He declared He was by no means indifferent to the horrible situation, but would shortly make quick work of it in judgment. And now He assures him that, though summary judgment should be visited upon Israel, yet He would not make a full end of them, but would preserve a remnant for Himself. Nor does Romans 11. 4 in anywise conflict with this, providing we change the word 'answer' to 'oracle' (as the Greek requires!), for God was not replying to an objection, but making known to Elijah things to come.

It will thus be seen that we take an entirely different view from the popular interpretation not only of verse 18, but of the whole passage. Every writer we have consulted regards these verses as expressing the Lord's displeasure against a refractory servant, that He dealt with him in judgment, *setting him aside* from the honoured position he had occupied by appointing Elisha in his stead. But apart from the gentle rebuke implied in His question, 'What doest thou here, Elijah?', there is nothing to signify the Lord's displeasure, but much to the contrary. Rather do we regard these verses as a record of God's comforting answer to the prophet's despondency. Elijah felt that the forces of evil had triumphed: the Lord announces that the worship of Baal should be utterly destroyed, v. 17 and cf. 2 Kings 10. 25-28. Elijah grieved because he 'only was left': the Lord declares 'I will *leave* Me seven thousand in Israel.' So desperate was the situation, they sought to take the life of Elijah: The Lord promises that Elisha shall complete his mission. Thus did Jehovah most tenderly silence his fears and reassure his heart.

With the verses which have been before us, we like to link those words of Christ to His apostles, 'Henceforth I call you not servants; for the servant knoweth not what his lord doeth: but I have called you friends; *for* all things that I have heard of My Father I have *made known* unto you,' John 15. 15 – indicative of the intimate fellowship they enjoyed with Him. Thus it was with Elijah. The Lord of hosts had condescended to make known unto him things to come, which certainly had not been the case if he were estranged from Him. It was like what we read of in Genesis 18. 17, 'And the Lord said, Shall I hide from Abraham that thing which I do?' No, He did not, for Abraham was 'the *friend* of God,' James 2. 23. Blessed indeed is it to see how the Lord had restored Elijah's soul to the most intimate communion with Himself: recovering him from his gloom and reinstating him in His service.

'So he departed thence, and found Elisha the son of Shaphat, who was plowing with twelve yoke of oxen before him, and he with the twelfth: and Elijah passed by him, and cast his mantle upon him,' v. 19. Here is good evidence that the Lord *had* restored the soul of His servant. Elijah raised no objection, made no delay, but responded promptly. Obedience must ever be the test of our relations with God: 'If ye love Me, keep My commandments,' John 14. 15. In this instance it involved a difficult journey of some one hundred and sixty miles – the distance between Horeb and Abel-meholah, v. 16 and cf. 4. 12 – most of it across the desert; but when God commissions it is for us to comply. There was no jealous resentment that another should fill his place: as soon as Elisha was encountered Elijah cast his mantle upon him – indicative of his investiture with the prophetic office and a sign of friendship that he would take him under his care and tuition. So indeed the young farmer understood it, as is evident from his response. 'And he left the oxen, and ran after Elijah, and said, Let me, I pray thee, kiss my father and my mother, and then I will follow thee,' v. 20. The Spirit of God moved him to accept the call, so that he at once relinquished all his worldly expectations. See how easily the Lord can stir men up to undertake His work in the face of great discouragements. 'Had he consulted with flesh and blood, he would have been very unwilling to be in Elijah's situation, when thus hunted in those dangerous times, and when there was nothing but persecution to be expected. Yet Elisha chose to be a servant to a prophet rather than master of a large farm, and cheerfully resigned all for God. The prayer of Divine grace can remove every objection and conquer every prejudice' (Robert Simpson). 'And he said unto him, Go back again: for what have I done to thee?' v. 20. Very beautiful is this: there was no self-importance, but rather total self-renunciation. Like John the Baptist (who came in his *spirit*: Luke 1. 17) he was sent to usher in another, and his language here was tantamount to 'he must increase, I must decrease.' Blessed humility!

'And he returned back from him, and took a yoke of oxen and slew them, and boiled their flesh with the instruments of the oxen, and gave unto the people, and they did eat. Then he arose, and went after Elijah and ministered unto him,' v. 21. What a lovely finishing touch to the picture! Certainly Elisha did not look upon Elijah as one who had been set aside by the Lord! What comfort for the Tishbite now to have for his companion one of so dutiful and affectionate disposition; and what a privilege for this young man to be under so eminent a tutor! And what is the next reference to him in Scripture? This, 'And the word of the Lord came to Elijah the Tishbite, saying, Go down to meet Ahab king of Israel,' 1 Kings 21. 17, 18: how completely that disposes of the popular idea that God had discarded him from His service. Plainly he had been thoroughly reinstated and was back again on the same old terms with his Master. That is why we have entitled this chapter 'Elijah's Recovery.'

CHAPTER TWENTY-NINE

Naboth's Vineyard

The contents of 1 Kings 20 have presented quite a problem to most of those who have written thereon. It opens with the statement, 'And Benhadad the king of Syria gathered all his host together: and there were thirty and two kings with him, and horses and chariots: and he went up and besieged Samaria, and warred against it.' So confident of victory was he that he sent messengers to Ahab saying, 'Thy silver and thy gold is mine; thy wives also and thy children,' v. 3. Having seen something of the accumulated and aggravated sins of Ahab, we might well suppose the Lord would give success to this enterprise of Benhadad's and use him to humiliate and punish Ahab and his apostate consort. But this expectation is not realized. Strange as that appears, our surprise is greatly increased when we learn that a prophet came unto Ahab saying, 'Thus saith the Lord, Hast thou seen all this great multitude? behold, I will deliver it into thine hand this day; and thou shalt know that I am the Lord,' v. 13. In the immediate sequel we behold the fulfilment of that prediction: 'The king of Israel went out, and smote the horses and chariots, and slew the Syrians with a great slaughter,' v. 21: thus the victory was not with Benhadad but with Ahab.

Nor does the above incident stand alone, for the next thing we read of is: 'And the prophet came to the king of Israel, and said unto him, Go, strengthen thyself, and mark, and see what thou doest: for at the return of the year the king of Syria will come up against thee,' v. 22. This seems passing strange: that the Lord should come to the help of such a one as Ahab. Again the prediction was fulfilled, for Benhadad came with such immense forces that the army of Israel appeared 'like two little flocks of kids, but the Syrians filled the country,' v. 27. Once more, a prophet came to Ahab saying, 'Thus saith the Lord, Because the Syrians have said, The Lord is God of the hills, but He is not God of the valleys, therefore will I deliver all this great multitude into thine hand, and ye shall know that I am the Lord,' v. 28. The outcome was that 'The children of Israel slew of the Syrians a hundred thousand footmen in one day,' v. 29. But because he allowed Benhadad to go free, another prophet announced unto Ahab, 'Thy life shall go for his life,' v. 42.

God's time to destroy Ahab and all who followed him in idolatry had not yet come. It was through Hazael and not Benhadad the Divine vengeance was to be wrought. But if the hour of retribution had not then arrived, why was Benhadad permitted thus to menace the land of Samaria? Ah, it is the answer to that question which casts light upon the above problem. The 'day of the Lord' is deferred because God is long-suffering to His elect, 'not willing that any should perish, but that all should come to repentance,' 2 Pet. 3. 9, 10. Not until Noah and his family were safely in the ark did the windows of heaven open and pour down their devastating flood. Not until Lot was delivered from Sodom did fire and brimstone fall upon it : 'I cannot do anything (said the destroying angel) till thou be come thither,' Gen. 19. 22. And so it was here : not until Elijah and his helper had completed their work, not until all the 'seven thousand' whom Jehovah reserved for Himself had been called, would the work of judgment be effected.

Following upon the account of Elisha's call to the ministry the inspired narrative supplies us with no description of the activities in which they engaged, yet we may be sure that they redeemed the time. Probably in distant parts of the land they sought to instruct the people in the worship of Jehovah, opposing the prevailing idolatry and general corruption, labouring diligently though quietly to effect a solid reformation. It would seem that, following the example of Samuel, 1 Sam. 10. 5-10; 19. 20, they established schools here and there for fitting young men unto the prophetic office, instructing them in the knowledge of God's Law and preparing them to become expounders of it unto the people, and also to lead in psalmody – an important service indeed. We base this view on the mention of 'the sons of the prophets that were at Bethel' and 'at Jericho,' 2 Kings 2. 3, 5. Thus it was that Elijah and Elisha were able to proceed for a year or two unmolested in their work, for being engaged in defending himself and his kingdom from powerful enemies, Ahab was too fully occupied to interfere with them. How wondrous are God's ways: kings and their armies are but pawns to be moved here and there as He pleases.

In what has been before us we may see what varied means the Lord employs to protect His servants from those who would injure them. He knows how to ward off the assaults of their enemies, who would oppose them in their pious efforts to be good. He can make all things smooth and secure for them, that they may proceed without annoyance in discharging the duties which He has assigned them. The Lord can easily fill the heads and hands of their opponents with such urgent business and solicitations that they have enough to do to take care of themselves without harassing His servants in their work. When David and his men were hard pressed in the wilderness of Maon and it appeared they were doomed, 'There came a messenger unto Saul, saying, Haste thee, and come; for the Philistines have invaded the land. Wherefore Saul returned from pursuing after David, and went against the Philistines,' 1 Sam. 23. 27, 28. How incapable we are of determining why God permits one nation to rise up against another, against this one rather than that!

The two prophets continued their work in preaching to the people and instructing their younger brethren for some time, and in view of the promise in 19. 18 we may conclude the blessing of the Lord rested upon their labours, and that not a few were converted. Gladly would they have remained in this quiet and happy occupation, only too glad to escape the notice of the court. But the ministers of God are not to expect a smooth and easy life. They may be thus indulged for a brief season, especially after they have been engaged in some hard and perilous service, yet they must hold themselves in constant readiness to be called forth from their tranquil employment to fresh conflicts and severer duties, which will try their faith and demand all their courage. So it was now with Elijah. A fresh trial awaited him, a real ordeal, nothing less than being required to confront Ahab again, and this time pronounce his doom. But before considering the same we must look at that which occasioned it.

'And he laid him down upon his bed, and turned away his face, and would eat no bread,' 1 Kings 21. 4. The reference is unto Ahab. Here lay the king of Israel in a room of the palace, in a fit of dejection. What had occasioned it? Had some invader overcome his army? No, his soldiers were still flushed with victory over the Syrians. Had his false prophets suffered another massacre? No, the worship of Baal had now recovered from the terrible disaster of Carmel. Had his royal consort been smitten down by the hand of death? No, Jezebel was still very much alive, about to lead him into further evil. What then had brought about his melancholy? The context tells us. Adjoining the royal residence was a vineyard owned by one of his subjects. A whim suddenly possessed the king that this vineyard must become his, so that it might be made an attractive extension to his own property, and he was determined to obtain it at all costs. The wealthy are not satisfied with their possessions but are constantly lusting after more.

Ahab approached Naboth, the owner of this vineyard, and offered to give him a better one for it or to purchase it for cash. Apparently that was an innocent proposal: in reality it was a subtle temptation. 'The land shall not be sold for ever (outright): for the land is Mine,' Lev. 25. 23; 'So shall not the inheritance of the children of Israel remove from tribe to tribe: for every one of the children of Israel shall keep himself to the inheritance of the tribe of his fathers,' Num. 36. 7. Thus it lay not within the lawful power of Naboth to dispose of his vineyard. But for that, there could have been no harm in meeting the equitable offer of Ahab, nay it had been discourteous, even churlish, to refuse his sovereign. But however desirous Naboth might be of granting the king's request, he could not do so without violating the Divine

Law which expressly forbade a man's alienating any part of the family inheritance. Thus a very real and severe test was now presented to Naboth: he had to choose between pleasing the king and displeasing the King of kings.

There are times when the believer may be forced to choose between compliance with human law and obedience to the Divine Law. The three Hebrews were faced with that alternative when it was demanded that they should bow down and worship an image set up by Nebuchadnezzar, Dan. 3. 14, 15. Peter and John were confronted with a similar situation when the Sanhedrin forbade them preach any more in the name of Jesus, Acts 4. 18. When the government orders any of God's children to work seven days in the factories, they are being asked to disobey the Divine statute, 'Remember the Sabbath day to keep it holy.' While rendering to Caesar the things which Caesar may justly require, under no circumstances must we fail to render unto God those which He demands of us, and if we should be bidden to rob God, our duty is plain and clear: the inferior law must yield to the higher – loyalty to God takes precedence over all other considerations. The examples of the three Hebrews and the apostles leave no room for doubt on this point. How thankful we should be that the laws of our country so rarely conflict with the Law of God.

'And Naboth said to Ahab, The Lord forbid it me, that I should give the inheritance of my fathers unto thee,' 21. 3. He started back with horror from such a proposal, looking upon it with alarm as a temptation to commit a horrible sin. Naboth took his stand on the written Word of God and refused to act contrary thereto, even when solicited to do so by the king himself. He was one of the seven thousand whom the Lord had reserved unto Himself, a member of the 'remnant according to the election of grace.' Hereby do such identify themselves, standing out from the compromisers and temporizers. A 'Thus saith the Lord' is final with them: neither monetary inducements nor threats of punishment can move them to disregard it. 'Whether it be right in the sight of God to hearken unto you more than unto God, judge ye,' Acts 4. 19, is their defence when browbeaten by the powers that be. Settle it in your mind, my reader, it is no sin, no wrong, to defy human authorities if they should require of you anything which manifestly clashes with the Law of the Lord. On the other hand, the Christian should be a pattern to others of a law-abiding citizen, so long as God's claims upon him be not infringed.

Ahab was greatly displeased by Naboth's refusal, for in the thwarting of his desire his pride was wounded, and so vexed was he to meet with this denial that he sulked like a spoiled child when his will is crossed. The king so took to heart his disappointment that he became miserable, took to his bed and refused nourishment. What a picture of the poor rich! Millionaires and those in high office are not to be envied, for neither material wealth nor worldly honours can bring contentment to the heart. Solomon proved that: he was permitted to possess everything the natural man craved, and then found it all to be nothing but 'vanity and vexation of spirit.' Is there not a solemn warning here for each of us? How we need to heed that word of Christ's, 'Take heed, and beware of covetousness: for a man's life consisteth not in the abundance of the things which he possesseth,' Luke 12. 15. Coveting is a being dissatisfied with the portion God has given me and lusting after something which belongs to my neighbour. Inordinate desires always lead to vexation, unfitting us to enjoy what is ours.

'But Jezebel his wife came to him, and said unto him, Why is thy spirit so sad that thou eatest no bread? And he said unto her, Because I spake unto Naboth the Jezreelite, and said unto him, Give me thy vineyard for money; or else, if it please thee, I will give thee another vineyard for it: and he answered, I will not give thee my vineyard,' vv. 5, 6. How easy it is to misrepresent the most upright. Ahab made no mention of Naboth's conscientious grievance for not complying with his request, but speaks of him as though he had acted only with insubordination and obstinacy. On hearing that statement, Jezebel at once revealed her awful character: 'Dost thou now govern the kingdom of Israel? arise, and eat bread, and let thine heart be merry: I will give thee the vineyard of Naboth,' v. 7. As Matthew Henry expressed it, 'Under pretence of comforting her afflicted husband, she feeds his pride and passion, blowing the coals of his corruptions.' She sympathized with his unlawful desire, strengthened his feeling of disappointment, tempted him to exercise an arbitrary power, and urged him to disregard the rights of another and defy the Law of God. Are you going to allow a subject to balk you? Be not so squeamish: use your royal power: instead of grieving over a repulse, revenge it.

The most diabolical stratagem was now planned by this infamous woman in order to wrest the inheritance of Naboth from him. First, she resorted to forgery, for we are told 'she wrote letters in Ahab's name, and sealed them with his seal, and sent the letters unto the elders and to the nobles that were in his city, dwelling with Naboth,' v. 8. Second, she was guilty of deliberate hypocrisy. 'Proclaim a fast,' v. 9, so as to convey the impression that some horrible wickedness had been discovered, threatening the city with Divine judgment unless the crime were expiated – history contains ample proof that the vilest crimes have often been perpetrated under the cloak of religion. Third, she drew not the line at out-and-out perjury, suborning men to testify falsely: 'Set Naboth on high among the people (under colour of giving him a fair trial by legal prosecution), and set two men, sons of Belial, before him, to bear witness against him, saying, Thou didst blaspheme God and the king,' v. 10 – thus even in 'the place of judgment wickedness was there,' Eccl. 3. 16.

Here was a woman who sowed sin with both hands. She not only led Ahab deeper into iniquity, but she dragged the elders and nobles of the city into the mire of her Devil-inspired crime. She made the sons of Belial, the false witnesses, even worse than they were before. She became both a robber and a murderess, filching from Naboth both his good name and heritage. The elders and nobles of Israel were base enough to carry out her orders – sure sign was this that the kingdom was ripe for judgment: when those in high places are godless and conscienceless, it will not be long ere the wrath of the Lord falls on those over whom they preside. At the instigation of those nobles and elders, Naboth was 'carried forth out of the city and stoned with stones that he died,' v. 13 – his sons also suffering a similar fate, 2 Kings 9. 26, that the entail might be cut off.

Let it be well attended to that this unprincipled woman, so full of limitless ambition and lust of power, is not only an historical personage, but the predictive symbol of a nefarious and apostate system. The letters to the seven churches in Revelation 2 and 3 supply a prophetic outline of the history of Christendom. That of Thyatira, which portrays Romanism, makes mention of 'that woman Jezebel,' 2. 20, and striking are the parallels between this queen and the monstrous system which has its headquarters at the Vatican. Jezebel was not a Jewess, but a heathen princess, and Romanism is not a product of Christianity but of paganism. Scholars tell us her name has a double meaning (according to its Zidonian and Hebrew significations): 'a chaste virgin' – which is what Rome professes to be: and 'a dunghill' – what Rome *is* in God's sight. She reigned in power as Israel's queen, Ahab being merely her tool: kings are the puppets of Rome. She set up an idolatrous priesthood. She slew the Lord's servants. She employed dishonest and fiendish methods to obtain her ends. She met with a terrible end.

As Jezebel was a prophetic symbol of that Satanic system known as the Papacy, Naboth was a blessed type of the Lord Jesus. First, he possessed a vineyard: so also did Christ, Matt. 21. 33. Second, as Naboth's vineyard was desired by one who had no respect for God's Law so was Christ's, Matt. 21. 38. Third, each was tempted to disobey God and part with his inheritance, Matt. 4. 9. Fourth, each refused to heed the voice of the Tempter. Fifth, each was falsely accused by those who sought his death. Sixth, each was charged with 'blaspheming God and the king,' Matt. 26. 65; Luke 23. 1, 2. Seventh, each was put to death by violent hands. Eighth, each was slain 'outside' the city, Heb. 13. 12-14. Ninth, the murderers of each were charged with their crime, 1 Kings 21. 19; Acts 2. 22, 23. Tenth, the murderers of each were destroyed by Divine judgment, 1 Kings 21. 19-23; Matt. 21. 41; 22. 7.

'And it came to pass, when Jezebel heard that Naboth was stoned, and was dead, that Jezebel said to Ahab, Arise, take possession of the vineyard of Naboth the Jezreelite, which he refused to give thee for money: for Naboth is not alive, but dead. And it came to pass, when Ahab heard that Naboth was dead, that Ahab rose up to go down to the vineyard of Naboth the Jezreelite, to take possession of it,' vv. 15, 16. Jezebel was permitted to carry out her vile scheme and Ahab to acquire the coveted vineyard. By his action he testified his approval of all that had been done, and thus became sharer of its guilt. There is a class of people who refuse personally to commit crime, yet scruple not to use their employees and hired agents to do so, and then take advantage of their villainies to enrich themselves. Let such conscienceless rascals and all who consider themselves shrewd in sharing unrighteous gains know that in God's sight they are partakers of the sins of those who did the dirty work for them and will yet be punished accordingly. Many another since the days of Ahab and Jezebel has been allowed to reach the goal of his lusts even at the price of fraud, lying, dishonesty and cruel bloodshed. But in due course each shall discover that 'The triumphing of the wicked is short, and the joy of the hypocrite but for a moment,' Job. 20. 5.

Meanwhile the Lord God had been a silent spectator of the whole transaction with respect to Naboth. He knew its atrocity, however disguised by the impious semblance of religion and law. As He is infinitely superior to kings and dictators, so He is qualified to call them to account; and as He is infinitely righteous, He *will* execute judgment upon them without respect to persons. Scarcely had that horrible crime been committed than Ahab is reckoned with. 'And the word of the Lord came to Elijah the Tishbite, saying, Arise, go down to meet Ahab king of Israel, which is in Samaria: behold, he is in the vineyard of Naboth, whither he is gone down to possess it. And thou shalt speak unto him, saying, Thus saith the Lord, Hast thou killed, and also taken possession? And thou shalt speak unto him, saying, Thus saith the Lord, In the place where dogs licked the blood of Naboth shall dogs lick thy blood, even thine,' vv. 17-19. Here was the prophet's ordeal: to confront the king, charge him with his wickedness, and pronounce sentence upon him in God's name.

CHAPTER THIRTY

The Sinner Found Out

'And it came to pass, when Ahab heard that Naboth was dead, that Ahab rose up to go down to the vineyard of Naboth the Jezreelite, to take possession of it,' 1 Kings 21. 16. The coveted object (see v. 2) should now be seized. Its lawful owner was dead, brutally murdered by Ahab's acquiescence, and being king, who was there to hinder him enjoying his ill-gotten gain? Picture him delighting himself in his new acquisition, planning how to use it to best advantage, promising himself much pleasure in this extension of the palace grounds. To such lengths are men allowed to go in their wickedness that at times onlookers are made to wonder if there be such a thing as justice, if after all might be not right. Surely, if there were a God who loved righteousness and possessed the power to prevent flagrant unrighteousness, we should not witness such grievous wrongs inflicted upon the innocent, and such triumphing of the wicked. Ah, that is no new problem, but one which has recurred again and again in the history of this world, a world which lieth in the Wicked One. It is one of the mystery elements arising out of the conflict between good and evil. It supplies one of the severest tests of our faith in God and His government of this earth.

Ahab's entering into possession of Naboth's vineyard reminds us of a scene described in Daniel 5. There we behold another king, Belshazzar, surrounded by the nobility of his kingdom, engaged in a great feast. He gives orders that the golden and silver vessels which his father had taken out of the temple of Jerusalem should be brought to him. His command was obeyed and the vessels were filled with wine, his wives and concubines drinking from them.

Think of it: the sacred utensils of Jehovah's house being put to such a use! How passing strange that a worm of the dust should be suffered to go to such fearful lengths of presumption and impiety! But the Most High was neither ignorant of nor indifferent unto such conduct. Nor can a man's rank exempt him from or provide him any protection against the Divine wrath when God is ready to exercise it. There was none in Samaria who could prevent Ahab's taking possession of Naboth's vineyard, and there was none in Babylon who could hinder Belshazzar desecrating the sacred vessels of Israel's temple, but there was One above who could and did bring each of them to judgment.

'Because sentence against an evil work is not executed speedily, therefore the heart of the sons of men is fully set in them to do evil,' Eccl. 8. 11. Since retribution does not promptly overtake evildoers, they harden their hearts still further, becoming increasingly reckless, supposing that judgment will never fall upon them. Therein they err, for they are but treasuring up unto themselves 'wrath against the day of wrath and revelation of the righteous judgment of God,' Rom. 2. 5. Note well that word, 'revelation.' The 'righteous judgment of God' is now more or less in abeyance, but there is a set time, an appointed 'Day,' when it shall be made *fully manifest*. The Divine vengeance comes slowly, yet it comes none the less surely. Nor has God left Himself without plain witness of this. Throughout the course of this world's history He has, every now and then, given a clear and public proof of His 'righteous judgment,' by making an example of some notorious rebel and evidencing His abhorrence of him in the sight of men. He did so with Ahab, with Belshazzar, and with others since then, and though in the great majority of instances the heavens may be silent and apparently impervious, yet those exceptions are sufficient to show 'the heavens *do* rule,' and should enable the wronged to possess their souls in patience.

'And the word of the Lord came to Elijah the Tishbite, saying, Arise, go down to meet Ahab king of Israel, which is in Samaria: behold, he is in the vineyard of Naboth, whither he is gone down to possess it,' vv. 17, 18. A living, righteous and sin-hating God had observed the wickedness to which Ahab had been a willing party, and determined to pass sentence upon him, employing none other than the stern Tishbite as His mouthpiece. In connection with matters of less moment, junior prophets had been sent to the king a short time before, 20. 13, 22, 28, but on this occasion none less than the father of the prophets was deemed a suitable agent. It called for a man of great courage and undaunted spirit to confront the king, charging him with his horrid crime and denouncing sentence of death upon him in God's name. Who so well qualified as Elijah for this formidable and perilous undertaking? Herein we may perceive how the Lord reserves the hardest tasks for the most experienced and mature of His servants. Peculiar qualifications are required for special and important missions, and for the development of those qualifications, a rigid apprenticeship has to be served. Alas, that these principles are so little recognized by the churches today.

But let us not be misunderstood at this point. It is not natural endowments, intellectual powers, and educational polish we make reference to. It was vain for David to go forth against the Philistine giant clad in Saul's armour: he knew that, and so discarded it. No, it is spiritual graces and ministerial gifts of which we speak. It was strong faith and the boldness it imparts which this severe ordeal called for: faith not in himself but in his Master. Strong faith, for no ordinary had sufficed. And that faith had been tried and disciplined, strengthened and increased in the school of prayer and on the battlefield of experience. In the wilds of Gilead, in the loneliness of Cherith, in the exigencies of Zarephath, the prophet had dwelt much in the secret place of the Most High, had learned to know God experimentally, had proved His sufficiency. It was no untried novice that Jehovah called upon to act as His ambassador on this solemn occasion, but one who was 'strong in the Lord and in the power of His might.'

On the other hand, we must be careful to place the crown where it properly belongs and ascribe unto God the honour of furnishing and sustaining His servants. We have nothing but what we have received, 1 Cor. 4. 7, and the strongest are as weak as water when

He withdraws His hand from them. He who calls us must also equip, and extraordinary commissions require extraordinary endowments, which the Lord alone can impart. Tarry ye in Jerusalem, said Christ to the apostles 'until ye be endued with power from on high,' Luke 24. 49. Bold sinners need to be boldly reproved, but such firmness and courage must be sought from God. Said He to another of His prophets, 'All the house of Israel are impudent and hard-hearted. Behold, I have made thy face strong against their faces, and thy forehead strong against their foreheads. As an adamant harder than flint have I made thy forehead: fear them not, neither be dismayed at their looks,' Ezek. 3. 7-9. Thus, if we behold Elijah complying promptly with this call, it was because he could say, 'But truly I am full of power by the Spirit of the Lord, and of judgment, and of might, to declare unto Jacob (Ahab) his transgression,' Micah 3. 8.

'Arise, go down to meet Ahab king of Israel, which is in Samaria: behold, he is in the vineyard of Naboth, whither he is gone down to possess it.' Ahab was not in his palace, but God knew where he had gone and the business with which he would be engaged. The eyes of the Lord are in *every* place, beholding the evil and the good,' Prov. 15. 3: nothing can be concealed from Him. Ahab might pride himself that none should ever reprove him for his diabolical conduct, and that now he could enjoy his spoils without hindrance. But sinners, whether of the lowest or the highest rank, are never secure. Their wickedness ascends before God, and He often sends after them when they least expect it. Let none flatter themselves with impunity because they have succeeded in their iniquitous schemes. The day of reckoning is not far distant, even though it should not overtake them in this life. If these lines should be read by one who is far from home, no longer under the eye of loved ones, let him know that he is still under the observation of the Most High. Let that consideration deter him from sinning against Him and against his neighbour. Stand in awe of God's presence, lest some fearful sentence from Him be pronounced upon you, and be brought home to your conscience with such power that you will be a terror to yourself and to all around you.

'And thou shalt speak unto him, saying, Thus saith the Lord, Hast thou killed, and also taken possession? And thou shalt speak unto him, saying, Thus saith the Lord, In the place where dogs licked the blood of Naboth shall dogs lick thy blood, even thine,' v. 19. With no smooth and soothing message was the prophet now sent forth. It was enough to terrify himself: what then must it have meant to the guilty Ahab! It proceeded from Him who is King of kings and Lord of lords, the supreme and righteous Governor of the universe, whose omniscient eye is witness to all events and whose omnipotent arm shall arrest and punish all evil doers. It was the word of Him who declares, 'Can any hide himself in secret places that I shall not see him? saith the Lord. Do not I fill heaven and earth?' Jer. 23. 24. For 'His eyes are upon the ways of man, and He seeth all his goings. There is no darkness, nor shadow of death, where the workers of iniquity may hide themselves,' Job 34. 21, 22. It was a word of denunciation, bringing to light the hidden things of darkness. It was a word of accusation, boldly charging Ahab with his crimes. It was a word of condemnation, making known the awful doom which should surely overtake the one who had blatantly trampled upon the Divine Law.

It is just such messages which our degenerate age calls for. It is the *lack of them* which has brought about the terrible condition which the world is now in. Mealy-mouthed preachers deceived the fathers, and now their children have turned their backs on the churches. 'Behold, a whirlwind of the Lord is gone forth in fury, even a grievous whirlwind: it shall fall grievously upon the head of the wicked,' Jer. 23. 19. The figure is an awful one: a 'whirlwind uproots trees, sweeps away houses, and leaves death and desolation in its wake. Who among God's people can doubt that such a whirlwind is now going forth? 'The anger of the Lord shall not return, until He have executed, and till He have performed the thoughts of His heart: in the latter days ye shall consider it perfectly,' 23. 20. And why? What is the root cause thereof? This: 'I have not sent these prophets, yet they ran: I have not spoken to them, yet they prophesied,' v. 21: false prophets, preachers never called of God, who uttered 'lies' in His name,

v. 25. Men who rejected the Divine Law, ignored the Divine holiness, remained silent about Divine wrath. Men who filled the churches with unregenerate members and then amused them with speculations upon prophecy.

It was false prophets who wrought such havoc in Israel, who had corrupted the throne and called down upon the land the sore judgment of God. And throughout the past century the false prophets have corrupted Christendom. As far back as fifty years ago Spurgeon lifted up his voice and used his pen in denouncing the 'Downgrade movement' in the churches, and withdrew his tabernacle from the Baptist Union. After his death things went rapidly from bad to worse and now 'a whirlwind of the Lord' is sweeping away the flimsy structures the religious world erected. Everything is now in the melting pot and only the genuine gold will survive the fiery trial. And what can the true servants of God do? Lift up their voices, 'Cry aloud, and spare not,' Isa. 58. 1. Do as Elijah did: fearlessly denounce sin in high places.

A message pleasant to deliver? No, far from it. A message likely to be popular with the hearers? No, the very reverse. But a message sorely needed and criminally neglected. Did the Lord Jesus preach a sermon in the temple on the love of God while its sacred precincts were being made a den of thieves? Yet this is what thousands of those who pose as His servants have been doing for the last two or three generations. With flaming eye and scourge in hand, the Redeemer drove out from His Father's House the traffickers who defiled it. Those who were the true servants of Christ refused to use carnal methods for adding numbers of nominal professors to their membership. Those who were the true servants of Christ proclaimed the unchanging demands of a holy God, insisted on the enforcing of a Scriptural discipline, and resigned their pastorates when their flocks rebelled. The religious powers-that-be were glad to see the back of them, while their ministerial brethren, so far from seeking to strengthen their hands, did all they could to injure them and cared not if they starved to death.

But those servants of Christ were few in number, a negligible minority. The great bulk of 'pastors' were hirelings, time-servers, holders of an easy and lucrative job at any price. They carefully trimmed their sails, and deliberately omitted from their preaching anything which would be distasteful unto their ungodly hearers. The people of God in their congregations were famished, though few of them dared to take their pastors to task, following the line of least resistance. And the very passage from which we have quoted above declares, 'but *if they had* stood in My counsel, and had caused My people to hear My words, then they should have *turned them* from their evil way, and from the evil of their doings,' Jer. 23. 22. But they did not, and therefore 'a whirlwind of the Lord is gone forth in fury, even a grievous whirlwind.' Can we wonder at it? God will not be mocked. It is the churches who are responsible for it, and there is no denomination, no party, no circle of fellowship that can plead innocence.

'And Ahab said to Elijah, Hast thou found me, O mine enemy?' v. 20. With what consternation must the king have beheld him! The prophet would be the last man he wished or expected to see, believing that Jezebel's threat had frightened him away so that he would be troubled by him no more. Perhaps Ahab thought that he had fled to some distant country or was in his grave by this time: but here he stood before him. The king was evidently startled and dismayed by the sight of Elijah. His conscience would smite him for his base wickedness, and the very place of their present meeting would add to his discomfort. He therefore could not look on the Tishbite without terror and fearful foreboding that some dire threat of vengeance was at hand from Jehovah. In his fright and annoyance he cried, 'Hast thou found me?' Am I now tracked down? A guilty heart can never be at peace. Had he not been conscious of how ill he deserved at the hands of God, he would not have greeted His servant as 'O mine enemy.' It was because his heart condemned him as an enemy of God that he was so disconcerted at being confronted by His ambassador.

'And Ahab said to Elijah, Hast thou found me, O mine enemy?' Such a reception is all that the faithful servant of God must expect at the hands of the wicked, especially from unregenerate religious professors. They will regard him as a disturber of the peace, a troubler of those who wish to be comfortable in their sins. They who are engaged in evil-doing are annoyed at him who detects them, whether he be a minister of Christ or a policeman. The Scriptures are detested because they denounce sin in every form. Romanism hates the Bible because it exposes her hypocrisies. The impenitent look upon those as their *friends* who speak smooth things to them and help them to deceive themselves. 'They hate him that rebuketh in the gate, and they abhor him that speaketh uprightly,' Amos 5. 10. Hence it was that the apostle declared, 'If I yet pleased men, I should not be the servant of Christ,' Gal. 1. 10 – how few servants of Christ are left! The minister's duty is to be faithful to his Master, and if he pleases *Him*, what matter it though he be despised and detested by the whole religious world? Blessed are they whom men shall revile for Christ's sake.

At this point we would say to any young man who is seriously contemplating entering the ministry, Abandon such a prospect at once if you are not prepared to be treated with contempt and made 'as the filth of the world, the off-scouring of all things,' 1 Cor. 4. 13. The public service of Christ is the last place for those who wish to be popular with their fellows. A young minister once complained to an older one, 'My church is making a regular door-mat of me,' to which he received the reply, 'If the Son of God condescended to become the Door surely it is not beneath you to be made a door-mat.' If you are not prepared for elders and deacons to wipe their feet on you, shun the ministry. And to those already in it we would say, Unless your preaching stirs up strife and brings down persecution and contumacy upon you, there is something seriously lacking in it. If your preaching is the enemy of hypocrisy, of carnality, of worldliness, of empty profession, of all that is contrary to vital godliness, then you must be regarded as the enemy of those you oppose.

'And he answered, I have found thee.' Elijah was not a man who wore his heart on his sleeve. It took a good deal more than a frown to deter, or an angry word to peeve him. So far from being 'hurt' and turning away to sulk, he replied like a man. He took up Ahab on his own terms and said, 'Yes, I have found thee.' I have found thee as a thief and murderer in another's vineyard. It is a good sign when the self-convicted one denounces God's servant as his 'enemy,' for it shows the preacher has hit the mark, his message has gone home to the conscience; 'Be sure your sin will find you out,' Num. 32. 23, says God, and so Adam, Cain, Achan, Ahab, Gehazi, Ananias proved. Let none think they shall escape Divine retribution: if punishment be not inflicted in this life, it most certainly will be in the next, unless we cease fighting against God and flee to Christ for refuge. 'Behold, the Lord cometh with ten thousands of His saints, to execute judgment upon all, and to convince all that are ungodly among them of all their ungodly deeds which they have ungodly committed, and of all their hard speeches which ungodly sinners have spoken against Him,' Jude 14, 15.

CHAPTER THIRTY-ONE

A Dreadful Message

'And Ahab said to Elijah, Hast thou found me, O mine enemy?
And he answered, I have found thee: because thou hast sold
thyself to work evil in the sight of the Lord,' 1 Kings 21. 20. We
have already considered Ahab's question and the first part of the
prophet's reply; we turn now to look at the solemn charge which
he preferred against the king. 'Because thou hast *sold thyself to
work evil* in the sight of the Lord.' Here we may observe how
essential it is that we note particularly each word of Holy Writ,
for if we read this verse carelessly we shall fail to distinguish
sharply between it and an expression used in the New Testament,
which, though similar in sound, is vastly different in sense. In
Romans 7. 14 we find the apostle declares, 'But I am carnal, *sold
under sin.*' That statement has puzzled quite a few, and some have
so misunderstood its force that they have confounded it with the
prophet's terrible indictment against Ahab. It may be somewhat
of a digression, yet numbers of our readers will probably welcome
a few expository comments upon the difference in meaning of
these two expressions.

It will be noted that Romans 7. 14 begins with the affirmation,
'For we know that the Law is spiritual,' which among other things
means, it legislates for the soul as well as the body, its demands
reaching beyond the mere outward act to the motive which
prompted it and the spirit in which it is performed; in a word,
it requires *inward* conformity and purity. Now as the apostle
measured himself by the high and holy requirements of God's
law, he declared, 'but I am carnal.' That was not said by way of
self-extenuation, to excuse his coming so far short of the Divine

standard set before us, but in self-condemnation because of his lack of conformity thereto. That is the sorrowful confession of every honest Christian. 'I am carnal' expresses what the believer is in himself by nature: though born from above, yet the 'flesh' in him has not been improved to the slightest degree. Nor is that true of the believer only when he has suffered some fall: he is always 'carnal,' for there is no getting rid of the old nature; though he is not always conscious of this humiliating fact. The more the Christian grows in grace the more does he realize his carnality – that the 'flesh' pollutes his holiest exercises and best performances.

'Sold under sin.' This does not mean that the saint gives up himself to be the willing slave of sin, but that he finds himself in the case or experience of a slave, of one whose master requires him to do things against his own inclinations. The literal rendering of the Greek is 'having been sold under sin,' that is, at the Fall, in which condition we continue to the end of our earthly course. 'Sold' so as to be under the power of sin, for the old nature is never made holy. The apostle speaks of what he finds himself, what he is before God, and not of what he appeared in the sight of men. His 'old man' was thoroughly opposed to God's Law. There was an evil principle in him against which he struggled, from which he longed to be delivered, but which continued to exert its fearful potency. Notwithstanding the grace he had received, he found himself far, far from being perfect, and in all respects unable to attain thereunto, though longing after it. It was while measuring himself by the Law, which requires perfect love, that he realized how far short he came of it.

'Sold under sin': indwelling corruption holds the believer back. The more spiritual progress he is enabled to make, the more he discovers his handicap. It is like a man journeying uphill with a heavy load on his back: the farther he proceeds the more conscious does he become of that burden. But how is this to be harmonized with 'sin shall not have dominion over you,' Rom. 6. 14? Thus: though indwelling sin tyrannizes the believer, it by no means prevails over him totally and completely. Sin reigns over the sinner, having an absolute and undisputed dominion over him, but not so with the saint. Yet it so far plagues as to prevent his attaining unto perfection, which is what he craves: see Philippians 3. 12. From the standpoint of the new nature and as God sees him in Christ, the believer is spiritual; but from the standpoint of the old nature and as God sees him in himself, he is 'carnal.' As a child of Adam he is 'sold under sin,' as a child of God he 'delights in the Law of God after the inward man,' Rom 7. 22. The acts of a slave are indeed his own acts, yet not being performed with the full consent of his will and delight of his heart they are not a fair test of his disposition and desires.

Vastly different was the case of Ahab from that which we have briefly sketched above: so far from being brought into captivity against his will, he had 'sold himself to work evil in the sight of the Lord.' Deliberately and without limit, Ahab wholly gave himself up unto all manner of wickedness in open defiance of the Almighty. As Balaam 'loved the wages of unrighteousness,' 2 Pet. 2. 15, and therefore freely hired himself unto Balak to curse the people of God, as Judas coveted the silver of the chief priests, sought them out and covenanted to betray the Saviour unto them, Matt. 26. 14, 15, so this apostate king 'sold himself to work evil' without compunction or reserve. His horrible crime in respect of Naboth was no detached act contrary to the general tenor or course of his life, as David's sin in the matter of Uriah had been, but was simply a specimen of his continual rebellion against God. 'Having sold himself to work evil in the sight of the Lord, as if in contempt and defiance of Him, he was openly, constantly, and diligently employed in it as a slave in his master's business,' (Thomas Scott).

'Thou hast sold thyself to work evil in the sight of the Lord.' His downward course commenced when he *married Jezebel*, v. 25, a heathen, an idolater, and the consequences of that horrible union are recorded for our learning. They stand out as a red light, a danger signal, a solemn warning to the people of God today. The Law expressly forbade an Israelite to marry a Gentile, and the New Testament just as definitely prohibits a Christian from marrying a worldling. 'Be ye not unequally yoked together with unbelievers: for what fellowship hath righteousness with unrighteousness? and what communion hath light with darkness?' 2 Cor. 6. 14. It is at his or her peril that any Christian wilfully treads under foot this Divine commandment, for deliberate disobedience is certain to incur the marked displeasure of God. For a child of His to enter the state of wedlock with an unbeliever is to make Christ have concord with Belial, 2 Cor. 6. 15. When a Christian man marries a worldling, a son of God becomes united to a daughter of Satan. What a horrible combination!

In no uncertain tones did Elijah denounce Ahab for his defiant union with Jezebel and all the evils it had brought in its train. 'Thou hast sold thyself to work evil in the sight of the Lord.' That is the prime business of God's servant: to make known the indignation and judgment of Heaven against sin. God is the enemy of sin. He is 'angry with the wicked every day,' Psa. 7. 11. His wrath is revealed against all ungodliness and unrighteousness of men, Rom. 1. 18. That wrath is the antagonism of holiness to evil, of consuming fire to that which is incapable of sustaining it. It is the business of God's servant to declare and make known the awful case and course of the sinner, that those who are not for Christ are against Him, that he who is not walking with God is fighting against Him, that he who is not yielding himself to His service is serving the Devil. Said the Lord Jesus, 'Whosoever committeth sin is the servant of sin,' John 8. 34, complying with the orders of his master, the slave of his lusts, yet the willing slave, delighting therein. It is not a service which has been forced upon him against his desires, but one into which he has voluntarily sold himself and in which he voluntarily remains. And therefore it is a criminal servitude for which he must be judged.

This, then, was the ordeal which confronted Elijah, and in essence it confronts every servant of Christ today. He was the bearer of an unwelcome message. He was required to confront the ungodly king and tell him to his face precisely what he was in the sight of a sin-hating God. It is a task which calls for firmness of mind and boldness of heart. It is a task which demands that the glory of God shall override all sentimental considerations. It is a task which claims the support and co-operation of all God's people. Let them do and say nothing to discourage the minister in the faithful discharge of his office. Let them be far from saying, 'Prophesy not unto us right things: speak unto us smooth things, prophesy deceits,' Isa. 30. 10. Rather, let the people of God pray earnestly that the spirit of Elijah may rest upon their ministers, that they may be enabled to open their mouths 'with all boldness,' Acts 4. 29, that they may keep back nothing which is profitable, that they may shun not to declare all the counsel of God, Acts 20. 20, 27. Let them see to it that there be no failure to hold up their hands in the day of battle, Ex. 17. 12. Ah, my reader, it makes a tremendous difference when the minister knows he has the support of a praying people. How far is the pew responsible for the state of the pulpit today?

'Behold, I will bring evil upon thee,' v. 21. It is the business of God's servant not only to paint in its true colours the course which the sinner has chosen to follow, but to make known the inevitable consequence of such a course. First and negatively, they who have sold themselves to work evil in the sight of the Lord 'have sold themselves for *nought*,' Isa. 52. 3. Satan has assured them that by engaging in his service they shall be greatly the gainers, that by giving free rein to their lusts they shall be merry and enjoy life. But he is a liar, as Eve discovered at the beginning. Of those who sell themselves to work evil it may be inquired, 'Wherefore do ye spend money for that which is not bread? and your labour for that which satisfieth not?' Isa. 55. 2. There is no contentment of mind, no peace of conscience, no real joy of heart to be obtained by indulging the flesh, but rather the wrecking of health and the storing up of misery. Oh, what a wretched bargain is this: to sell ourselves 'for nought'! To squander our substance in riotous living and then come to woeful want. To render full obedience to the dictates of sin and receive only kicks and cuffs in return. What madness to serve such a master!

But the servant of God has a still more painful duty to perform, and that is to announce the positive side of the consequences of selling ourselves to work evil in the sight of the Lord. Sin pays terrible wages, my reader. It is doing so at this present moment in the world's history. The horrors of war, with all the untold suffering and anguish they entail, is the wages of sin now being paid out to the nations, and those nations which have sinned against the greatest light and privileges are the ones receiving the heaviest instalments. And is it not meet it should be so? Yes, a 'just recompence of reward,' Heb. 2. 2, is what the Word of Truth designates it. And identically the same principle pertains to the individual: unto every one who sells himself to work evil in the sight of the Lord His rejoinder is, 'Behold, I will bring evil upon thee,' dire judgment which shall overwhelm and utterly consume. This, too, is the duty of God's servant: solemnly to declare unto every rebel against God, irrespective of his rank, 'O wicked man, thou shalt surely die,' Ezek. 33. 8, and that same verse goes on to tell us that God will yet say unto the watchman that failed in his duty, 'his blood will I require at thine hand.' Oh, to be able to say with Paul, 'I am pure from the blood of all men,' Acts 20. 26.

'And will make thine house like the house of Jeroboam the son of Nebat, and like the house of Baasha the son of Ahijah, for the provocation wherewith thou has provoked Me to anger, and made Israel to sin. And of Jezebel also spake the Lord, saying, The dogs shall eat Jezebel by the wall of Jezreel. Him that dieth of Ahab in the city the dogs shall eat; and him that dieth in the field shall the fowls of the air eat,' vv. 22-24. The mills of God grind slowly but they grind exceeding small. For many years Ahab defied Jehovah but now the day of reckoning was nigh at hand, and when it dawned, Divine judgment would fall not only upon the apostate king and his vile consort but upon their family as well; so that his evil house should be utterly exterminated. Is it not written, 'the name of the wicked shall rot,' Prov. 10. 7? We are here supplied with an awe-inspiring illustration of that solemn principle in the governmental dealings of God: 'visiting the iniquity of the fathers upon the children,' Ex. 20. 5. Behold here the justice of God in making Ahab reap as he had sown: not only had he consented unto the death of Naboth, 21. 8, but the sons of Naboth also had been slain, 2 Kings 9. 26, hence Divine retribution was visited not only upon Ahab and Jezebel but on their children too.

'And will make thine house like the house of Jeroboam the son of Nebat, and like the house of Baasha the son of Ahijah.' In declaring that He would make the house of Ahab like unto that of two other wicked kings who preceded him, God announced the total destruction of his descendants, and that by a violent end. For the house of Jeroboam – whose dynasty lasted barely twenty-four years – we read, 'He smote all the house of Jeroboam: he left not to Jeroboam any that breathed, until He had destroyed him, 1 Kings 15. 29; while of Baasha – whose dynasty lasted only just over a quarter of a century – we are told, 'He left him not one male, neither of his kinsfolks, nor of his friends,' 1 Kings 16. 11. Probably one reason why the fearful doom which overtook the families of his predecessors as here specifically mentioned, was to emphasize still further the enormity of Ahab's conduct – that he had failed to take to heart those recent judgments of God. It greatly aggravates our sins when we refuse to heed the solemn warnings which history records of the unmistakable judgments of God upon other evildoers, as the guilt of our generation is so much the greater through disregarding the clarion call made by the war of 1914-18 for the nations to turn from their wickedness and return to the God of their fathers.

And what was the effect produced upon Ahab by this message from Jehovah? Disconcerted and displeased he was on first beholding the prophet, yet when he heard the awful sentence he was deeply affected: 'he rent his clothes, and put sackcloth upon his flesh, and fasted, and lay in sackcloth, and went softly,' v. 27. He made no effort to silence Elijah by self-vindication. His conscience smote him for approving the murderous act, for seizing the booty though not killing the owner thereof. He knew well that connivance at wickedness by those in authority, who ought to restrain it, is justly visited upon themselves as their own deed; that the receiver of stolen goods is as bad as the thief. He was abashed and abased. God can make the stoutest sinner to tremble and the most arrogant humble himself. But all is not gold that glitters. There may be a great outward show of repentance without the heart being changed. Many have been made afraid of God's wrath who would not part with their sins. It is to be carefully noted there is no hint that Ahab put away Jezebel or restored the worship of the Lord.

That which is recorded here of Ahab is both solemn and instructive. Solemn, because it sounds a warning against being deceived by appearances. Ahab made no effort to justify his crimes nor did he lay violent hands on Elijah. Nay more: he humbled himself, and by his outward acts acknowledged the justice of the Divine sentence. What more could we ask? Ah, that is the all-important point. External amendment of our ways, though good in itself, is not sufficient: 'rend your heart, and not your garments,' Joel 2. 13, is what a holy God requires. A hypocrite may go far in the outward performance of holy duties. The most hardened sinners are capable of reforming for a season: Mark 6. 20; John 5. 35. How many wicked persons have, in times of danger and desperate illness, abased themselves before God, but returned to their evil ways as soon as restored to health. Ahab's humiliation was but superficial and transient, being occasioned by fear of judgment and not a heart hatred of his sins. Nothing is said of his restoring the vineyard to Naboth's heirs or next of kin, and where righting of wrongs is absent we must always seriously suspect the repentance. Later we find him saying of a servant of God, 'I *hate* him,' 22. 8, which is clear proof that he had undergone no change of heart.

Instructive also is the case of Ahab, for it throws light on God's governmental dealings with individuals in this life. Though the king's repentance was but superficial, yet inasmuch as it was a public or visible humbling of himself before God, He was so far owned and honoured, and an abatement of His sentence was obtained: 'Because he humbleth himself before Me, I will not bring the evil in his days, but in his son's days,' v. 29 – he was spared the anguish of witnessing the slaughter of his children and the complete extermination of his house. But there was no repeal of the Divine sentence upon himself. Nor was the king able to avoid God's stroke, though he made attempt to do so, 22. 30. The Lord had said 'in the place where dogs licked the blood of Naboth shall dogs lick thy blood,' 21. 19, and we are told 'so the king died, and was brought to Samaria; and they buried the king in Samaria. And one washed the chariot in the pool of Samaria; and the dogs licked up his blood; and they washed his armour, according unto the word of the Lord,' vv. 37, 38. He who sells himself to sin must receive the wages of sin. For the doom which overtook Ahab's family see 2 Kings 9. 25; 10. 6, 7, 13, 14, 17.

'And of Jezebel also spake the Lord, saying. The dogs shall eat Jezebel by the wall of Jezreel,' 21. 23. No vain threats were those which the prophet uttered, but announcements of Divine judgment which were fulfilled not long after. Jezebel outlived her husband for some years but her end was just as Elijah had foretold. True to her depraved character we find that on the very day of her death 'she painted her face, and tired her head, and looked out at a window' to attract attention, 2 Kings 9. 30. It is solemn to observe that God takes note of such things, not with approbation but abhorrence; and it is equally solemn to learn from this passage that those women who paint their faces and go to so much trouble in artificially dressing their hair and seeking to make themselves conspicuous, belong to the same class as this evil queen or 'cursed' creature, v. 34. She was thrown out of the window by some of her own attendants, her blood sprinkling the wall, and her corpse being ruthlessly trampled under foot. A short time after, when orders were given for her burial, so thoroughly had the dogs done their work that naught remained but 'the skull and the feet and the palms of her hands,' 2 Kings 9. 35. God is as faithful and true in making good *His threatenings* as He is in fulfilling His promises.

CHAPTER THIRTY-TWO

Elijah's Last Task

After the death of Ahab the judgments of God began to fall heavily upon his family. Of his immediate successor we are told, 'Ahaziah the son of Ahab began to reign over Israel in Samaria the seventeenth year of the reign of Jehoshaphat king of Judah, and reigned two years over Israel. And he did evil in the sight of the Lord, and walked in the way of his father, and in the way of his mother, and in the way of Jeroboam the son of Nebat, who made Israel to sin: For he served Baal, and worshipped him, and provoked to anger the Lord God of Israel, according to all that his father had done,' 1 Kings 22. 51-53. Unspeakably solemn is that. The three and a half years' famine, the exposure of Baal's impotence, the slaying of his prophets there on Carmel, and the awe-inspiring dealings of God with his father, were all known to Ahaziah, but they produced no salutary effect upon him, for he refused to take them to heart. Heedless of those dire warnings he went on recklessly in sin, continuing to 'serve Baal and worship him.' His heart was fully set in him to do evil, and therefore was he cut off in his youth; nevertheless even in his case mercy was mingled with justice, for 'space for repentance' was granted him ere he was removed from this scene.

'Then Moab rebelled against Israel after the death of Ahab,' 2 Kings 1. 1. In fulfilment of Balaam's prophecy, Num. 24. 17, David had conquered the Moabites so that they became his 'servants,' 2 Sam. 8. 2, and they continued in subjection to the kingdom of Israel until the time of its division, when their vassalage and tribute was transferred to the kings of Israel, as those of Edom remained to the kings of Judah – the tribute which the Moabites rendered unto the king of Israel being 'a hundred thousand lambs and a hundred thousand rams with their wool,' 2 Kings 3. 4. But after the death of Ahab they revolted. Therein we behold the Divine providence crossing Ahaziah in his affairs. This rebellion on the part of Moab should be regarded in the light of 'when a man's ways please the Lord, He maketh even his enemies to be at peace with him,' Prov. 16. 7–but when our ways displease Him, evil from every quarter menaces us. Temporal as well as spiritual prosperity depends entirely on God's blessing. When any behave ill to us it should make us at once examine our conduct toward God. To make His hand more plainly apparent, He frequently punishes the wicked after the similitude of their sins. He did so to Ahab's son. As he had turned from the Lord, Moab was moved to rebel against him.

What has just been pointed out concerns the *governmental* dealings of God and illustrates an important principle in His 'ways' with a nation: by which we mean, it treats of that which relates to time and not to eternity, to the workings of Divine providence and not to the sphere of salvation. Nations as such have only a temporal existence, though the individuals which comprise them have an eternal destiny. The prosperity or adversity of a nation is determined by its attitude and conduct toward God: directly so by those who have His living Oracles in their hands, indirectly so with the heathen – in their case being determined by their conduct toward His people. The Old Testament supplies us with so many examples of this that he who runs may read. The attitude of a nation towards God is to be gauged not so much by the general deportment of its people as by the character of its governors or government. The two are of course intimately related, for where a majority of the subjects are pious, they will not tolerate wickedness in high places, and on the other hand, when those who lead and rule set an evil example, it cannot be expected that those who follow will excel them in righteousness. Whatever be the particular form of government in a country, or whichever party be in power, it is the character and enactments of its executives that are the deciding factor, for they are the ones holding the positions of chief responsibility in the sight of God.

In avowedly 'Christian' countries like Great Britain and the U.S.A., it is the churches which regulate the pulse of the nation. They act as the 'salt' upon the corporate body, and when their ways please the Lord, He gives them favour in the eyes of those round about them. When the Holy Spirit is unhindered, His power is manifested, not only in calling out the elect, but in subduing sin in the non-elect and by causing the machine of state to support godliness, as was more or less noticeably the case a hundred years ago. But when error comes into the churches and discipline is relaxed, the Spirit is grieved and His power is withheld, and the evil effects of this become more and more apparent in the country by a rising tide of lawlessness. If the churches persist in a downward course, then the Spirit is quenched and 'Ichabod' is written over them, as is the case today. Then it is that the restraining hand of God is removed and an orgy of licentiousness comes in. Then it is the government becomes an empty title, for those in power have no power except what the people have delegated to them, and therefore they act in accord with the depraved desires of the masses. This then is ever the order: turning from the true God, turning to false gods, and then the disturbance of the peace – either social revolution or international war.

Ahaziah 'served Baal and worshipped him and provoked to anger the Lord God of Israel.' The Lord God is a jealous God, jealous of His truth, jealous of His honour, and when those calling themselves His people turn unto other gods, His wrath is kindled against them. How many false gods have been worshipped in Christendom during the last few decades! What a travesty of the Divine character has been set forth by the major portion of Protestantism – a 'god' whom no one fears. What a mangling of the Gospel has there been in the 'orthodox' sections of christendom, whereby 'another Jesus,' 2 Cor. 11. 4, has displaced the Christ of Holy Writ. Little wonder that, in the inevitable reaction, the multitudes have made gods of mammon and pleasure and that the nation puts its trust in its armed forces instead of the arm of the Lord. Here and there was an Elijah who raised his voice in testimony to the living God and in denouncing modern forms of

Baal worship, but who gave ear to them? Certainly not the churches, for they closed their pulpits against them so that, like the Tishbite of old, they were forced into isolation and virtual retirement; and now it seems their last task before God calls them hence is to pronounce sentence of death upon the whole apostate system.

'And provoked to anger the Lord God of Israel . . . Then Moab rebelled against Israel.' Though those two statements are separated by the ending of the first book of Kings and the beginning of the second, yet the connection between them is too obvious to be missed. It is the connection of cause and effect, the latter making manifest the former. For many years Moab had been tributary to Israel but now it threw off the yoke. And have we not lived to witness a similar thing with the British Empire? One country after another has severed ties with Britain and become independent. The Bible is no defunct book recording historical events of the remote past, but a living book, enunciating vital principles applicable to every age and describing things as they are today. History repeats itself, not only because human nature is fundamentally the same in all ages, but also because the 'ways' of God, the principles of His government, remain unchanged. As the Lord God was provoked by Ahaziah, so He has been provoked by the churches, the politicians and the people of Great Britain, and as His anger was evidenced by His moving Moab to seek her independence, so His displeasure is now seen in His causing one dependency after another to break away from the 'Mother country.'

'And Ahaziah fell down through a lattice in his upper chamber that was in Samaria, and was sick,' v. 2. First, we would note that this verse opens with the word 'And,' which appears to intimate the king's response or rather lack of response to what is recorded in the previous verse. What is *not* found here is solemn and informative, revealing as it does the character of Ahaziah. There was no turning to the Lord for guidance and help. There was no humbling of himself before God and inquiring why this disturbance had entered his realm. Nothing happens by chance, and the curse causeless does not come, Prov. 26. 2, therefore the king's duty was to fast and pray and ascertain what it was that had displeased the Lord. No, we take that back: it would have been downright mockery for him to have done any such thing. There was no need to inquire of the Lord: the king *knew* quite well what was wrong – he was serving and worshipping Baal, and until his idols were abolished it would be nothing but play-acting, a pious farce, for him to call upon the name of the Lord. Does the reader agree? *Does he?* Does she? If not, carefully re-read this paragraph. If you concur, is not the application to our own national situation clearly apparent? Unspeakably solemn – yes; indescribably awful – yes. But if we face facts, things as they really are, the conclusion is unescapable.

Let us call attention to another factor which is absent from verse 2. Ahaziah not only failed spiritually but naturally too. What ought to have been his reaction to this revolt of Moab? Why, to have dealt with it with a firm hand and nipped it in the bud. That was obviously his duty as king. Instead he followed the line of least resistance and devoted himself to pleasure. Instead of taking his place at the head of his army and putting down this rebellion by force, he seems to have luxuriated in the palace. Must we not say in such circumstances, that God had given him up to a spirit of madness! He shrank in cowardly fear from the camp and the dangers of the field, and leaving Moab to do as she pleased, without attempting her re-subjugation, led a life of self-indulgence. Perhaps he recalled the fate which had so recently overtaken his father on the battlefield and decided that 'discretion is the better part of valour.' But there is no escaping the hand of God when He is determined to smite: we are just as liable to meet with an 'accident' in the shelter of our home as if we were exposed to the deadliest weapons on the battlefield.

'And Ahaziah fell down through a lattice in his upper chamber that was in Samaria, and was sick.' Here was where mercy was mingled with justice: here was where 'space for repentance' was granted the idolatrous king. O how long-suffering is God! Ahaziah's fall did not prove immediately fatal, though it placed him on a bed of sickness, where he had opportunity to 'consider his ways.' And how often the Lord deals thus, both with nations and with individuals. The Roman empire was not built in a day, nor was it destroyed in a day. Many a blatant rebel against Heaven has been pulled up suddenly in his evil career. An 'accident' overtook him, and though it may have deprived him of a limb, yet not of his life. Such may have been the experience of someone who reads these lines. If so, we would say to him with all earnestness, Redeem the time that is now left you. You might now be in hell, but God has given you a further season (brief at the most) to think of eternity and prepare for it. O that His goodness may lead you to repentance! Today, if ye will hear His voice, harden not your heart. Throw down the weapons of your warfare against Him and be reconciled to Him, for how shall you escape the everlasting burnings if you neglect His so-great salvation?

'And he sent messengers and said unto them, Go, inquire of Baal-zebub the god of Ekron whether I shall recover of this disease,' v. 2. First, God had crossed him in his affairs, and then He smote him in his body. We have called attention to what this evil king did not do, now we turn to consider the course which he actually followed. Neither of those judgments softened him, and having lived without God in prosperity, so in adversity he despised His chastening hand. Saul in his extremity had inquired of a witch, only to hear of his immediate doom. So Ahaziah now had recourse to the demon-gods of the heathen. He was evidently uneasy at the present state of his health, so sent some of his servants to ascertain of an idolatrous oracle whether or no he should recover from this affliction – proof that his soul was in a worse state than his body. The 'Baalim' was a general epithet for the false gods, each having his own peculiar office and district, hence the distinguishing titles of Baal-zebub, Baal-peor, Baal-zephon, Baal-berith. 'Baal-zebub' was the idol of Ekron, a city of Philistia, a country noted for 'sooth-sayers,' Isa. 2. 6.

This 'Baal-zebub' signifies 'The lord of a fly or flies,' probably because, since their country was infested with flies (as modern travellers still report), they supposed he protected them from the diseases which they spread. In Matthew 12. 24 we find our Lord terming Beelzebub (the Greek form of spelling) 'the prince of the demons,' which intimates that under various names and images evil spirits were actually worshipped as gods by the heathen – as is plainly stated in 1 Corinthians 10. 20: 'the things which the Gentiles sacrifice they sacrifice to *demons* and not to God.' It would appear that at the time of Ahaziah the priests of Baal had through their incantations of evil spirits acquired celebrity for their knowledge of future events, much as the oracle of Delphi was held in high repute in Greece some years later. Believing that the idol at Ekron could foresee and foretell things to come, Ahaziah paid him homage. The exceeding sinfulness of such practices is placed beyond dispute by such passages as Leviticus 20. 6, 27; Deuteronomy 18. 10; 1 Chronicles 10. 13. Thus those who consult fortune-tellers, astrologers and 'spiritualists' are guilty of a fearful sin, and expose themselves unto the powers of evil.

'When a king of Israel sent to inquire of a heathen oracle, he proclaimed to the Gentiles his want of confidence in Jehovah: as if the only nation favoured with the knowledge of the true God had been the only nation in which no God was known. This was peculiarly dishonourable and provoking to Jehovah' (Thomas Scott). The action of Ahaziah was indeed a deliberate and public rejection of the Lord, a defiant choice of those ways which had called down the wrath of Heaven upon his father. It could not pass unnoticed, and accordingly He who is King of kings, as well as the God of Israel, specifically calls him to account. Elijah was sent to meet the king's messengers as they went speeding on their way from Samaria, with the announcement of certain death: 'But the angel of the Lord said to Elijah the Tishbite, Arise, go up to meet the messengers of the king of Samaria, and say unto them, Is it not because there is not a God in Israel that ye go to inquire of Baal-zebub the god of Ekron?' v. 3. Nothing escapes the observation of Him with whom we have to do. His eyes are ever upon all the ways of men, whether they be monarchs or menials: none are too high or independent to be above His control, and none are too low or insignificant to be overlooked by Him. All we do or say or think is perfectly known to the Lord, and in that Day we shall be called upon to render a full account.

'But the angel of the Lord said to Elijah the Tishbite, Arise, go up to meet the messengers of the king of Samaria, and say unto them, Is it not because there is not a God in Israel, that ye go to inquire of Baal-zebub the god of Ekron,' v. 3. The Hebrew is more expressive and emphatic than the English: 'Is it because there is no God, none in Israel' that you turn for information to the emissaries of Satan? Not only had the true and living God made Himself known to Israel, but He was in *covenant relationship* with them. This it is which explains 'the angel of the Lord' addressing Himself to Elijah on this occasion, emphasizing as it did that blessed relationship which the king was repudiating – it was the Angel of the Covenant, Ex. 23. 23, etc. As such, Jehovah had given clear demonstration of Himself to Ahaziah in his own lifetime.

'Now therefore thus saith the Lord, Thou shalt not come down from that bed on which thou art gone up, but shalt surely die,' v. 4. Having reproved the awful sin of Ahaziah, the servant of God now pronounces judgment on him. Here then was the last and solemn task of Elijah, to pass the capital sentence upon the apostate king. Unto the widow of Zarephath God had made him 'the savour of life unto life,' but unto Ahab and now to his son he became 'the savour of death unto death.' Varied indeed are the tasks assigned unto the ministers of the Gospel, according as they are called upon to comfort God's people and feed His sheep, or warn the wicked and denounce evildoers. Thus it was with their great Exemplar: both benedictions and maledictions were found on His lips; though most congregations are far more familiar with the former than the latter. Yet it will be found that His 'Blesseds' in Matthew 5 are balanced by an equal number of 'Woes' in Matthew 23. It should be duly noted that those 'woes' were uttered by the Lord Jesus at *the close* of His public ministry, and though the end of the world may not be at hand (no one on earth knows) yet it seems evident that the end of the present 'order' of things, 'civilization,' is imminent, and therefore the servants of Christ have a thankless task before them today. O that grace may preserve them 'faithful unto death'!

CHAPTER THIRTY-THREE

The Minister of Vengeance

'And Elijah departed,' 2 Kings 1. 4. At his Master's bidding, the prophet had gone forth to meet the servants of Ahaziah and delivered what the Lord had commissioned him, and had sent them back with this message to their king, and then took his leave of them. His departure was not for the purpose of concealing himself but to return to his communion with God. It was to 'the top of a hill,' v. 9, that he retired: typically it spoke of moral separation from, and elevation above, the world. We have to betake ourselves to 'the secret place of the Most High' – and this is not to be found near the giddy and bustling crowds – if we are to 'abide under the shadow of the Almighty,' Psa. 91. 1; it is from the mercyseat *His* voice is heard speaking, Num. 7. 89. On a previous occasion we have seen Elijah making for the mountaintop as soon as his public work was completed, 1 Kings 18. 42. What an object lesson is there here for all the servants of Christ: when they have delivered their message, to retire from the public eye and get alone with God, as their Saviour before them was wont to do. The 'top of the hill' is also the place of observation and vision: O to make spiritual observatories of our private rooms!

There is nothing in the sacred narrative which indicates the nationality of these messengers of Ahaziah. If they were Israelites they could scarcely be ignorant of the prophet's identity when he so suddenly accosted them and so dramatically announced the doom of their master. If they were foreigners, imported from Tyre by Jezebel, they were probably ignorant of the mighty Tishbite, for some years had elapsed since his last public appearance. Whoever they were, these men were so impressed by that commanding figure and his authoritative tone, so awed by his knowledge of their mission and so terrified by his pronouncement, that they at once abandoned their quest and returned to the king. He who could tell what Ahaziah thought and said could evidently foretell the outcome of his sickness: they dared not proceed on their journey to Ekron. That illustrated an important principle. When a servant of God is energized by an ungrieved Spirit, his message carries conviction and strikes terror into the hearts of his hearers: just as Herod 'feared' John the Baptist, Mark 6. 20, and Felix 'trembled' before Paul, Acts 24. 25. But it is not talking to the wicked about the *love of God* which will produce such effects, nor will such conscience-soothers be owned of Heaven. Rather is it those who declare, as Elijah of Ahaziah, 'Thou shalt surely die.'

'And when the messengers turned back unto him, he said unto them, Why are ye now turned back?' v. 5. It must have been both a surprise and a shock to the king when his servants returned unto him so quickly, for he knew that sufficient time had not elapsed for them to have journeyed to Ekron in Philistia and back again. His question expresses annoyance, a reprimand for their being remiss in discharging his commission. Kings in that day were accustomed to receive blind obedience from their subjects, and woe be unto those who crossed their imperial wills. This only serves to emphasize the effect which the appearance and words of Elijah made upon them. From the next verse we learn that the prophet had bidden them, 'Go turn again unto the king that sent you' and repeat my message unto him. And though their so doing meant placing their lives in jeopardy, nevertheless they carried out the prophet's order. How they put to shame thousands of those professing to be the servants of Christ who for many years past have studiously withheld that which their auditors most needed to hear and criminally substituted a message of 'Peace, peace' when there was no peace for them, and that in days when a faithful proclamation of the truth had not endangered their persons. Surely these messengers of Ahaziah will yet rise up in judgment against all such faithless time-servers.

'And they said unto him, There came a man up to meet us and

said unto us, Go, turn again unto the king that sent you and say unto him, Thus saith the Lord, Is it not because there is not a God in Israel that thou sendest to inquire of Baal-zebub the god of Ekron? therefore thou shalt not come down from that bed on which thou art gone up, but shalt surely die,' v. 6. From their omission of his name and by referring to Elijah simply as 'a man' it seems clear that these messengers of the king were ignorant of the prophet's identity. But they had been so overawed by his appearance and the solemnity of his manner, and were so convinced his announcement would be verified, that they deemed themselves warranted in abandoning their journey and returning to their master. Accordingly they delivered a plain straightforward account of what had occurred and faithfully reported Elijah's pronouncement. They knew full well that such a message must prove most unwelcome to the king, yet they made no attempt to alter its tone or soften it down. They shrank not from telling Ahaziah to his face that sentence of death had gone out against him. Again we say, How these men put to shame the temporizing, cowardly and pew-flattering occupants of the pulpit. Alas, how often is more sincerity and fidelity to be found among open worldlings than in those with the highest spiritual pretensions.

'And he said unto them, What manner of man was he which came up to meet you and told you these words?' v. 7. No doubt the king was fairly well convinced as to who it was that had dared to cross their path and send him such a message, but to make quite sure he bids his servants describe the mysterious stranger: what was his appearance, how was he clothed, and in what manner did he address you? How that illustrates one of the chief traits of the unregenerate: it was not the *message* which Ahaziah now inquired about, but the *man* who uttered it – yet surely his own conscience would warn him that no mere man could be the author of such a message. And is not this the common tendency of the unconverted: that instead of taking to heart *what* is said, they fix their attention on *who* says it. Such is poor fallen human nature. When a true servant of God is sent and delivers a searching word, people seek to evade it by occupying themselves with his personality, his style of delivery, his denominational affiliation – anything secondary as long as it serves to crowd out that which is of supreme moment. Yet when the postman hands them an important business letter they are not concerned about his appearance.

'And they answered him, He was a hairy man, and girt with a girdle of leather about his loins,' v. 8. We do not regard this as a description of his person so much as of his attire. Concerning John the Baptist, who came 'in the spirit and power of Elijah,' Luke 1. 17, it is recorded that he 'had his raiment of camel's hair and a leathern girdle about his loins,' Matt. 3. 4. Thus we understand that the outward garment of Elijah was made of skins, cf. Heb. 11. 37, girded about by a strip of undressed leather. That the prophets had some such distinguishing garb is clear from Zechariah 13. 4, by the false prophets assuming the same in order to beguile the people: 'a garment of hair to deceive.' In that era when instruction was given to the eye as well as the ear, by symbols and shadows, that uncouth dress denoted the prophet's mortification to the world, and expressed his concern and sorrow for the idolatry and iniquity of his people, just as the putting on of 'sackcloth' by others signified humility and grief. For other references to the symbolic meaning of the prophet's dress and actions compare 1 Kings 11. 28-31; 22. 11; Acts 21. 10, 11.

'And he said, It is Elijah the Tishbite,' v. 8. There could be no mistake: the king knew now who it was that had sent such a solemn message to him. And what effect was produced upon him? Was he awed and humbled? Did he now bewail his sins and cry unto God for mercy? Far from it. He had learned nothing from his father's awful end. The severe affliction under which he was suffering softened him not. Even the near approach of death made no difference. He was incensed against the prophet and determined to destroy him. Had Elijah sent him a lying and flattering word, that had been acceptable, but the truth he could not bear. How like the degenerate generation in which our lot is cast, who had rather be bombed to death in places of amusement than be found on their faces before God. Ahaziah was young and arrogant, not at all disposed to receive reproof or endure opposition to his will, no matter from what quarter it proceeded, no, not even from Jehovah Himself. The message from Elijah, though in God's name and by His express command, enraged the monarch beyond measure, and instantly he resolves on the death of the prophet, though he had done nothing more than his duty.

'Then the king sent unto him a captain of fifty with his fifty. And he went up to him: and behold, he sat on the top of a hill. And he spake unto him, Thou man of God, the king hath said, Come down,' v. 9. Ahaziah was at no loss to find wicked men ready to execute the most desperate and impious orders. This company of soldiers went forth promptly to seize the Lord's servant. They found him sitting composedly upon an eminence. The spirit of the captain evidenced that his heart was thoroughly in his task, for he insolently addressed Elijah as 'thou man of God,' which was by way of derision and insult. It was as though he had said, Thou claimest Jehovah as thy Master, we come to thee in the name of a greater than he: King Ahaziah says, Come down! Fearful effrontery and blasphemy was that! It was not only an insult to Elijah, but to Elijah's God, an insult which was not suffered to go unchallenged. How often in the past have the wicked made a mock at sacred things and turned the very terms by which God designates His people into epithets of reproach, sneeringly dubbing them 'the elect,' 'saints,' etc. That they do so no longer is because the fine gold has become dim; godliness is no more a reality and a rebuke to the impious. Who would think of designating the average clergyman a 'man of God?' Rather does he wish to be known as 'a good mixer,' a man of the world.

'And Elijah answered and said to the captain of fifty, If I be a man of God, then let fire come down from heaven, and consume thee and thy fifty,' v. 10. There was no personal vindictiveness in the terrible reply of Elijah, but a consuming zeal for the glory of God, which had been so blatantly insulted by this captain. The king's agent had jibed at his being a 'man of God,' and now he should be furnished with summary proof whether or no the Maker of heaven and earth owned the prophet as His servant. The insolence and impiety of this man who had insulted Jehovah and His ambassador should meet with swift judgment. 'And there came down fire from heaven and consumed him and his fifty,' v. 10. Sure sign was this that Elijah had not been actuated by any spirit of revenge, for in such a case God had not responded to his appeal. On an earlier occasion the 'fire of the Lord' had fallen upon and consumed the sacrifice, 1 Kings 18. 38, but here it falls on sinners who had slighted that sacrifice. So shall it again be when 'the Lord Jesus shall be revealed from heaven with His mighty angels, in flaming fire taking vengeance on them that know not God and that obey not the Gospel of our Lord Jesus Christ,' 2 Thess. 1. 7, 8.

Surely so manifest an interposition of God would serve as a deterrent, if not to the abandoned king yet to his servants, so that no further attempt would be made to apprehend Elijah. But no: 'Again also he sent unto him another captain of fifty with his fifty. And he answered and said unto him, O man of God, thus hath the king said, Come down quickly,' v. 11. It is hard to say which, on this occasion, was the more remarkable, the madness of the wounded Ahaziah when the report of the awful event reached him, or the presumption of this officer and his soldiers. This second captain took no warning from what had befallen the first and his soldiers. Was the calamity which overtook them attributed to chance, to some lightning or fireball happening to consume them, or was he recklessly determined to brave things out? Like his predecessor he addressed the prophet in the language of insulting derision, though using more peremptory terms than the former: 'Come down quickly.' See once more how sin hardens the heart and ripens men for judgment. And who maketh *thee* to differ? To what desperate lengths might the writer and the reader have gone if the mercy of God had not interposed and stopped us in our mad career! O what praise is due unto sovereign grace which snatched me as a brand from the burning!

'And Elijah answered and said unto them, If I be a man of God, let fire come down from heaven and consume thee and thy fifty,' v. 12. Proof had already been given that Jehovah was omniscient, v. 4, now they should know He is omnipotent. What is man in the hands of his Maker? One flash of lightning and fifty-one of His enemies become burnt stubble. And if all the hosts of Israel, yea the entire human race, had been assembled there, it had needed no other force. Then what folly it is for him whose breath is in his nostrils to contend with the Almighty: 'Woe unto him that striveth with his Maker,' Isa. 45. 9. Some have blamed Elijah for destroying those men, overlooking the fact that *he* could no more bring down fire from heaven than *they* can. Elijah simply announced on these occasions what God had Himself determined to do. Nor was it to please the prophet that the Lord acted, or to gratify any vindictive passion in Himself, but to show forth His power and justice. It cannot be said the soldiers were innocent, for they were performing no military duty, but openly fighting against Heaven – as the language of the third captain indicates. This has been recorded as a lasting warning for all ages, that those who mock at and persecute God's faithful ministers will not escape His punishment. On the other hand, those who have befriended them shall by no means lose their reward.

'And he sent again a captain of the third fifty with his fifty,' v. 13. What fearful obstinacy is there here. Deliberately hardening his heart, Ahaziah strengthened himself against the Almighty and makes one more attempt to do the prophet harm. Though on his death-bed, and knowing the Divine judgment which had befallen two companies of his soldiers (as v. 14 intimates), yet he persists in stretching forth his hand against Jehovah's anointed, and exposes to destruction another of his captains with his body of men. So true are those words of Holy Writ, 'Though thou shouldest bray a fool in a mortar among wheat with a pestle, yet will not his foolishness depart from him,' Prov. 27. 22. And why is this? Because 'the heart of the sons of men is full of evil, and madness is in their heart while they live,' Eccl. 9. 3. In view of such unerring declarations, and with such examples as Pharaoh, Ahab and Ahaziah before us, we ought not to be in the least surprised or startled by what we see and read of what is taking place in the world today. Saddened and solemnized we should be, but not staggered and nonplussed.

'And the third captain of fifty went up, and came and fell on his knees before Elijah, and besought him and said unto him, O man of God, I pray thee, let my life and the life of these fifty thy servants be precious in thy sight. Behold, there came fire down from heaven and burnt up the two captains of the former fifties with their fifties: therefore let my life now be precious in thy sight,' vv. 13, 14. This man was of a different disposition from the two who had preceded him: even in the military forces God has a remnant according to the election of grace. Daring not to attempt anything against Elijah, he employed humble submission and fervent entreaties, with every expression of respect. It was an affecting appeal, a real prayer. He attributed the death of the previous companies to its true cause and appears to have had an awful sense of the justice of God. He owns that their lives lay at the prophet's mercy and begs they may be spared. Thus did Jehovah provide not only for the security but also the honour of Elijah, as He did for Moses when Pharaoh had threatened to put him to death, Ex. 11. 8. The appeal of this captain was not in vain. Our God is ever ready to forgive the humble suppliant, however rebellious he may have been, and the way to prevail with Him is to bow before Him.

'And the angel of the Lord said unto Elijah, Go down with him: be not afraid of him,' v. 15. This clearly demonstrates that Elijah waited for the Divine impulse and was entirely guided by it in the former instances of severity. Neither God nor His servant could have any pleasure in taking away the lives of those who approached them in a becoming manner. It was to punish them for their scorn and impiety that the others had been slain. But this captain came with fear and trembling, not with ill-will to the prophet nor contempt for his Master. Accordingly he found mercy and favour: not only were their lives preserved, but the captain succeeds in his errand – Elijah shall go with him to the king. Those who humble themselves shall be exalted, whereas those who exalt themselves shall be abased. Let us learn from Elijah's example to deal kindly toward those who may have been employed against us, when they evidence their repentance and entreat our clemency. Mark it was 'the angel of the Lord' who again addressed the prophet: but what a test of his obedience and courage! The Tishbite had greatly exasperated Jezebel and her party, and now her reigning son must have been furious at him. Nevertheless he might safely venture into the presence of his raging foes seeing that the Lord had bidden him do so, with the assurance, 'Be not afraid.' They could not move a finger against him without God's permission. God's people are quite safe in His hands, and faith may ever appropriate the triumphant language of Psalm 27. 1-3.

'And he arose and went down with him unto the king,' v. 15, readily and boldly, not fearing his wrath. He made no objection and indicated no fear for his safety: though the king was enraged and would be surrounded by numerous attendants, he committed himself to the Lord and felt safe under His promise and protection. What a striking instance of the prophet's faith and obedience to God. But Elijah did not go to confront the king until bidden by the Lord to do so, teaching His servants not to act presumptuously by recklessly and needlessly exposing themselves unto danger: but as soon as He required it he went promptly, encouraging us to follow the leadings of Providence, trusting God in the way of duty and saying, 'The Lord is my helper, I will not fear what man shall do unto me,' Heb. 13. 6.

'And he said unto him, Thus saith the Lord,' etc. v. 16. Elijah now repeats to the king, without any alteration, what he had said to his servants. Without fear or mincing the matter, the prophet spoke God's word plainly and faithfully to Ahaziah; in the name of Him in whose hands are both life and death, he reproved the monarch for his sin and then pronounced sentence on him. What an awful message for him to receive: that he should go from his bed to hell. Having discharged his commission, the Tishbite departed without molestation. Enraged as were Jezebel and her party, the king and his attendants, they were as meek as lambs and as silent as statues. The prophet went in and out among them with perfect safety, receiving no more harm than Daniel when cast into the lions' den, because he trusted in God. Let this cause us to go forth firmly but humbly in the discharge of our duty. 'So he died according to the word of the Lord which Elijah had spoken,' v. 17.

CHAPTER THIRTY-FOUR

Elijah's Departure

The departure of Elijah from this world was even more striking and remarkable than had been his entrance upon the stage of public action, yet the supernatural character of his exit was but the fitting finale to such a meteoric course. No ordinary career was his, and no commonplace end to it would have seemed suitable. Miracle had attended him wherever he had gone, and a miracle brought about his departure from this scene. He had ministered during stormy times; again and again did he call down Divine judgments upon the heads of evil-doers, and at the last a 'whirlwind' carried *him* away from this earth. In answer to his prayer 'the fire of the Lord' had fallen upon Mount Carmel, and again on those who sought to take his life, 2 Kings 1. 12, and at the close 'a chariot of fire and horses of fire' parted him asunder from Elisha. At the beginning of his dramatic career he declared, 'The Lord God of Israel, before whom I stand,' 1 Kings 17. 1, and at its conclusion he was mysteriously rapt into His immediate presence without passing through the portals of death. Before looking more closely at that startling exit, let us briefly review his life, summarize its principal features, and seek to mark its leading lessons.

The life of Elijah was not the career of some supernatural being who tabernacled among men for a brief season: he was no angelic creature in human form. It is true that nothing is recorded of his parentage, his birth or early life, but the concept of any super-human origin is entirely excluded by that expression of the Holy Spirit's, 'Elijah was a *man*, subject to like passions as we are,' James 5. 17. He, too, was a fallen descendant of Adam harassed by the same depraved inclinations, subject to the same temptations, annoyed by the same devil, meeting with the same trials and oppositions as both writer and reader experience. Yet did he trust in the same Saviour, walk by the same faith, and have all his needs supplied by the same gracious and faithful God as it is our privilege to do. A study of his life is particularly pertinent today, for our lot is cast in times which closely resemble those which he encountered. Varied and valuable are the lessons which his life illustrated and exemplified, the chief of which we have sought to point out in this book. Our present task is to summarize the leading points among them.

1. *Elijah was a man who walked by faith and not by sight,* and walking by faith is not a mystical or nebulous thing but an intensely practical experience. Faith does more than rest upon the bare letter of Scripture: it brings the living God into a scene of death, and enables its possessor to endure by 'seeing Him who is invisible.' Where faith is really in exercise, it looks beyond distressing and distracting circumstances and is occupied with Him who regulates all circumstances. It was faith in God which enabled Elijah to sojourn by the brook Cherith, there to be fed by the ravens. The sceptic supposes that faith is mere credulity or a species of religious fanaticism, for he knows not of the sure foundation on which it rests. The Lord had told His servant, 'I have commanded the ravens to feed thee there,' and the prophet 'judged Him faithful who had promised,' and therefore he was not put to confusion. And that is recorded for *our* encouragement. Faith looks beyond the promise to the Promiser, and God never fails those who trust alone in Him and rely fully upon Him.

It was faith which had moved Elijah to sojourn with the desolate widow of Zarephath, when she and her son were at the point of starvation. To natural instincts it seemed cruel to impose himself upon her, to carnal reason it appeared a suicidal policy. But Jehovah had said 'I have commanded a widow woman to sustain thee there' and the prophet 'staggered not at the promise of God through unbelief.' Ah, faith looks to and counts upon the living God with whom nothing is too hard. Nothing, my reader, honours God so much as faith in Himself, and nothing so dishonours Him as our unbelief. It was by faith that Elijah returned to Jezreel and bearded the lion in his den, telling Ahab to his face his impending doom, and announcing the awful judgment which would surely seize upon his wife. 'Faith cometh by hearing, and hearing by the word of God,' Rom. 10. 17: Elijah heard, believed and acted. Yes, *acted*, for a faith without works is but a dead and worthless one. Obedience is nothing but faith in exercise, directed by the Divine authority, responding to the Divine will.

2. *Elijah was a man who walked in manifest separation from the evil around him.* Alas, the policy prevailing in Christendom today is to walk arm in arm with the world, to be a 'good mixer' if you wish to win the young people. It is argued that we cannot expect them to ascend to the spiritual plane, so the only way for the Christian to reach and help them is by descending to theirs. But such reasoning as 'Let us do evil that good may come' finds no support in the Word of God, but rather emphatic refutation and condemnation. 'Be not unequally yoked together with unbelievers,' 2 Cor. 6. 14, 'have no fellowship with the unfruitful works of darkness,' Eph. 5. 11, are the peremptory demands. 'Know ye not that the friendship of the world is enmity with God? whosoever therefore will be a friend of the world is the enemy of God,' James 4. 4 – as true in this twentieth century as in the first, for it is never right to do wrong. God has not called His people to 'win the world to Christ': rather does He require them, by their lives, to witness against it.

Nothing is more marked about Elijah than his uncompromising separation from the abounding evil all around him. We never find him fraternizing with the people of his degenerate day, but constantly reproving them. He was indeed a 'stranger and pilgrim' here. No doubt many considered him selfish and unsociable, and probably charged him with assuming an 'I am holier than thou' attitude. Ah, Christian reader, you must not expect mere religionists, empty professors, to appreciate your motives or understand your ways: 'the world knoweth us not,' 1 John 3. 1. God leaves His people here to witness for Christ, and the only way to do that is to walk with Christ. Thus we are bidden to 'go forth therefore unto Him without the camp, bearing His reproach,' Heb. 13. 13: we cannot walk with Christ except we be where His Spirit is – outside the apostate mass, apart from all that dishonours and disowns the Lord Jesus; and that inevitably involves 'bearing His reproach.'

3. *Elijah was a man of marked elevation of spirit.* Possibly that expression is a new one to some of our readers, yet its meaning is more or less obvious. That which we make reference to was symbolized by the fact that the prophet is seen again and again 'on the mount.' The first mention of him, 1 Kings 17. 1, tells us that he was 'of the inhabitants of Gilead,' which was a hilly section of the country. His memorable victory over the false prophets of Baal was upon mount Carmel. After his slaughter of them at the brook Kishon, and his brief word to the king, we are told that 'Ahab went up to eat and drink' whereas Elijah 'went up to the top of Carmel,' 18. 42 – which at once revealed their respective characters. When the Lord recovered him from his lapse we read that he 'went in the strength of that meat forty days and forty nights unto Horeb the mount of God,' 1 Kings 19. 8. After he had delivered his message to Ahaziah, it is recorded, 'behold, he sat on the top of a hill,' 2 Kings 1. 9. Thus Elijah was markedly the man of the mount. Now there is a mystical or spiritual significance in that, apparent unto an anointed eye, which we have termed elevation of spirit.

By elevation of spirit we mean heavenly-mindedness, the heart being raised above the poor things of this world, the affections being set upon things above. This is ever one of the effects or fruits of walking by faith, for faith has God for its object, and He dwells on high. The more our hearts are occupied with Him whose throne is in heaven, the more are our spirits elevated above the earth. The more our minds are engaged with the perfections of Him who is altogether lovely, the less will the things of time and sense have power to attract us. The more we dwell in the secret place of the Most High, the less will the baubles of men charm us. The same feature comes out prominently in the life of Christ: He was pre-eminently the Man of the Mount. His first sermon was delivered from one. He spent whole nights there. He was transfigured upon 'the holy mount.' He ascended from the mount of Olives. 'They that wait upon the Lord shall renew their strength; they shall mount up with wings as eagles,' Isa. 40. 31 – their bodies on earth, their hearts in heaven.

4. *Elijah was a mighty intercessor*. Let it be pointed out that none but one who walks by faith, who is in marked separation from evil around him, and who is characterized by elevation of spirit or heavenly-mindedness, is qualified for such holy work. The prevalency of Elijah's intercession is recorded not only for our admiration but emulation. Nothing is more calculated to encourage and embolden the Christian in his approaches to the throne of grace than to mark and recall how frail mortals like himself, unworthy and unprofitable sinners, supplicated God in the hour of need and obtained miraculous supplies from Him. God delights for us to put Him to the test, and therefore has He said, 'All things are possible to him that believeth,' Mark 9. 23. Wondrously was that exemplified in the life of Elijah, and so should it be in ours too. But we shall never have power in prayer while we give way to an evil heart of unbelief, or fraternize with religious hypocrites, or while we are absorbed with the things of time and sense. Faith, fidelity and spirituality are necessary qualifications.

In answer to the intercession of Elijah the heavens were shut up for three years and a half, so that it rained not at all. This teaches us that the supreme motive behind all our supplications must be the glory of God and the good of His people – the chief lessons inculcated by Christ in the family prayer. It also teaches that there are times when the servant of God may request his Master to deal in judgment with his enemies. Drastic diseases call for drastic remedies. There are times when it is both right and necessary for a Christian to ask God to bring down His chastening rod on His backslidden and wayward people. We read that Paul delivered unto Satan certain ones who had made shipwreck of the faith that they might learn not to blaspheme, 1 Tim. 1. 20. Jeremiah called on the Lord to 'Pour out Thy fury upon the heathen that know Thee not, and upon the families that call not on Thy name,' 10. 25.

The Lord Jesus interceded not only for 'His own,' but also *against* Judas and his family, Psa. 109.

But there is a brighter side to the efficacy of Elijah's intercession than the one contemplated in the preceding paragraph. It was in answer to his prayer that the widow's son was restored to life, 1 Kings 17. 19, 22. What a proof was *that* that nothing is too hard for the Lord: that in response to believing supplication He is able and willing to reverse what unto sight seems the most hopeless situation. What possibilities to trustful and importunate prayer does that present! Man's extremity is indeed God's opportunity – to show Himself strong on our behalf. But let it not be forgotten that behind the prophet's intercession there was a higher motive than the comforting of the widow's heart: it was that his Master might be glorified – vindicated in the claims made by His servant. Ah, that is so important, though generally overlooked. Christian parents reading this chapter are most desirous that their children should be saved, and pray daily for that end. Why? Is it only that they may have the comforting assurance *their* loved ones have been delivered from the wrath to come? Or, is it that *God* may be honoured by their regeneration?

It was in response to Elijah's intercession that the fire came down from heaven and consumed the sacrifice. Here, too, his petition was based on the plea for the Lord to vindicate His great and holy name before the vast assembly of His vacillating people and the heathen idolaters: 'let it be known this day that Thou art God in Israel,' 1 Kings 18. 36. As we pointed out in an earlier chapter, that 'fire of the Lord' was not only a solemn type of the Divine wrath smiting Christ when bearing the sins of His people, but it was also a dispensational foreshadowing of the public descent of the Holy Spirit on the day of Pentecost attesting God's acceptance of the sacrifice of His Son. Thus the practical lesson for us is believingly to pray for more of the Spirit's power and blessing, that we may be favoured with further manifestations of His presence with and in us. That we are warranted in so making request is evidenced by that word of our Lord, 'If ye then, being evil, know how to give good gifts unto your children, how much more shall your heavenly Father give the Holy Spirit to them that ask Him?' Luke 11. 13. Pray for faith to lay hold of that promise.

So, too, it was in answer to the prophet's intercession that the terrible drought was ended: 'He prayed again, and the heaven gave rain, and the earth brought forth her fruit,' James 5. 18. The spiritual meaning and application of that is obvious. For many years past the churches have been in a parched and languishing condition. This was evident from the varied expedients they resorted to in the attempt to 'revive' and strengthen them. Even where carnal means were not employed with the object of attracting outsiders, religious 'specialists' in the form of 'successful evangelists' or 'renowned Bible teachers' were called in to aid in extra meetings – as sure a sign of the churches' ill-health as the summoning of a doctor. But artificial stimulants soon lose their efficacy, and unless his health is restored by ordinary means, leave the patient worse than before. So it has been with the churches, until their dry and dead condition is apparent even to themselves. Yet, unless the end of the world be upon us, showers of blessing will yet descend (though possibly in different parts of the earth than formerly), and they will come (at their appointed time) in answer to some Elijah's prayer!

5. *Elijah was a man of intrepid courage*, by which we mean not a natural bravery but spiritual boldness. That distinction is an important one, yet it is rarely recognized. Few today seem capacitated to discriminate between what is of the flesh and what is wrought by the Spirit. No doubt the prevailing habit of defining Bible terms by the dictionary rather than from their usage in Holy Writ, adds much to the confusion. Take for example the grace of spiritual patience: how often is it confounded with an even and placid temperament, and because they possess not such a natural disposition, many of the Lord's people imagine they have no patience at all. The patience of which the Holy Spirit is the Author is not a calm equanimity which never gets irritated by delays, nor is it that gentle graciousness which bears insults and injuries without retaliation or even murmuring – rather is *that* much closer akin to *meekness*. How many have been puzzled by those words,

'Let us run with patience the race set before us,' Heb. 21. 1? They create their own difficulty by assuming that 'patience' is a passive rather than an active grace.

The 'patience' of Christians is not a passive virtue but an active grace, not a natural endowment but a supernatural fruit. It signifies endurance: it is that which enables the saints to persevere in the face of discouragements, to hold on his way despite all opposition. In like manner, Christian 'courage' is not a constitutional endowment but a heavenly enduement: it is not a natural quality but a supernatural thing. 'The wicked flee when no man pursueth (a guilty conscience filling them with terror), but the righteous are bold as a lion,' Prov. 28. 1. He who truly fears God is fearless of man. That spiritual courage or boldness has shone forth in many a weak, timid, shrinking woman. Those who would have trembled at the prospect of walking alone through a cemetery on a dark night, shrank not from confessing Christ when a fiery death was the certain sequel. The boldness of Elijah in denouncing Ahab to his face, and in confronting single-handed his army of false prophets, must not be attributed to his natural constitution but ascribed to the operations of the Holy Spirit.

6. *Elijah was a man who experienced a sad fall*, and this also is recorded for our instruction: not as an excuse for us to shelter behind, but as a solemn warning to take to heart. Few indeed are the recorded blemishes in Elijah's character, yet he did not attain to perfection in this world. Remarkably as he was honoured by his Master, yet sin had not been eradicated from his being. Glorious indeed was the 'treasure' which he bore about, nevertheless God saw fit to make it manifest that an '*earthen vessel*' carried the same. Strikingly, it was in his faith and courage he failed, for he took his eye off the Lord for a brief season and then fled in terror from a woman. What force does that give to the exhortation, 'Wherefore let him that thinketh he standeth take heed lest he fall,' 1 Cor. 10. 12! We are just as dependent upon God for the maintenance of our spiritual graces as we are for the bestowment of them. But though he fell, Elijah was not utterly cast down. Divine grace sought him, delivered him from his despondency, restored him to

the paths of righteousness, and so renewed him in the inner man that he was as faithful and courageous afterward as he had been formerly.

7. *Elijah was a man who had a supernatural exit from this world.* As this will be the subject of the closing chapter, we will not now anticipate our remarks thereon.

CHAPTER THIRTY-FIVE

The Chariot of Fire

After Elijah's interview with king Ahaziah we read no more of him till we come to the closing scene of his earthly career, but from the hints conveyed by the Divine record in 2 Kings 2 we gather that his last days here were not idle ones. If not engaged in anything spectacular and dramatic, he was employed in doing what was good and useful. It would seem that both he and Elisha not only instructed the people in private but also founded and superintended seminaries or schools of the prophets in various parts of the land. By training them to read and teach the Word of God, those young men were prepared for the ministry and to carry on the work of reformation in Israel, and therein the prophets were well employed. Such sacred activity, though less striking to the senses, was of far greater importance, for the effect produced by witnessing supernatural wonders, though stirring at the time, soon wears away, whereas the truth received in the soul abides for ever. The time spent by Christ in training the apostles produced more lasting fruit than the prodigies He performed in the presence of the multitudes.

Elijah had now almost finished his course. The time of his departure was at hand, how then does he occupy his last hours? what does he do in anticipation of the great change impending? Does he shut himself up in a cloister that he may not be disturbed by the world? Does he retire to his chamber that he may devote his last moments to devout meditation and fervent supplication, making his peace with God and preparing to meet his Judge? No, indeed, he had made his peace with God many years before and had lived in blessed communion with Him day after day. As for getting ready to meet his Judge, he had not been so mad as to post-pone that all-important task till the last. He had, by Divine grace, spent his life in walking with God, in performing His bidding, in trusting in His mercy, and in experiencing His favour. Such a man is always getting ready for the great change. It is only the foolish virgins that are without oil when the Bridegroom comes. It is only the worldling and ungodly who put off preparation for eternity till their last moments.

'Dust thou art, and unto dust shalt thou return,' Gen. 3. 19: out of the ground was man's body taken, and because of sin, unto the ground it shall revert. More than three thousand years had passed since that sentence was pronounced against the fallen race, and Enoch had been the only person who was exempted from it: why he, rather than Noah, Abraham, Samuel, should have been so honoured we know not, for the Most High does not always deign to give a reason in explanation of His conduct. He ever does as He pleases, and the exercise of sovereignty marks all His ways. In the saving of souls – exempting sinners from merited condem-nation and conferring unmerited blessings – He divideth to every man severally as He will,' 1 Cor. 12. 11, and none can say Him nay. Thus it is in connection with those whom He spares from the grave. Another was now on the point of being transported bodily to Heaven, but why such peculiar honour should be conferred upon Elijah rather than any other of the prophets we cannot say, and it is idle to speculate.

'And it came to pass, when the Lord would take up Elijah into heaven by a whirlwind, that Elijah went with Elisha from Gilgal,' 2 Kings 2. 1. That the prophet had received previous notification of the Lord's gracious intention to give him a supernatural exit from this world appears by his conduct in going from place to place by Divine direction. 'Gilgal' marked the starting-point of his final journey, and most suitably so. It had been the first stopping-place of Israel after they crossed the Jordan and entered the land of Canaan, Josh 4. 19. It was there the children of Israel pitched their camp and set up the tabernacle. It was there they had 'kept the passover' and 'did eat of the old corn of the land' instead of the manna on which they had so long been miraculously fed, Josh 5. 10-12. 'And Elijah said unto Elisha, Tarry here, I pray thee; for the Lord hath sent me to Bethel,' 2. 2. Various conjectures have been made as to why Elijah would have Elisha now part company with him: that he wished to be alone, that modesty and humility would hide from human eyes the great honour to be bestowed upon him, that he would spare his companion the grief of final departure, that he would test the strength of his attachment and faith – we incline to this last.

'And Elisha said unto him, As the Lord liveth, and as thy soul liveth, I will not leave thee. So they went down to Bethel,' v. 2. When first called by Elijah he had declared, 'I will follow thee,' 1 Kings 19. 20. Did he really mean it? Would he cleave to the prophet unto the end? Elijah tried his faith, to determine whether his avowal was actuated by a fleeting impulse or if it were a stead-fast resolution. Elisha had meant what he said, and refused now to forsake his master when given the opportunity to do so. He was determined to have the benefit of the prophet's company and instruction as long as he could, and clave to him probably in hope of receiving his parting blessing. 'So they went down to Bethel,' which means 'the house of God.' This was another place of hallowed memory, for it was the spot where Jehovah had first appeared unto Jacob and given him the vision of the mystic ladder. Here the 'sons of the prophets' at the local school came and informed Elisha that the Lord would remove his master that very day. He told them he knew that already, and bade them hold their peace, v. 3, for they were intruding.

'And Elijah said unto him, Elisha, tarry here, I pray thee; for the Lord hath sent me to Jericho,' v. 4. As the Saviour 'made as though He would have gone further,' Luke 24. 28, when putting to the proof the affection of His disciples on the way to Emmaus, so the prophet told his companion to 'tarry ye here,' at Bethel – the place of such sacred memories. But as the two disciples had 'con-strained' Christ to abide with them, so nothing could tempt Elisha to forsake his master. 'So they came to Jericho,' which was on the border of the land from which Elijah was departing. And the sons of the prophets that were at Jericho came to Elisha and said unto him, 'Knowest thou that the Lord will take away thy master from thy head today? and he answered, Yea, I know it; hold ye your peace,' v. 5. The force of this seems to be: What is the use of clinging so tenaciously to your master? He will be taken from you on the morrow, why not stay here with us! But like the great apostle at a later date, Elisha 'conferred not with flesh and blood,' but adhered to his resolution. Oh, that like grace may be granted both writer and reader when tempted to follow not the Lord fully.

'And Elijah said unto him, Tarry, I pray thee, here; for the Lord hath sent me to Jordan,' v. 6. Much ground had now been covered; was Elisha tiring of the journey or would he continue to the end? How many run well for awhile and then grow weary of well-doing? Not so Elisha. 'And he said, As the Lord liveth, and as thy soul liveth, I will not leave thee. And they two went on,' v. 6. How that reminds us of Ruth's decision: when Naomi bade her, 'Return thou after thy sister-in-law,' she replied, 'Intreat me not to leave thee, or to return from following after thee: for whither thou goest, I will go; and where thou lodgest, I will lodge,' 1. 16. 'And they two went on,' leaving the school of the prophets behind them. The young believer must not suffer even happy fellowship with the saints to come in between him and his own individual communion with the Lord. How richly Elisha was rewarded for his fidelity and constancy we shall see in the sequel.

'And fifty men of the sons of the prophets went, and stood to view afar off: and they two stood by Jordan,' v. 7, probably because they expected to witness Elijah's translation into heaven, a favour, however, which was granted only to Elisha. Nevertheless they were permitted to witness a remarkable miracle: the dividing asunder of the waters of Jordan so that the prophet and his companion passed over dryshod. How the *sovereignty of God* is displayed everywhere! The multitudes witnessed Christ's miracle of multiplying the loaves and the fishes, but not even all of the twelve beheld His transfiguration on the mount. It had pleased God to make these young prophets acquainted with the supernatural exit of His servant from this world, yet they were not permitted to be actual spectators of the same. Why, we know not, but the fact remains, and from it we should take instruction. It illustrates a principle which is revealed on every page of Holy Writ and is exemplified all through history: that God makes distinction not only between man and man but also between His saints, between one of His servants and another, distributing His favours as it pleases Him. And when any dare to challenge His high sovereignty, His answer is, 'Is it not lawful for Me to do what I will with Mine own?' Matt. 20. 15.

'And Elijah took his mantle, and wrapped it together, and smote the waters and they were divided hither and thither, so that they two went over on dry ground,' v. 8. This dividing of the Jordan was a fitting prelude to the prophet's rapture on high. As Matthew Henry pointed out, it was 'the preface to Elijah's translation into the heavenly Canaan, as it had been to the entrance of Israel into the earthly Canaan,' Josh. 3. 15-17. Elijah and his companion might have crossed the river by ferry, as other passenges did, but the Lord had determined to magnify His servant in his exit from the land, as He had Joshua in his entrance thereto. It was with his *rod* Moses had divided the sea, Ex. 14. 16, here it was with his *mantle* Elijah divided the river – each the insignia or badge of his distinctive office. That there is a deeper meaning and broader application to this remarkable incident scarcely admits of a doubt. The 'Jordan' is the well-known figure of death: Elijah is here a type of Christ, as Elisha is to be regarded as representative of all who cleave to and follow Him. Thus we learn that a safe and comfortable way through death has been provided for His people by the Lord Jesus Christ.

'And it came to pass, when they were gone over, that Elijah said unto Elisha, Ask what I shall do for thee, before I be taken away from thee,' v. 9. Here is proof that Elijah had been *testing* his companion when he bade him 'tarry' at the previous stopping-places, for certainly he had not offered such an invitation as this had he been contravening his express desire. The prophet was so pleased with Elisha's affection and attendance that he determined to reward him with some parting blessing. And what a testing of his character was this, 'Ask what I shall do for thee'! One of the Puritans has called attention to the significance of Elijah's *'before I be taken from thee,'* for it had been useless for Elisha to invoke his master afterward. 'He was not to be prayed unto as a "mediator of intercession" as Papists blasphemously teach concerning saints and angels.' Christ is the only one in heaven who intercedes for God's people on earth. How attentively we need to read the language of Holy Writ: that single word 'before' gives the lie to one of the cardinal errors of Rome.

'And Elisha said, I pray thee, let a double portion of thy spirit be upon me,' v. 9. Here was his noble answer to Elijah's 'What shall I do for thee?' Rising above both the lusts and sentiments of the flesh, he asked not anything nature might have coveted, but that which was spiritual, seeking not his own aggrandizement but the glory of God. We do not think he asked for something superior to what his master had enjoyed, but a portion 'double' that which was communicated to the other prophets. He was to take Elijah's place on the stage of public action: he was to be the leader of 'the sons of the prophets' (as v. 15 intimates), and therefore he wished to be equipped for his mission. Rightly did he 'covet earnestly the best gifts': he asked for a double portion of the spirit of prophecy – of wisdom and grace, of faith and strength – that he might be 'thoroughly furnished unto all good works.'

'And he said, Thou hast asked a hard thing,' v. 10. Elisha had asked not for riches or glory, wisdom or power, but for a double portion of the spirit that rested on and wrought through his master. In terming it 'a hard thing' Elijah appears to have emphasized the great *value* of such a bestowment: it was as though he said, That is much for you to expect. We regard Matthew Henry's comment as a pertinent one: 'Those are best prepared for spiritual blessings that are most sensible of their worth and their own unworthiness to receive.' Elisha felt his own weakness and utter insignificance for such a work as that to which he was called, and therefore he desired to be qualified for his eminent office. 'Nevertheless, if thou *see* me when I am taken from thee, it should be so unto thee; but if not, it shall not be so,' v. 10. This is very blessed: his request would be granted and he was to know it by the sign mentioned: a sight of Elijah's translation would be the proof that his request was agreeable to the will of God and a pledge of his desire being gratified: but in order thereto his *eye* must continue *fixed upon* his master! Chronologists reckon that the ministry of Elisha lasted at least twice the length of his predecessor's and apparently he wrought double the number of miracles.

The grand moment had arrived. Elijah had fully discharged the commission God had given him. He had preserved his garments from being spotted by the apostate religious world. Now his conflict was over, his course run, his victory won. He had no home or resting place here, so he pressed onward to his heavenly rest. 'And it came to pass, as they still went on, and talked, that, behold, there appeared a chariot of fire, and horses of fire, and parted them both asunder; and Elijah went up by a whirlwind into heaven,' v. 11. It is to be carefully noted that God did not send His chariot for Elijah while he was in Samaria. No, the land of Israel was polluted and Ichabod was written over it. It was on the far side of Jordan, in the place of separation, that this signal honour was conferred upon the prophet. As the souls of the saints are conveyed to Paradise by the angels, Luke 16. 22, so we believe it was by celestial beings, the highest among them, that Elijah was taken to heaven. 'Seraphim' signifies 'fiery,' and God is said to make His angels 'a flaming fire,' Psa. 104. 4, while 'cherubim' are called 'the chariots of God,' Psa. 68. 17 and cf. Zech. 1. 8; 6. 1. 'Elijah was to remove to the world of angels, and so angels were sent to conduct him thither' (Matthew Henry), that he might ride in state and triumph to the skies like a conqueror.

In the translation of Elijah we have clear testimony to the fact that there is a reward for the righteous. Often this appears to be flatly contradicted by the experiences of this life. We behold the wicked flourishing like the green bay-tree, while the child of God has a bare temporal subsistence; but it shall not always be thus. Elijah had peculiarly honoured God in a day of almost universal apostasy, and now God was pleased highly to honour him. As he had taught men, at the constant hazard of his life, the knowledge of the only true God, so he would now teach them by his being taken alive into heaven that there is a future state, that there is a world beyond the skies into which the righteous are admitted, where they shall henceforth dwell with God and all the angelic hosts in glory everlasting. Future bliss shall infinitely compensate present sacrifices and sufferings: he that humbleth himself shall be exalted. Elijah's supernatural exit from this world also demonstrated the fact that the human body is capable of immortality! It could not witness to the truth of resurrection, for he never died; but his corporeal removal to Heaven furnished indubitable evidence that the body is capable of being immortalized and of living in celestial conditions.

In the translation of Elijah we see how much better are God's ways than ours. In an hour of despondency the prophet had wanted to leave this world before God's time had come for him to do so, and by a way far inferior to that which He had appointed: under the juniper tree he had requested that he might die, saying, 'It is enough; now, O Lord, take away my life,' 1 Kings 19. 4. Had he been granted his desire, how much he had lost! How much better than to be taken away by death in a fit of impatience! And this is recorded for our instruction, pointing as it does a lesson we all need take to heart. It is the part of wisdom to leave ourselves and all our affairs in God's gracious hands, trusting Him fully and being willing for Him to use His own measures and methods with us. We are certain to sustain serious loss if we determine to have our own way: 'He gave them their request; but sent leanness into their soul,' Psa. 106. 15. The mature Christian will assure his younger brethren that today he thanks God for refusing the answers he once craved. God denies thy request now because He has ordained something better for thee.

In the translation of Elijah we have both a pledge and a type of the supernatural exit from this world which *every* child of God experiences. In the course of these chapters we have pointed out again and again that though in certain respects the character and career of Elijah was an extraordinary one, yet in its broad outlines he is to be regarded as a representative saint. Thus it was in connection with the final event. No ordinary departure from this world was his, and vastly different from the common end to earthly existence experienced by the wicked is that of the righteous. Death as the wages of sin has been abolished for the redeemed. For them physical dissolution is but the body being put to sleep: as for the soul it is conveyed by angels into God's immediate presence, Luke 16. 22, which is certainly a supernatural experience. Nor shall all God's people even 'sleep,' 1 Cor. 15. 51. That generation of them alive on the earth at the return of the Saviour shall have their bodies 'changed,' that they may be 'fashioned like unto His glorious body,' Phil. 3. 21, and shall be caught up together with the resurrected saints to 'meet the Lord in the air,' 1 Thess. 4. 17. Thus a supernatural exit from this world is assured to all the ransomed hosts of God.